CW00801518

Musashi's
Dokkodo

(The Way of Walking Alone)

Musashi's
Dokkodo

(The Way of Walking Alone)

Half Crazy, Half Genius
Finding Modern Meaning in the
Sword Saint's Last Words

By Miyamoto Musashi

Edited by Lawrence A. Kane and Kris Wilder
with Alain Burrese, Lisa A. Christensen, and Wallace Smedley
Foreword by Dan Anderson

Copyright © 2015 by Lawrence Kane and Kris Wilder

Cover photo by Lawrence Kane
Cover design and interior layout by Kami Miller

All rights reserved. No part of this publication may be reproduced, distributed or transmitted in any form or by any means, including photocopying, recording, or other electronic or mechanical methods, without the prior written permission of the publisher, except in the case of brief quotations embodied in critical reviews and certain other noncommercial uses permitted by copyright law. For permission requests, write to the publisher, addressed "Attention: Permissions Coordinator," at the address below:

Stickman Publications, Inc.
Burien, WA 98146
www.stickmanpublications.com

ISBN-13: 978-0692563496
ISBN-10: 0692563490

Disclaimer

Information in this book is distributed "As Is," without warranty. Nothing in this document constitutes a legal opinion nor should any of its contents be treated as such. Neither the authors nor the publisher shall have any liability with respect to information contained herein. Further, neither the authors nor the publisher have any control over or assume any responsibility for websites or external resources referenced in this book.

Praise for Musashi's Dokkodo ...

"Here's something you don't see every day: A detailed analysis of a short list of life-principles offered by a sword-saint just before he died. The authors divide themselves into five archetypes—monk, warrior, teacher, insurance executive, and businessman, and reflect in extensive detail upon the meaning of Miyamoto Musashi's final written words. It's fascinating stuff. Not a meal to be consumed and digested in a hurry, but one that needs to be addressed more leisurely to make the most of the varied flavors in it."

— **Steve Perry**
New York Times bestselling author

~~

"The writings of the Japanese sword-saint Miyamoto Musashi have guided martial artists for hundreds of years. This modern examination of his 21 precepts shines new light on his teachings. The authors begin with the startling assertion that Musashi was, by modern standards, a psychopath. It doesn't take much argument on their part to see they're right. Musashi pursued a life of killing without any apparent conscience and many of his precepts seem impossibly harsh in the modern world. And yet... if we can look beyond their apparent inhumanity, we get an invaluable guide for the modern martial artist.

"I would recommend this book, along with Musashi's *Book of Five Rings*, to those facing a big test or simply wishing to enter more deeply into the martial way. The five contributors—all high-level martial artists—make a fine job of examining the precepts and deriving the messages that apply today. They offer perspectives from backgrounds as diverse as a monk, a warrior, a teacher, an insurance executive and a businessman. There's difference of opinion that provides scope and depth in each assessment, allowing the reader, in the end, to infer his or her own meaning from Musashi's words.

"Congratulations to the authors—they've made classic samurai wisdom accessible to the modern martial artist like never before."

— **Goran Powell**
award winning author of *Chojun*, *A Sudden Dawn*,
Matryoshka, and *Waking Dragons*

~~

"I am not familiar with martial arts so I had never heard of Miyamoto Musashi. However, I do like books that promote self-improvement and philosophy. When I first saw this book I initially thought it would not be something I was interested in. However, I was intrigued by the approach that the authors had taken to do such a unique and personal interpretation of Musashi's 21 precepts. The precepts themselves offer priceless advice to anyone, not just those in martial arts. And the authors approach make this a fresh and fun read. Well done!"

— **Kate Vitasek**
Faculty, Graduate and Executive Education, University of Tennessee

~~

"Reading *Musashi's Dokkodo* was like convening around a warm fire with a hot mug of cappuccino and a wizened group of philosophical mentors. It was akin to talking to five therapists. The unique viewpoints, examples and stories were cleverly wrought, causing me to laugh out loud and experience 'a-ha' moments. I could read this multiple times and get to deeper levels of awareness. The five point perspective inspired deep introspection. I have been elevated to higher and deeper levels of personal and professional growth by reading this book."

— **Laela Erickson**
Senior Business Development Executive

~~

"*Musashi's Dokkodo* is a very unique book which critically and creatively analyzes the precepts of a two sword psycho-killer and seeks to learn positive lessons even from such a mind. Anyone who has read *The Book of Five Rings* will agree that Musashi is one of the most influential martial artists of all time. If he was indeed a psychopath, the question should be, 'What does that say about those of us who choose to follow his precepts, or at least consider them?' This is a question I rarely thought about until reading this book.

"I thoroughly enjoyed *The Book of Five Rings* in the way I enjoyed Sun Tzu's *Art of War*. I had always thought that these were warriors, and for those of us who are training to be warriors of a sort, this was line of thinking was perfectly acceptable. Except, the battles most of us fight are within ourselves. We are not living in feudal Japan. Musashi fought his 60 famous duels to the death in order to better his skills and sharpen his warrior's mind. That is what was necessary. And, he only fought, sword to sword, against proven warriors as well (or so the stories go).

"This book about Miyamoto's precepts—based on 5 different points of view—analyzes the thinking that made Miyamoto successful, allowing him to conquer his inner demons along with his combative foes. What is most fascinating about this approach is that although these authors are martial artists, they also live in and work in different fields. If this were merely a book by and for martial artists, it would still be interesting, but arguably not as important or even as provocative. It is from deeper analysis that these precepts become internalized, and therefore, most usable.

"The authors of Musashi's Dokkodo should be commended for opening a door to new paths, allowing us to understand the thinking of a psycho killer, and yet appreciate how much we have evolved in the martial arts—by fighting our inner demons instead of our human enemies. After all, most of us train for peace."

— Ron Breines
Associate Professor, University of Maryland;
martial arts instructor
(*Kakuto Ryu Jujutsu*/Karate-*Jutsu*, Okinawa *Meibukan Goju Ryu*);
certified firearms/self-defense tactical instructor

~~

"I was never sure if Musashi was a genius, or had one oar out of the water, or was like a guy on the loading docks pontificating about how the company 'should be run.' One thing is for sure, he was a killer—and he was good at it. Now the question is, 'How well do those attributes translate into modern life?' There are a lot of modern wannabe warriors running around who like to claim they understand ol' Miyamoto. As there are corporate types who pretend *The Book of Five Rings* is a business model. Thing is there's a lot of stuff he said that is off the deep end and, yet, there's some solid advice there too. The questions are: One, which one is which? Two, what advice can you apply to modern life and what do you need to drop faster than an annoyed scorpion. *Musashi's Dokkodo* takes the refreshing approach of five modern people, from different backgrounds, offering you insights into what advice can help you versus which advice will sting you."

— Marc MacYoung
www.nononsenseselfdefense.com

~~

"One of the more limiting quotes I've ever heard went something like, 'Those that can, do. Those that can't, teach.'" Perhaps, though, there is a kernel of truth in this, but from the opposite direction some of the best doers, for lack of a better word, were absolutely horrible teachers. They simply could not get across the phenomenal skill sets they possessed to other people.

"Miyamoto Musashi was one of the greatest doers to ever live. Arguably the greatest known swordsman of all time, his actions speak for themselves. That said, he was also a rather gifted teacher. His treatise The Book of Five Rings is essential reading in many quarters from war colleges to business. But he also passed on a lesser known tome, Dokkodo, which is translated as 'The Way of Walking Alone.' This short work is a list of twenty-one precepts he wrote to his protégé one week before he died. It is masterful and profound, for such a small work.

"The book you're about to read is how these precepts are viewed through the different lenses and experiences of people with expertise in different professional areas of society. Ranging from a warrior to a businessman to a monk, each person will have a different take on the same precept. Sometimes there are only subtle differences. Sometimes wildly different takes result. Oftentimes you the reader will disagree with the particular interpretation. This is a good thing. We should argue what Musashi meant, particularly given more modern takes on morality and ethics.

"So, read on, and make sure to bring an open mind."

— M. Guthrie
Federal Air Marshal

Contents

FOREWORD

Dan Anderson's martial arts career began at the age of 14 under the tutelage of Loren Christensen in Vancouver, Washington. Dan achieved his 1st degree Black Belt on January 7, 1970 at the age of 17. For the next 10 years Anderson committed himself to becoming a karate tournament champion, eventually becoming rated in the national top 10 ratings four years in a row. He began his writing career with the book *American Freestyle Karate: A Guide to Sparring*, first published in 1981. He has since authored 20 books on karate and Filipino Martial Arts as well as producing 25 DVDs on the subjects.

In 1980, Dan began training in the second martial art that would shape his research and career from that time forward, Modern Arnis under Remy A. Presas. Since then Dan has been personally accepted as a student of Manong Ted Buot, a student Balintawak Eskrima's founder, Anciong Bacon. In 2006, Dan traveled to the Philippines to teach at both the 3rd World Filipino Martial Arts Festival and the 1st Remy A. Presas memorial Training Camp, one of a handful of westerners to teach at these events. It was during this trip where he became a founding member of the Worldwide Family of Modern Arnis. His branch of Modern Arnis, the MA80 System Arnis/Eskrima was also recognized by the International Modern Arnis Federation Philippines as a valid branch of the Remy Presas' art.

In 2008, Dan Anderson received the *Gat Andres Bonafacio* award from the Philippine Classical Arnis society. In 2012 Dan Anderson tested for and passed the examination for 9th dan in karate by the American Karate Black Belt Association. Dan Anderson currently teaches karate and Filipino Martial Arts at the Dan Anderson Karate School in Gresham, Oregon. He is aided by his wife, Marie, and his daughter, Amanda.

This is a most uncommon book that you hold in your hands.

Miyamoto Musashi is the stuff of legend. Known as Japan's greatest swordsman, there has been much written about him coming from the oral lore of that country. He won his first duel at the age of 13. He ended up killing over 60 adversaries before retiring to a life of solitude. Musashi in Japan is much like the icons of the Wild, Wild West of American history; Wild Bill Hickok, Bat Masterson, Billy the Kid and so on. How much of his story is fact and how much of it is fiction?

He has been revered as Japan's "sword saint" and yet at the same time been dismissed by one of the leading swordsmen of the 19th century, Yamaoka Tesshu (1836 – 1888).* As there has been very little written of Musashi that can be verified with any historical accuracy, who really knows what he was like. In the introduction Kane and Wilder have presented a viewpoint of him in 21st century terms based on his *conduct* rather than his legend. The results differ from the stuff of legend and are disturbing.

This is a most uncommon book that you hold in your hands. Musashi wrote two books. His first book was *Go Rin No Sho* (*The Book of Five Rings*), a treatise on the martial arts strategy that he formulated over the years based on his combat experience. That book has been the subject of many translations and commentaries, much like *The Art of War* by Sun Tzu, and has been studied by literally thousands and thousands of martial artists across the globe. The volume you hold in your hands is his second book, *Dokkodo* (*The Way of Walking Alone*), a much lesser known work of Musashi's. Compared to his book of strategy, *Go Rin no Sho*, in present day publishing terms *Dokkodo* is more of a pamphlet or booklet than a book.

One week or two prior to his death Musashi wrote out a series of 21 precepts regarding life for his favorite student Terao Magonojō and left it at that. Unlike L. Ron Hubbard's *The Way to Happiness* and other works like it wherein the author goes on to further elaborate on each precept, Musashi wrote *Dokkodo* in line-item form and left it at that. It might be said that Magonojō was so familiar with Musashi that he needed very little to go on. It might also be said that Musashi thought that since he had to come to these conclusions himself over a lifetime of experience so too should Magonojō, so he wrote very little expecting his disciple to do some life research himself. Who knows?

This is a most uncommon book that you hold in your hands. Musashi's last work is examined by no less than five people from very different walks of life: a monk, a warrior, a teacher, a businessman, and an insurance executive. Each one has expertise

---

* Founder of the *Itto Shoden Muto-ryu* school of swordsmanship, Tesshu was known for his calligraphy as much as for his fighting prowess. An elite bodyguard for Shogun Tokugawa Yoshinobu, after the Meiji Restoration Tesshu hung up his swords to become governor of the Imari Prefecture. His exploits are described in the book *The Sword of No Sword: Life of the Master Warrior Tesshu* by John Stevens.

in their walk of life. How do each of these individuals read Musashi's last work? What is their take on it? Their views are not the usual martial artist's take on it. These are areas of life which martial arts may have very little or no impact on. What does Japan's warrior strategist have to say to them?

Read on. Find how they view Musashi's writings. They agree and disagree, both with Musashi and each other, but they all have one thing in common—this book caused them to think about life and their relationship to it.

What is my own reaction to this book? Here are the writings of a man in the twilight of his life attempting to lay down a foundation of life for a favored student. I think to myself, "What might he have written differently if he'd done this ten, twenty, or thirty years earlier?"

This book makes me reflect on what I thought was important at various points of my life and what I think now at age sixty three. With life experience I view things quite differently than when I was a hot-blooded karate competitor. Thirty odd years, six children and twelve grandchildren will do that. What is *Dokkodo*? I feel these are the writings of a man who has reflected on the excesses of his life and wishes to guide his student down a different path, a less turbulent life path than the one he took.

Explore each precept from your own point of view, your own life experience, and find out what Miyamoto Musashi, arguably the greatest swordsman Japan has ever produced, has to say to *you*.

Yes, this is a most uncommon book that you hold in your hands.

Dan Anderson
October, 2015

INTRODUCTION

Musashi, the Myth and the Man
The Truth behind the Legend

"Saints have no moderation, nor do poets, just exuberance." — Anne Sexton

In 1935 novelist Eiji Yoshikawa (1892 – 1962) changed the martial arts world when he published his epic *Musashi*, a fictionalized account of the adventures of Miyamoto Musashi which was serialized in the newspaper *Asahi Shimbun*. The legendary swordsman was well known to practitioners of classical Japanese swordsmanship, but virtually no one had heard of Musashi beyond that fellowship. Certainly he was not the mythic figure we think we know today, one who has been portrayed in books, movies, manga, and comics to the point where he has become a household name far beyond the traditional martial arts community.

Yoshikawa was a talented writer, one who ignited the imaginations of his readership. Once he created the mystique of Musashi it caught fire, growing in the same way that virtually all myths are born and developed. Suddenly Musashi was larger than life, a figure whose methods of thought, strategy, and tactics were adopted across a wide spectrum of Japanese society, especially amongst military leaders and captains of industry. They studied his ancient treatise on strategy *Go Rin No Sho*, intuiting relevance and meaning in modern life. Before long Musashi's legend spread beyond the shores of Japan, making an impact on people from all walks of life all across the world. In fact, his treatise *Go Rin No Sho* has been translated into English at least a dozen different times where it was published under the title *The Book of Five Rings* and various derivations thereof.* It has also been printed in languages as diverse as Arabic, Chinese, Greek, German, Indonesian, French, Lithuanian, Spanish, and Thai.

If Musashi had not written this exposition *Go Rin No Sho* and Yoshikawa subsequently publicized it centuries later, it is likely that Japan's most famous swordsman would have been relegated to the dustbins of history along with most other luminaries of his period, known only by historians and historical re-enactors. Nevertheless, Musashi retired to a cave near the end of his life, put down his swords, and took up a pen. And, Yoshikawa brought those ancient writings back to life. In the process he is largely responsible for making Musashi the venerable sword saint that he is today.

When legendary figures pass away, we tend to turn them into saints, though not necessarily in a spiritual manner. Nevertheless, we do it much in the same way that religious institutions deify noteworthy members of their organizations. The formula works this way: First, while the future saint is still alive society does not acknowledge his or her brilliance. These individuals are often branded eccentrics, mavericks, or rabble-rousers. Secondly, after they die we discover their message, recognize their contributions, and adopt them as our own. Thirdly, we canonize them, putting special emphasis on their remarkable deeds and honorable behaviors while ignoring or brushing over any questionable or contemptuous acts they may have performed. "No, he wasn't crazy, just a little quirky. Perhaps a touch eccentric, but what genius isn't? Think of all the contributions he made to..." we might say to ourselves. Once that justification has taken root and been accepted by the masses, the last stage of canonization takes place when we as a society turn them into saints. And then we build statues of them, name things after them, and pay homage to their memories.

And so it was with Musashi. Roughly three hundred years after his death in 1645, Musashi suddenly became an icon and a hero. His name is synonymous with samurai ethos, as ubiquitous as *katana*, *bushido*, and *shogun*. In fact, he is often called *kensei*, the "sword saint" of Japan. Musashi is, without doubt, a larger-than-life figure. However, he was not just a mythic hero; he was a real

---

* Sporting subtitles such as *The Classic Guide to Strategy*, *A Classic Text on the Japanese Way of the Sword*, and *The Definitive Interpretation of Miyamoto Musashi's Classic Book of Strategy*, among many, many others.

person too… In studying his writings it is important to remember that. Before he became the symbol of a bygone era, arguably the greatest swordsman who ever lived, Musashi was a real person, and an imperfect one at that. His icon is an affair of the heart, but to understand his reality requires an analysis of the mind. Who is to say that we cannot hold a perspective about him that blends both heart and mind?

Today we know that Miyamoto Musashi (1584 – 1645) was born Shinmen Takezō. He grew up in the Harima Province of Japan and slew his first opponent, Arima Kihei, in a duel he fought at the tender age of thirteen. Over a lifetime of blood and strife he killed more than sixty samurai warriors in fights or duals during the feudal period where even a minor battle injury could lead to infection and death, a miraculous feat. He was the founder of the unconventional *Hyōhō Niten Ichi-Ryu* style of swordsmanship, which translates as "Two Heavens as One," or more simply "Two-Sword Style." Like most samurai, he was a highly trained martial artist, a veritable killing machine, but he was also skilled in the peaceful arts as well, an exceptional poet, calligrapher, and artist. Two years before he died, Musashi retired to a life of seclusion in a cave where he codified his winning strategy in *Go Rin No Sho* which, in English, means *The Book of Five Rings*.

At an early age, Musashi exhibited the traits of a saint. Legends state that when he was only eight years old he left home to learn calligraphy, poetry, and other arts, leaving almost everything behind. Impressive, right? Perhaps, but let's try to separate the man from the myth for a moment. In Japanese society *tatemae* (official truth/outward story) often varies from *honne* (secret truth/inward story). Was leaving home the first steps along a path toward enlightenment in an ascetic lifestyle or simply a young man running away from an abusive father?

At the age of thirteen Musashi challenged a famous swordsman, Arima Kihei, to a duel and defeated him using a stick in lieu of a sword. Was this a heroic battle as it is customarily portrayed (*tatemae*) or did Musashi through grit, determination, anger, and a burning desire for glory ambush Kihei, knock him to the ground, and savagely beat him to death (*honne)*? Clearly we cannot know with certainty what actually occurred, yet we are hard pressed to think of a less elegant or more brutal way to murder another human being than to pummel them with a hunk of wood. Imagine a young man standing over a hapless swordsman lying on the ground and repeatedly slamming a bludgeon into his victim's face until he stops breathing. Then, he keeps pounding on the samurai's bloody pulp of a face to ensure that he is not just unconscious but, in fact, dead. And then he walks away smiling afterward, knowing that his reputation has been enhanced…

In 1612, Musashi fought another famous duel, this time with Sasaki Kojirō.* Musashi showed up three hours late. When he finally arrived, both his adversary and the officials of the duel were irritated by his tardiness. Rather than carrying a steel blade he was once again armed with a wooden sword. This time it was a *bokken* that he had carved out of an oar. Furthermore, Musashi knew that Kojirō's sword was a little longer than a normal *katana*, so he spent the extra time to carve a wooden weapon that was just a little bit longer than that, giving him an additional advantage in reach.

By arriving late, showing contempt for the opponent and the moment and then doubling down by not even having the dignity to use a real sword for a life-or-death duel he rattled his adversary. Brilliant strategy don't you think? But, Musashi went even farther still… When Kojirō drew his sword to get things started he threw his *saya* (scabbard) aside in disgust, prompting Musashi to further unnerve him by commenting something along the lines of, "If you have no more use for your scabbard, you are already dead."

Musashi had won even before the fight began because he had stacked the deck in his favor so effectively. Not only did he use psychological tricks, but he also wielded a longer weapon, something which many overlook in his victory.

Remember the scene in the Bruce Lee movie *Enter the Dragon* where he tricked an opponent onto a boat and then left him floating without an oar? That was inspired by another of Musashi's dirty tricks. He may or may not have truly been the greatest swordsman of his period, perhaps even of all time, but we know for certain that Musashi was one of the most successful. An unconventional thinker, he often fought with two swords instead of one, he made extensive use of misdirection and psychological

---

* The duel has been immortalized with an impressive, larger than life sculpture of the two warriors battling on a small island in the Kanmon Straits, close to Shimonoseki. Kojirō is depicted with his long sword whereas Musashi is armed with his *bokken*. At the time of the battle the island was called *Funa-jima*, but afterwards it was renamed *Ganryū*, after Kojirō's style of swordsmanship, an interesting historical oddity since Musashi won the battle.

warfare, and nearly always cheated in one way or another in order to win. In fact, he was downright brilliant at his job, which like most warriors who live in tumultuous times ultimately boils down to killing people efficiently.

Unlike others of his era, however, Musashi took the time to write about what he had done, the things he had accomplished, and the strategies that made him successful in his endeavors. That's a vital factor in what we know and think about him today. After all, he's not the only one who lived an amazing life during that time period, but he is one of the few who documented his perspectives on what he had seen and done for posterity.

The Book of Five Rings, Musashi's most famous writing, is a work where life experience meets genius. One surefire way to know whether or not you hold genius in your hands when you read it is to have the work span your lifetime regarding its impact. If, for example, you read the classic science-fiction book *A Wrinkle in Time* by Madeleine L'Engle as a child it's magical. To re-read it later in life brings back those magical feelings. That's the mark of a truly well-written book, but is it genius? No, not so much… Let's contrast this with Musashi's work. To read *The Book of Five Rings* in your youth and then peruse it again in mid-life, the sensation is not a recounting of emotion but rather a newer and deeper understanding of what has been presented. This is what you're looking for. In fact, *The Book of Five Rings* is often placed alongside The *Art of War* by Sun Tzu, *On War* by General Carl von Clausewitz, *Infantry Attacks* by Field Marshal Erwin Rommel, and *Patterns of Conflict* by Colonel John Boyd. Each of these works has materially influenced military thinking, directly or indirectly influencing modern combat despite the fact that they were written decades or even centuries ago.

In this sense, Musashi truly was a combative genius. Small wonder that our patron sword saint crossed over to become an icon, a legend… But what drove him? What brought him there?

While he never wrote a book that we know of, Musashi's father Munisai was a famous martial artist in his own right. His very name means, "A man unequaled." After defeating a famous swordsman of the Yoshioka family in front of the *shogun*, Ashikaga Yoshiaki, he was honored with the title, *hi no shita heihojutsusha*, which translates as, "The greatest fighter/tactician under the sun."

He was also reported to be self-assured, aggressive, aloof, and domineering. And, he firmly believed that his son was arrogant. It is easy to see that this combination of the autocrat and the arrogant would not mix well. Night and day; oil and water... And, to be certain, it didn't.

Musashi's father treated him poorly, ostensibly in order to bend him to his will. It didn't work. When he could no longer abide the strict rules of Munisai's household and treatment that he felt was beneath his station, Musashi ran away from home.* He was only eight years old at the time. It is reasonable to assume that he returned to his birthplace now and again, as it was a place of refuge after all, but once he had made his reputation by killing Kihei he left his hometown never to return. We do not know if he ever spoke to a family member again, but it's likely a safe bet that he did not.

With no meaningful relationships in his young life, he set out to "barrow the battlefield," a term used by swordsmen wanting to prove themselves in combat and win a position within that domain. The cause, the lord under whose banner he fought, even the reason for war was not horribly important, but rather proving oneself by killing others was paramount.

Let's think about this: No meaningful relationships, a self-selected loner, intense focus to the point of obsession, and a willingness to kill. Of course we love Musashi, he is Clint Eastwood, Chuck Norris, Jason Statham, and Bruce Lee all rolled into one badass mercenary who roamed the land with a three-foot razor blade searching out prey to slaughter... Wait a minute, on a movie screen that's that makes for a rousing good time, but in real life it sounds an awful lot like something a psychopath might do.

Was Musashi a functional psychopath? We believe the answer to that question is a definitive yes. Surprised? You shouldn't be. Let's examine some of his behaviors: To begin, Musashi was ruthless. He sought out other men to murder. He didn't kill to defend his life, his property, or even his liege-lord; he killed simply to test his skill in battle. He killed to improve his reputation and status in life. He killed because he could. And, he was very good at it.

---

* There are numerous (and conflicting) stories of Musashi's childhood. In some accounts his father died when he was eight, in others his father abandoned him when he was that age, but we believe this to be the most likely explanation of what actually occurred.

Musashi was fearless, another common attribute of functional psychopaths. Fearlessness can be good or bad, it's not the trait so much as how it is used and perceived. An example of this might be the "Zodiac Killer" who terrorized Northern California in the late 60's and early 70's. The Zodiac Killer, in at least one documented instance, walked up to his victims in broad daylight and shot them to death. Then he taunted police with cryptic messages. Fearless for certain, but not in a good way... Contrast this with members of elite military units or law enforcement operators who overcome long odds and complete hazardous assignments in part due to fearlessness that lets them focus on the job despite the dangers they face. It's not that they never get scared but rather that they never let their fears stop them. Musashi clearly embraced the adage, "A samurai never fears death."

The ability to be and stay mentally focused was a key to Musashi developing and honing his skills as a swordsman. This mental discipline led to the development of his innovative two-sword system, a style that was unheard of in the orthodox sword-schools of his time. In fact, Musashi's focus was similar to that of Michelangelo di Lodovico Buonarroti Simoni. It is said that while sculpting the famous renaissance artist would not bathe or change his clothes for weeks at a time. When Michelangelo would finally remove his footwear, layers of skin would fall off of his feet and remain with the boots. Just as Michelangelo's focus was so intense that it caused him to forget about simple hygiene, so was Musashi's. Wild unkempt hair, rumpled sweat-stained clothes, a disfiguring skin condition, and a thousand-yard stare were common descriptions of the master swordsman.

An absolute lack of conscience is another attribute of a psychopath. At no time does Musashi speak about being fair or just in his writings. His only focus was on how to win. He saw the world as a very utilitarian place. At no time did he ever express remorse either. It is our belief that Musashi never lost one moment of sleep over the people that he killed, the families that he disrupted, or the damage that he had done. Sure, he lived in a different time, was held to a different set of standards and ethics, but even in warrior societies it's not easy to wantonly go around killing people with no remorse. Insofar as we can tell the only remorse that Musashi ever experienced was not being even better, more efficient at slaughtering other human beings.

Musashi's actions throughout his life benefited himself first and foremost. Some might point to his writings as a deed designed to assist his disciples, and we would agree, but in many ways they were self-serving too. While his books may not have been propaganda per se, everything was described through the lens of his own perspective. Musashi's life was about himself, his swords, and finding increasingly efficient and effective ways to use them. He was detached from society, rarely stayed long term in the company of others. He did not depend on others, never formed any lasting romantic relationships, and lived alone the majority of his time. In fact, in his last writings he addressed the fact (in his opinion) that one should never be guided by love, filial or romantic.

In today's world we are able to obtain vast amounts of data about crimes and criminals over the internet. When we search for the information on serial killers, or read news reports of violent crimes, we can get information almost immediately. While early reports can be suspect, much of what is reported in the early minutes and hours ultimately proves to be accurate later on because reporters have an easy time finding relevant and meaningful information near instantly. Pick a criminal, any violent criminal, and perform a background check. Within moments we can find a history of antisocial behaviors. Sometimes they originate from nature, other times from nurture, but they're virtually always there. Every violent crime has a back story, and oftentimes the criminal has a history of antisocial behaviors that originates from his or (rarely) her childhood.

It is well known that Musashi's father was an autocrat, he dictated the terms of his household and his martial arts school. From our modern minds it must have been very hard to live in that household. This is speculation on the part of the authors, but requires consideration. Is it possible that Musashi's father, a teacher of martial arts and observer of people's temperaments, saw something in his son that was not desirable? Is it possible Musashi's father saw a nascent psychopath, yet his father only knew to call the behaviors arrogance since modern psychological science was unknown to him? Is it possible that this father chose to be hard on Musashi because it was the only way he knew how to squelch the undesirable conduct that his son exhibited? And finally, is it possible that his father's actions only fueled Musashi's antisocial behaviors?

So, what is a psychopath really? The Merriam-Webster Dictionary is a fine place to start with their brief and clear definition: "A person who is mentally ill, who does not care about other people, and who is usually dangerous or violent." This is a simple template in which everything we know about Musashi simply fits. However as much as we would like to make it that simple, placing Musashi into the category of functional psychopath still has some, well… wiggle room. Let's look at it this way: On July 22, 2011 Norwegian national Anders Behring Breivik killed eight people with a bomb and then hunted down and shot 69 participants of a Worker Youth League summer camp. Two court-appointed psychiatric teams who extensively examined Breivik in prison came to two different conclusions about the state of his mental health. If nothing else these differences prove that even what we might conclude as an "open and shut case" of insanity, of aberrant psychopathic behavior, may not be.

However, even though we are not psychologists and obviously spent no time examining Musashi in the flesh we stand by our conclusions. Musashi was a functional psychopath. To prove our point we use a checklist that comes from a guy who is a psychologist and far better versed in the subject matter than we will ever be, Dr. Kevin Dutton. He's also a writer and postdoctoral researcher at University of Oxford's Department of Experimental Psychology. His definition, which should sound eerily familiar to our earlier description of Musashi, includes the following elements:

- Ruthlessness
- Fearlessness
- Ability to be and stay mentally focused
- Lack of conscience

So, without question Musashi was a functional psychopath. While we believe that he was born predisposed to an antisocial personality disorder, we simultaneously acknowledge that Musashi was, beyond any shadow of a doubt, a genius. Can we separate the psychopath from the genius? Sure we can, but it is a bit of a challenge. Once we move past the acknowledgment that Musashi was a psychopath it places his writings in a different light.

When we read Musashi's writings, *Go Rin No Sho* or *Dokkodo*, we are reading the thoughts of a functional psychopath. Should we, therefore, accept his writings in totality? Clearly not. No more than we would never accept the policies of the Nazi party in total just because we like the way they addressed German citizens' access to healthcare. But, that's the point isn't it? We should feel free to embrace the uncomfortable, to move past the icon of Musashi constructed by Eiji Yoshikawa some seventy years ago.

Engage with the essentials of the master swordsman's teachings, his meaningful messages, all the while keeping a balance between the value of the icon and the reality of who he was as a man. In other words, he wrote about a different time and place, a different culture and ethic. There is merit in much of what he said, but his words are not a bible.

Many people know about Musashi's first book *Go Rin No Sho*, have even studied it in depth, but far fewer have perused his second one. On the occasion of Musashi giving away his possessions in preparation for his impending death, he wrote down his final thoughts about life in a treatise he called *Dokkodo* for his favorite student Terao Magonojō to whom *Go Rin No Sho* had also been dedicated. The title *Dokkodo* translates as, "*The Way of Walking Alone.*" It is a short essay that contains a mere 21 passages, yet it is just as profound as his longer dissertation.

The book you hold in your hands is our interpretation of that final work.

When reading famous historical writings readers are oftentimes subject to a single person's perspective about what an author from the past had to say. For instance, it might be the one person who spent the time and energy to translate an ancient work such as *Meditations* by Marcus Aurelius (Roman Emperor from 161 to 180 AD). Although the translator is unlikely to deliberately alter a statement or modify a meaning, there is always room for interpretation, opportunities for error. If the translator was an academic, for example, we get a scholarly view. If he or she was a military historian, on the other hand, the perspective would be different. Either way there's one lens, one point of view. We've tried to be more holistic here.

This translation of Musashi's precepts comes from the public domain, we saw no need to quibble with precise wording when each passage spans but a single sentence, yet this book contains five different interpretations of each precept of the *Dokkodo* written by five martial artists who come from very different walks of life. Each contributor was selected because he or she has lived a divergent existence from the others, yet shares the commonality of being a lifelong martial practitioner and published author.

We will address each of the 21 precepts in turn, taking the perspective of a monk (written by Franciscan Friar Kris Wilder), a warrior (written by former US Army Sniper Instructor Alain Burrese), a teacher (written by educator Wallace Smedley), an insurance executive (written by claims examiner Lisa Christensen), and a businessman (written IT strategist by Lawrence Kane), in our analysis. As you read this treatise you will see how some of these views agree with what Musashi has written, how we have found modern relevance from the legendary swordsman's final words, as well as where some of our views differ. Or, in some cases where one or more authors might have rejected Musashi's position entirely.

In this fashion you're not just reading a translation of Musashi's writing. You are scrutinizing his final words for deeper meaning. For all his faults, Musashi was a genius, one whose writings merit deep consideration. Our goal is to make you think; help you find modern meaning and application from *Dokkodo* for your own life as we have done for ours.

Enjoy!

PRECEPT 1

Accept everything just the way it is

"Acceptance looks like a passive state, but in reality it brings something entirely new into this world. That peace, a subtle energy vibration, is consciousness."

— Eckhart Tolle

Monk:

Standing on the front porch of my employer's home we watched the hail coming down, slamming into the orchard and ruining the apples that were his livelihood. Hail destroys the fruit; it makes the apples unsalable for the high-end market so after any significant hailstorm all of the unpicked fruit in the orchard has to become juice. Unfortunately, juice apples get such a low price that the return may not cover the year's operating costs, all of which in this instance was on loan from the growers' co-op. It was a dire situation.

I stood there next to my boss as the relentless hail showed no signs of letting up. I was angry that the crop been lost and let it be known. My boss, on the other hand, was silent and ignored my outrage. After a bit he shrugged his shoulders, looked at me, and said, "What are you going to do?" That response made me even more upset. In addition to raging against what nature was doing I was suddenly mad that he was not mad. His gaze still fixed on the storm, my boss ignored my invitation to dance with the anger saying, "There's nothing to be done but start to get the most out of what we have left." I was stunned by his stoicism.

I'd been shown this lesson many times in life, but as a child and later as a teen it was difficult to understand how accepting things for just what they are can actually bring clarity to life. How accepting things makes the world simpler. But, I get that now. You see, when you accept things as they are, it allows you to step into reality. The veil of fantasy that most of us shield ourselves with is torn into pieces and we can deal with things as they actually are, good, bad, or indifferent. The fact of the matter is that the world does not care about you or me, our hopes, our desires, or our dreams. And, the world of dreams, hopes, and desires that is constructed between our ears it is not necessarily a reflection of what is actually going on around us.

Musashi isn't the only famous person to point out this fact. Marcus Aurelius spoke to it in his journal *Meditations* where he wrote, "If you are distressed by anything external the pain is not due to the things itself but your estimate of it." That is some nice tight writing that deserves to be taken to heart. Let's face it, however, it takes effort to see everything the way it is, a real active effort. Musashi was anything but a pushover. Removing the idea of what you want something to be verses what it actually is can be compared to crossing a river gorge. You have to put aside the imposition of your will, your ego, and your desire to see something for other than what it is in order to have any chance of getting across the chasm.

It is a distortion to attempt to see anything for other than what it truly is. Sometimes this distortion is considerable, other times insignificant, but it is a distortion all the same. This is similar to the anthropomorphisms of animal behavior that most folks mistakenly believe. Animals work on instinct, not logic or higher reasoning, but we don't always look at their behaviors that way. For instance, what we may see as a cute way of showing that they love us that's not what's actually going on, it is truly something else entirely.

Think of a cat rubbing up against your leg. "Awww," you might say, "Kitty wants some pets." What the cat is actually doing is rubbing its smell on your leg just like it would on a tree trunk. It's not being cute; it's marking its territory. We just think of that behavior as cute. Everything has its nature and making an effort to see that nature in its unvarnished glory allows for truth. Truth in turn makes for clarity, which leads to good decision-making. With clarity you can chart a true path and uncover means to a real understanding or resolution of even the most challenging issues that you face throughout your life.

I drove my son across the country to college recently. The trip took two days. After a while he became horribly restless in the car, "I can't stand this anymore. This drive never ends! It needs to end... How are you doing this?" He looked at me intently trying to find out what the secret was, the reason I hadn't also gone stir crazy being locked up in the car with him. Not taking my eyes off the road I replied, "To get from here to there takes this much time and it's going to be this much time no matter how I feel about it so I've chosen to feel this way. Getting upset buys me nothing."

He looked at me in frustration because my statement didn't quite sort in his mind, but after a few minutes he decided to try to adjust to the reality of the long drive. After some more time, he actually began accepting things as they presented themselves. Soon he was in that simple place that allowed him to see the land, the sky, the cars we passed, and the funny billboards along the way. I watched as he began accepting the world as it was. And, I smiled, realizing that I was now in a more mature position myself. I had shown my son what my boss had shown me.

Warrior:

I have to agree with Musashi on this, as it really is the only way for a warrior, or anyone else for that matter, to live life. In fact, this precept reminds me of something co-authors Lawrence Kane and Kris Wilder wrote in *The Big Bloody Book of Violence: The Smart Person's Guide for Surviving Dangerous Times*. In their excellent book, the pair wrote, "Be a realist. It is vital to see the world as it truly is in order to keep yourself safe. Test your assumptions regularly, learning from a variety of reputable sources to hone in on the truth. And, importantly, be willing to change your thoughts or actions if you discover that you were wrong."

What "is" already is. That is the way it already exists. Refusing to accept the reality of the immediate moment is an exercise in futility, and something a warrior such as Musashi would refrain from attempting. Accepting everything just the way it "is" is simply being a realist, and as Kane and Wilder pointed out, a vital ingredient to keeping yourself safe. I have no doubt Musashi would agree with the passage I quoted from the *Big Bloody Book of Violence*, as he had more than his fair share of bloody violence in his lifetime.

This does not mean one must accept that what "is" must remain as it is, however. Nor does it suggest that you cannot create your own destiny and future. But it does reflect on the fact that we can only live in the present moment. No change will ever occur in the past, and no change can ever happen in the future. Because when the future arrives, it will be "now." The only actions we can take are now, and thus we should focus on the moment, not what may or may not be up ahead. I know this is getting a bit deep, and may feel esoteric, but realize that any future changes are caused by actions done in the now and are not realized until the future becomes the present. When you think about it this way, the only reasonable and practical thing a person can do is accept things just the way they are and live in the present moment to create future desired outcomes.

The acceptance of how things are really is a powerful concept, compounded when you fuse it with living in the present moment. Spencer Johnson actually wrote a short little book titled *The Precious Present*, which was later repackaged into the slightly longer *The Present*. In these works, Johnson shares how living in the present moment can make you happier and more successful, today. It's not difficult for me to picture Musashi as the old man in Johnson's story.

Accepting things the way they are is not passive. It doesn't resign you to leaving things the way they currently are; it's just accepting that that is how they are in the current moment. It's a starting point in reality, which is a must to create a variation in an uncertain course of events. Your alternatives to acceptance are avoidance and denial, neither of which embraces the warrior philosophy Musashi sets forth in his precepts and writings. And neither of which lend to effecting a positive change for the future.

Teacher:

I wish Musashi had used the term "see" instead of "accept." This simple change would make this precept into a statement that I could get 100% behind and say, "Yes, this is great advice."

However, in our culture the idea of simply accepting things as they are is not always considered a good thing. For example, if the local, State, or Federal Government makes a law that has a powerful negative impact on us personally, then advice like this becomes hard to take. In our culture we are supposed to remind the politicians that they work for us, not the other way around. Grassroots activism would never have accomplished anything if this mindset of accepting everything just the way it is were widespread. There is still that fine line of not wanting to be a busybody, but I think the point is still clear.

Nevertheless, we can still ask the question of context. Did Musashi mean accept *everything*?

My instinct says no.

He wrote this for his number one student, and as such certain things were probably foregone conclusions or points that did not need to be stated explicitly. I feel confident in this assumption because between myself and my longtime students, often things happen that seem like telepathy, but it is more truthfully a relationship that has reached a maturity where words are not necessary for full communication. A quick nod in the direction of some equipment in the room and the student who has been there for years will understand it to mean, "Go get that." The unspoken statement in that question is surmised from the context of the lesson. I don't need to tell them precisely which piece of equipment to bring, because they already know what I am asking for. They have been around long enough to be able to add two and two together. To a beginner, it may seem like a superpower, but it is just relationship.

We could and should assume the same holds true here. Not every detail needed to be spelled out.

In the example above regarding the political situation I described, simple acceptance is hard to do. But in a different context, say that of a self-defense situation, denial of circumstances or actions can be a very big problem. When things are about to go physical, you had better be seeing the situation as it is, and not as you think it should be.

When a person allows "why?" questions to roll through his or her mind, they are not acting in their own best interest. *Why* the guy is about to hit you is largely irrelevant when he is actually in the act of hitting you. It does not even compare in terms of importance to the fact that he *is* in the process of hitting you. Thoughts of "he wouldn't dare hit/stab/shoot me" are also a denial of facts and are very clear examples of not accepting things as they really are.

A step down the ladder is when we not only do not accept what is, but create a fantasy of what should be and conduct ourselves as if this is how the world works. The more you allow yourself to live in the fantasy world of how things should be, the less aware you are of what is really going on in the world that is. To me, that is the lesson here. It is easy to color a situation with our own biases.

There is a phenomenon called *confirmation bias*, and it is the act of mentally taking note of and remembering only those bits of information that confirm our preconceived notions. Information that is conflicting with what we already believe is ignored so quickly that one could even say it happens without thought. Confirmation bias is a real problem because we do not even know that we do it.

For me then, this precept makes more sense if read as, *"See everything just the way it is."* Do not cloud things with your personal biases or foregone conclusions. See things the way they really are, without judgment, without the pursuit of a desired end, and without games. See things the way that they really are so that you can conduct yourself accordingly. You will be happier, safer, and probably end up surrounded by people who love you and love being around you.

It's a win-win!

Insurance Executive:

I agree except for those times when I don't.

Boot is a six-pound Maltese dog, so white he looks like a cloud, so sweet you just have to rain kisses on his head, so funny he always makes us laugh, except when he gets into the cat box. He looks at Lexii's droppings the same way I see a bowl of M&Ms: Yum! Treats!

Is Boot's trait disgusting? Very much so. Is it easy to break him of getting into the box and walking around the house looking like a man with a cheap cigar in the corner of his mouth? No. In fact, I bought a book early on, titled *Training your Maltese*, and in one chapter the veteran Maltese trainer wrote that no matter how hard he tries, no matter how many tried-and-true training devices he employs, the Maltese still can't be broken from getting into the cat box.

So we've accepted that this icky trait is a less than charming part of Boot's nature. Now, acknowledging this doesn't mean I like it any better, but it helps—a little. Is there anything I can do? Sure, I can make an extra effort to maintain a clean cat box. It's a no brainer solution but it goes a long way toward helping me accept Boot's natural love for cat stogies. In the end, I accept the way he is and in a perfect world he should accept my role of taking away his treats. But judging by the look he gives me, I think I've grown more in this area than he has.

As is the case with Boot and his sick trait, we all have to do our best to accept things. My husband is a writer and I've accepted that he gets a little distant and grumpy when putting the final edits on a writing project. Actually, sometimes he gets a whole lot distant and moody, so it can be a real test for me to be understanding and accepting, especially when I'm not in the mood to be so. To give him credit, he knows when he's pushed the boundaries and he tries to put on a cheerful demeanor. Likewise, I know when his attitude is starting to get under my skin so I try my best to rein in my impatience.

When we can accept things in life just the way they are our stress level goes down, in some cases, a lot. But if we spend our day thinking about, dwelling on, sweating over, and complaining about the way things ought to be, it will quickly consume and destroy us.

Today we are bombarded with news stories, social media rants, and cell phone videos about increasing tensions between countries, ongoing war, and human tragedies all around the globe. Most often this is repeated over and over until the horrors fill our heads and adds even more stress to our days. While I might not have a choice whether to accept this growing tide of man's inhumanity to man and nature's vengeance, I can be cognizant of how much I permit into my home and ultimately into my psyche. While doing my best to control how much of this I will accept, I also look for ways to help where I can.

This is because I don't accept that there is nothing I can do as thousands of people are dying or being torn away from their homes by flood, soulless armies, and merciless diseases. I can choose to help anyway I can by lending a voice of protest and donating money to help those that desperately need it.

In the end, I will not accept everything just the way it is, but strive to change what I can, and not let those things I can't change destroy me.

Businessman:

Nobody ever woke up and said, "Today I want to dress up in an uncomfortable suit and tie, go sit in a noisy cubicle in a crowded workspace next to people I can't stand, push papers around my desk for hours upon hours on end, and be held accountable for things over which I have absolutely no control," yet this sort of work environment is so commonplace that it has been immortalized in Dilbert cartoons. Most of us in the business world have worked for a "pointy-haired boss" or two at some point in our careers, likely more than once, and while it's funny in the comic pages it's frustrating as hell in real life. We all need to earn a paycheck but most of us want to do it while interacting with congenial colleagues and working on something meaningful. In other words, we want to enjoy or at least not dislike what we do, use our time wisely, make a difference, and (hopefully) leave a legacy behind. Sadly the environment we find ourselves in rarely meets that description.

Let's face facts; unless we are fortunate enough to be the guy or gal in charge of a company, say the owner, president, or CEO, it is very difficult to affect meaningful change, especially in large corporations, government agencies, or educational institutions. This is not to say that progress is impossible for folks at the lower rungs of the group but rather that bureaucracy, once set in place, tends to be self-perpetuating. As organizations mature layers upon layers of process controls, policies, and middle management are put in place to assure that everything stays on the rails, that no one does anything illegal, unethical, or overly risky. In some ways this is goodness, of course, but in others it tends to forestall progress, velocity, and innovation to the detriment of both the organization and the individuals who work there.

While this can be extraordinarily frustrating for those un-empowered by lack of authority or influence, it honestly is the way of things. We may not like it, but we must accept it. Nevertheless, if we pick our battles wisely and work within the system we can often make a real difference despite all these challenges. But, we can only do it after learning how things truly work, how things really get done regardless of what policies or procedures dictate. It's not the organization charts, titles, RACI* diagrams or process flows that matter, its spheres of influence, the ability to understand how decisions are made, build relationships with the right people, and work the system to our mutual benefit. Here's

---

* RACI is an acronym that stands for Responsible, Accountable, Consulted, and Informed. It is a model that is frequently used in business to clearly lay out roles and responsibilities for activities that cross organizational boundaries so that everyone involved knows what they are supposed to do, nothing gets inadvertently missed, and there will be no duplication of efforts or arguments about who's in charge for each aspect of the work.

an example:

I work with a network engineer named Doug, a guy you won't find anywhere near the top of any organization chart but who wields extraordinary influence nonetheless. In large part this is because he's the smartest guy in the room at virtually any meeting he attends. More importantly, however, it's because our current CIO and vice president both used to manage the network organization before being promoted to the point where they reached their current positions. When Doug reported to people who reported to those two guys way back in day they both quickly realized his expertise and came to heavily lean upon him to make prudent business decisions. Since a significant network failure could grind factory production to a halt and get everyone in charge of IT fired in the process, we all take such things very seriously. As they moved on to new positions both the VP and CIO kept in touch with their favorite subject matter expert. Consequently if anyone suggests a change to the network that might introduce business or technology risk the first phone call goes to Doug. If he's not on board, nothing gets implemented. Knowing this, I was able to grease the skids to enable a significant strategic change that improved quality and reduced cost, a decision that never would have been approved if I had approached the guys at the top directly without first developing a good relationship with and tacit approval from Doug.

In just about every company, large or small, there's a "Doug," someone with vital subject matter expertise who wields significant influence beyond his or her official standing or station. This is but one example, of course, but it demonstrates that information rarely flows solely along lines defined by the organization chart. "Water cooler" conversations and other back-channel communications can be far more important than formal memos or meetings. Good ideas alone may not be enough without a champion to sponsor or promote them. Frankly, working both harder and smarter is oftentimes not enough either. Some of the hardest working people get nothing done because they do not know how to manipulate the system. This is why we all need to understand the way things are where we work, teach, or volunteer. And, we need to accept it even if we don't like it...

We need to know the players, understand the game, work within the constraints we are handed, and be able to succeed in spite of them. This means playing politics. If you're anything like me you hate that word, politics, but if you're anything like me that's because you don't really understand it. I certainly didn't. Through long experience, however, I have come to realize that who you know really is far more important than what you know… and that's not necessarily a bad thing. In fact, working the system for a good purpose is a good thing. For example, I once got an employee a well-deserved promotion during a companywide freeze on promotions. I took a lot of heat for it, but it was the right thing to do. And, it kept us from losing one of our top-performers to another company.

Politics are only bad when they're self-serving.

In order to win the office politics game it is vital to take the long view, always keeping in mind what we're trying to achieve. We must be certain to respond rather than react if interactions begin to get heated or our feelings get hurt. By leaving our egos at the door, keeping conversations professional, being willing to compromise, and giving others a face-saving way out we can get along with everyone better, which in turn means that they are more likely to respond to us in kind. We can then build alliances, work our spheres of influence, and advance our cause without generating any lasting ill-will.

That's the way it is in most businesses today. As Musashi sagely states, we need to accept it.

PRECEPT 2

Do not seek pleasure for its own sake

"I can think of nothing less pleasurable than a life devoted to pleasure."

— John D. Rockefeller

Monk:

Pleasures are not all created equal. There is a distinction in the form of pleasure that is being sought. For example, to go and get an ice cream cone on a hot day is a simple little pleasure in life. Rarely if ever do we need an ice cream cone for survival. Similarly, slathering a little butter on my toast is a wonderful thing. Filling a hot tub with ice cream and bathing in butter, on the other hand, is a pleasure for pleasures sake overindulgence… and a little creepy. Being a hedonist, simply seeking pleasure because it feels good, is a bucket full of cravings that can never be filled. The need for more is always present. So, seeking pleasure for its own sake is a path that can only lead to sadness, a feeling of incompleteness as the constant desire for "more" looms larger and larger.

Living a good life is a good thing. Living a great life is, well… great. But the definitions are where the screw turns. It is possible to live a good life? To enjoy a little ice cream *and* some butter on your toast? The fact is that many humans do just that, live a good life. On balance, they are balanced, and do the best they are capable of. But what about Musashi? Where did he draw the line? He was resolute in his austerity, living in the woods for much of his life, spending time in *daimyo's* castle occasionally, and then retiring to a cave in his later years. He clearly was living a monk-like existence yet many monks would consider his lifestyle extreme. Let's face it, the majority of monks have a nutritious meal and roof over their heads at the end of the day. The level of austerity that Musashi lived was harsh and deep, but wholly necessary for Musashi to be the person that he was.

It is my belief that pleasure is an internal choice that everyone needs to make of their own accord. If pleasure is defined by an external authority, the results are personal conflict and discord since external definitions of pleasure are not what truly resonates with any individual person. Audit your own life and seek simplicity in as many things as possible. Simplicity is as you choose it to be. One persons' version of simplicity may very not jive well with another person's version, but that's okay. Each person needs to explore this idea deeply. Find your own path to simplicity and you will be rewarded through the search as much as in the finding.

When you find your level, you will have found balance. The balance between what the world tells you that you must have to be happy and what you know you need (not want) to be happy. When you remove unnecessary things from your life, when you simplify, you will find new and profound levels of freedom. This brings liberty that is deep and personal. Musashi could live no other way. Of course, there are other manifestations of this burden-free form of life. Most religious orders have some form of minimalism on a personal level. The most extreme might be the anchorite sect. Anchorites were people who lived in seclusion for religious reasons, dedicating themselves to a holy site, a church more often than not, and in some instances were sealed into cells built in or around those churches. That, in my mind, is too much.

As for me, of course, simplicity is a vow that I have taken as a Franciscan, but one that is expressed in a modern way. An example of this is that my car is used. Not pre-owned, it is used... It does not have the gee-whiz technology that most vehicles come with today. At one time, while in the deep exploration of simplicity, I didn't even own a proper bed; my couch was where I slept. I lived with a toaster-oven and two of everything needed for a meal—two cups, two plates, two spoons, etc. That may seem overly austere, but let me assure you that there was an unbelievable level of freedom in that simplicity. I'm not in that stage in my life now, however. While I certainly don't live lavishly now, those several years could only be described as delicious.

So, seek your level, not that of others, and express your life as best you see fit. Seriously, give it a try... and watch the world open up to you.

Warrior:

It is interesting that Takeda Nobushige (1525 – 1561) wrote something similar in *The Ninety-Nine Articles*, which are precepts he wrote for the benefit of his son. In it he wrote, "One should not be excessive in refined pleasures. In Shih Chi it says, 'When the banquet is in full swing, there will be confusion. When pleasure is at its height, sorrow appears.' In the Tso Chuan it says, 'High living is like drinking poisoned *sake*: it is unthinkable.'"

Both men seem to look at pleasure negatively, and Musashi's stance to not seek pleasure for its own sake resembles Proverbs 21:17 from the New International Version of the Bible, which states, "Whoever loves pleasure will become poor, whoever loves wine and olive oil will never be rich."

Another Stoic, Epictetus (55 – 135 AD), also warned against pleasure in general when he wrote, "If you are struck by the appearance of any promised pleasure, guard yourself against being hurried away by it; but let the affair wait your leisure, and procure yourself some delay. Then bring to your mind both points of time: that in which you will enjoy the pleasure, and that in which you will repent and reproach yourself after you have enjoyed it; and set before you, in opposition to these, how you will be glad and applaud yourself if you abstain. And even thought it should appear to you a seasonable gratification, take heed that its enticing, and agreeable and attractive force may not subdue you; but set in opposition to this how much better it is to be conscious of having gained so great a victory."

Despite the fact that it's a common theme, I have to disagree with Musashi and the others when it comes to this precept, "Do not seek pleasure for its own sake" and the negativity toward pleasure in general. However, this is predicated upon a person's ability to condition their mind as to what pain and pleasure are linked to. This is due to the fact that what drives our behavior is instinctive reaction to pain and pleasure, not intellectual calculation.

Maybe it's because I've listened for years to Anthony Robbins saying, "What you link pain to and what you link pleasure to shapes your destiny." But the bottom line is I think Tony is right, and that pain and pleasure are the driving forces in our lives. We do things out of our need to avoid pain or our desire to gain pleasure. I also think Tony is right when he says, "The secret of success is learning how to use pain and pleasure instead of having pain and pleasure use you. If you do that, you're in control of your life. If you don't, life controls you."

This isn't necessarily a new concept either, because there is a quote attributed to Aristotle (384 – 322 BC) that states, "The aim of the wise is not to secure pleasure, but to avoid pain." The two have been linked for centuries, and I prefer to link pain and pleasure to the appropriate things in order to be led by the carrot rather than pushed by the stick. I believe it is perfectly acceptable, and actually preferable, to seek pleasure if you have aligned pleasure with the right activities and outcomes.

It's the alignment then that causes a problem, because whose morals determine which are the right activities and outcomes that we should seek as pleasurable? Would we then succumb to a hedonistic society that Musashi's precept seeks to steer us clear of? I don't know.

I'm not an advocate of wanton hedonism, but neither do I advocate following Musashi's second precept on its face value. We can direct our own associations to pain and pleasure and use this force to change our behaviors and accomplish great results. We can learn to condition our minds to link pain and pleasure to whatever we choose. We must then just ensure that what we choose is correct. And I'll let you ponder upon and choose just what that is.

Teacher:

It seems to be coded in the human DNA to seek pleasure and avoid pain. Everyone is drawn to the things that makes them happy, and is equally quick to avoid the things that cause pain.

How could this be a bad thing?

Well, for a start, our senses tend to dull. If it is spicy food which brings pleasure, a pleasure I overindulged in for far too many years, it seems that one must up the ante with the passage of time. I reached a point where jalapeno peppers were a snack and when I needed spicy I had to reach for the ghost pepper sauce.* Alcoholics go through the same thing. They get more and more wasted and eventually find that they need to consume more and more alcohol to get that blissful floating/falling feeling.

---

* Based on the Scoville heat unit rating, ghost peppers (otherwise known as *bhut jolokia* peppers) are roughly ten times stronger than habanera peppers, twenty times stronger than Thai green peppers, and 125 times stronger than jalapeno peppers. Chefs must wear gloves when working with them and use very small amounts in their recipes to avoid injury.

Our bodies cannot take these extremes. We were not designed for that. In my case, I ruined my guts and must live on rather bland, often flavorless food, or else suffer unspeakable pain. For the alcoholic, the liver fails and they suffer a slow debilitation leading to death.

Moreover, indulging in pleasures interferes with reaching goals. The students who go home and study, even though it means missing a party are better off in the long run than those who skip the study and attend the festivities. Keeping an eye on the goal, and working toward that goal every day involves sacrifice. This sacrifice can come in many forms.

In my teen years, I wanted to be a great martial artist. I wanted to be Bruce Lee or Chuck Norris, and I knew that if I were only dedicated enough, I could make it happen. Although it gives my students today quite a belly laugh to hear it, I have no shame in admitting that I didn't even go out on my first date until I was 20 or 21 years old. When my friends were pairing off and having fun, I was the weird kid saying, "No, I have to go to kung fu." It felt like a sacrifice having no social life, but to me it was more important that I was focusing on my training. I had an idea of where I wanted my life to go. And if I got side-tracked, somehow I knew it would mean that I would fail.

Sometimes it is hard to say "no" to things like parties and hangouts and fun times. Each person is different, everyone walks their own path. But, when you really have a goal you have to keep one thing in mind at all times: While you are pursuing that goal, someone else is too. And any time that you step down and decide that something else is more important in that moment, *they will pass you*. And the reason is simple, in that moment *they wanted it more than you did*.

No matter how much you want a particular goal, someone else wants it too. And the way of the world is that the prize usually goes to the most qualified.

The willingness to sacrifice, the ability to delay gratification is the key to achieving your dreams. I am reminded of the famous marshmallow experiments of the late 50s and early 60s. They took a group of four-year-old kids and left them alone in a room with a marshmallow on a plate. They told the kids that if the marshmallow was still there when they returned, the kid could have two marshmallows. Some of the kids just ate the marshmallow while others struggled terribly, but waited until they could have two treats. Years later, they tracked down the kids who were grown adults and discovered that the kids who were able to wait were much happier and much more successful by every measure they used. The patience and self-discipline they had demonstrated as children made them successful later in life.

Yes, I agree with most people that not seeking pleasure for its own sake is a good idea. Pleasure is good. But if we want to live a life of meaning we have to be able to set it aside in order to achieve our goals, whether these goals are athletic, academic, or professional. Being able to set aside wants for a higher goal is part of being a functional adult.

Insurance Executive:

People with fetishes or those with a particular mental illness deliberately seek the opposite of what is normally considered pleasure, and redefine it for themselves with misery, discomfort, and pain. The rest of us, however, seek what is ordinarily considered pleasure in our health, food, relationships with friends, partners/lovers, hobbies, and work.

As a martial artist, I take pleasure in training. Does it mean I wasted all those years if I'm never called upon to apply my skills for real? Absolutely not. The act of training for its own sake, the resultant fitness, friendships, discipline, and the satisfaction of knowing I succeed when the going gets tough, grueling, and sometimes painful, is a pleasure that is immeasurable.

My husband and I dine out often. We do it because it gives us pleasure (and we don't have to do dishes). It doesn't have to be fine dining with a bill close to the national debt. In fact, some of the best meals are reasonably priced, inexpensive even. Many of the food carts so popular in the cities nowadays have incredibly delicious and hard to find food. Pleasure from the dining experience isn't about the tab but about the food, the surroundings, the conversation, and the sense of satisfaction we feel after.

I design jewelry. It can be tedious work, a strain on my eyes and on my patience. Still, I derive great pleasure from the often microscopic physicality of it, the creative process, and the final product. When I sell my work, that too is a pleasure.

I enjoy many things from the perfectly brewed cup of freshly ground coffee, to smooth nitro beer, deep meditation, and a movie that makes me think about it long after the credits have ended.

The commonality in all these things is the moment, that is, being in the moment, right here, right now. If I were to think about Wednesday's workout in the middle of the one I'm doing on Monday, or if I were to think about Thanksgiving while eating sushi in July, or if I ponder my next creation while working on the jewelry project right in front of me now, I would miss the pleasure of being totally and completely present in the moment.

There is no harm in looking forward to experiencing pleasure—as that too can be a pleasurable experience. Likewise, there is no harm in deliberately planning "seeking pleasure"—a weekend at the beach, a finished project, meeting new people. But I don't think this type of seeking is what Musashi was referring to, anyway. I think he was telling us that pleasure is not just in the future; it is right here, right now. In other words, he is telling us not to spend all our time remembering past pleasures or longing for futures ones.

Buddha said, "Do not dwell in the past, do not dream of the future, concentrate the mind on the present moment." Mark Twain seemed to paraphrase Buddha when he wrote, "Don't live in the past, don't ponder about the future, stay at the present moment, now, always." Writers, such as Ralph Waldo Emerson, Wayne Dyer, Thich Nhat Hanh, and many others say the same thing. Happiness is found where you are right now. The past is gone and the future is, well, in the future. Therefore, enjoy and thus benefit from this very moment.

Take pleasure where you are and with what you have right now. Take pleasure that you can read (there are millions who can't). Take pleasure from where you're reading this: home, car, work break, commuter train, or in a park. Take pleasure in what you have: your health, your possessions, your job, your clothing, your family, and your friends. Many, many people don't have these things.

Go ahead and plan for the future and go ahead and reminisce on past pleasures. Then return to the moment and enjoy all you have at this very minute.

Businessman:

Business is about… well, business. A company, agency, or educational institution hires us to perform a particular function, something we're good at that adds value for the firm, and then compensates us for our efforts. In certain occupations such as sales they likely pay us for results, but more often than not we are remunerated simply for trying hard. Done right this is a reciprocal relationship, one where both parties benefit. The company gets good work that designs, builds, or supports products and services that customers are willing to pay for, while we get a nice salary and benefits for devoting our time and energies to the job. And, we usually learn something in the process; maybe even earn some acclaim or an occasional bonus too.

Sometimes, however, it's tempting to lose sight of the professional relationship we're supposed to be engaged in, to let personal desires override our fiduciary responsibility to our conscience and our company. This could be due to some real or perceived sleight, a promotion deserved but not earned, due respect not given, or even out of a sense that the folks in charge are egocentric Gordon Gekko wannabes, so why shouldn't we get our piece of the action too.* As tempting as it may be to stick it to the man, so to speak, such actions are beneath us. We all know that two wrongs do not make a right, so we also know that such thinking is misguided. If we are unhappy in a particular job it is far better to find a new one and leave rather than it is to stoop to unethical or illegal actions that can have serious consequences for our both our lives and our careers later on. Even if we never get caught, however, acting out inappropriately diminishes us human beings.

So, what does all this have to do with seeking pleasure for pleasure's sake? Quite a lot actually... There are many opportunities to take advantage of our companies, everything from accepting inadvisable gratuities from prospective suppliers that bear the appearance of impropriety, to booking boondoggle trips that could just as easily have been done via videoconference so that we can earn frequent flyer miles, to pilfering office supplies, to sexually harassing subordinates or coworkers, to other forms of theft, graft, or corruption. Unprincipled, self-serving behaviors are foolhardy. This holds true both for everyday life as well as for business.

---

* Gordon Gekko was the fictional character played by actor Michael Douglas (in the 1987 movie *Wall Street* and its 2010 sequel *Wall Street: Money Never Sleeps*) who became a symbol in popular culture for unrestrained greed.

Many organizations try to reign in these types of behaviors through ethics programs, policies, training, and the like, but while a company can enforce certain rules they cannot change the hearts and minds of those who work from them. That must come from within. For example, The Boeing Company's president and chief executive officer Harry Stonecipher was forced to resign on March 6, 2005 after getting caught having an affair with a female executive who reported to him.* The company's board determined that his actions were inconsistent with the aerospace giant's code of conduct, a set of policies that he himself had put in place.

Stonecipher isn't by any means the only chief executive who has had widely-publicized ethical lapses. On August 6, 2010 HP CEO Mark Hurd was forced to resign because of, "The conflict between his actions and the corporate code of conduct which he publicly championed in 2006 following a boardroom scandal." Mercedes-Benz USA CEO Ernst Lieb was fired on October 18, 2011 for, "Serious and repeated violations of the company's internal finance compliance rules." Lockheed-Martin's CEO Christopher Kubasik resigned on November 9, 2012 after admitting to an improper relationship with a subordinate. As you can see by these and hundreds of other headline-making examples, no matter what policies or procedures are promulgated by the folks in charge, thoughts and behaviors come from within, from either embracing or rejecting a personal code of ethics and morals that overrides the self-serving pleasures we are tempted with every day, actions that if we give in to them make us act more like animals than human beings.

Cleary everyone wants, and needs, a little pleasure in their life. We only live once, so we might as well enjoy it, right? But, we all know that there is a time for work and a time for play. That doesn't mean that work cannot be enjoyable but rather that it must be taken seriously even when we're having a good time at the office. It is necessary to prioritize and segment the things we do, acting responsibly in all our endeavors. In other words, it's vital to deliver results on the job, our careers depend on it, but it's equally imperative to do our jobs in a proper and ethical way. When faced with a moral dilemma I pause for a moment and ask myself the question, "Would I feel comfortable reading about this

---

* The company was ranked at number 25 on the Fortune® 500 at the time, so this event made headlines worldwide.

on the front page of *The Wall Street Journal*?" Even off the job our actions and interactions with others should be above board and beyond reproach.

A hedonistic lifestyle might feel good, but most of us are capable of greater things. To be successful in business we must focus on the job while we are at work.

PRECEPT 3

Do not, under any circumstances, depend on a partial feeling

"Mixed feelings, like mixed drinks, are a confusion to the soul."

— George Carman

Monk:

On my last trip to England I was able to visit some significant historical sites. A highlight of the trip was when I was able to put my nose inches from the protective glass that covered one of the most important documents in history, the Magna Carta, which was written in 1215 and signed by King John of England at Runnymede. I was gobsmacked. Here I was standing in front of THE *Magna Carta Libertatum* (Latin for "The Great Charter of the Liberties"), an underpinning of Western civilization. Among other things, inside this document was the kernel of the United States Constitution's Fifth Amendment.

The Fifth Amendment is famous for protecting people from self-incrimination. Simply put you are not required to answer any question that might incriminate you in a court of law. Publicly we look at people who "Plead the Fifth" and think, "They must be guilty." But, in actuality, we really don't know if they're guilty or not, we can't possibly know since the facts haven't been adjudicated yet. However, we have jumped to a conclusion already haven't we? Is this right? Is it fair? Is it mature?

Oftentimes opinionated individuals are considered bold, decisive, but that is really not the case. In fact, not having an immediate and conclusive opinion as soon as we hear about something is wise; it's not a sign of mental feebleness in any way, shape, or form. To hold one's decision until facts are known is a sign of having a mature thought process. Further, we need not have an opinion on everything.

Wisdom is based on and within life experience. Actors will lead a scene with a motion and then follow immediately with an emotion; it slows the moment, gives viewers an instant to prepare and then allows us to enter into the emotion they wish to portray. Nevertheless, the real world is reversed from that approach. The emotion ignites internally and then the action follows. Consequently being able to understand the emotion, the information that ignited the emotion, and the response that may be forthcoming is often difficult but the insight can be profound. It involves daily practice in both small and large moments. If you think that is easy I stand before you as living proof that the process is both challenging and full of failures.

Musashi in a short, ten-word sentence explains that going with your partial feeling is a path to failure and regret. Your initial feeling, your intuition, may not bring about the correct response. As his precept so aptly points out, the mind and the heart need to be of accord before you can proceed from intuition to action. It is much like the public opinion whenever a person pleads the Fifth. That presumption of guilt is an emotional decision, one that is sparked without engaging the mind or applying critical thought. In other words, it is a partial feeling. Similarly, a mental decision, one made of the mind without the heart, is a cold decision. It is born from the letter of the law with no gray area, no wiggle room, and no opportunity to consider the context of the event being judged. This too is a partial feeling.

Here's an example: Recently while talking with a martial arts friend he revealed that he was fighting with his son's school. A young boy had been expelled from that private school because he had brought his prescription medicines to school and was caught giving them to some of the other teens. Once discovered, the kid was expelled from the school for drugs. Makes sense, right? Drug-dealing and school don't mix. But what was seen at face value wasn't the whole truth…

The part of the story that clouds the event is that the boy who had the prescription is developmentally slow. He was exploited by the other kids because they said they would be his friends when he didn't have any, but "proof of friendship" required him to hand over some of his ADHD medications. You can see how this obfuscates the moment. After a weeklong involvement by parents, letters, phone calls, and meetings with many who had no real interest in the fight beyond the principle of it, the school's principal remained steadfast with her decision. The boy was to remain expelled from the private school. He was banned from the other private schools in the diocese as well, and since he had violated the school's policy his family also forfeited their tuition.

Did this decision fit with the letter of the law? Sure. Were there extenuating circumstances? Absolutely. But, were the extenuating circumstances taken into consideration? Absolutely not. The principal's decision had no heart. It was all head. And, it was an incomplete decision, justified legally perhaps, but brutal and lacking in the compassion that makes us human. It was made on a partial feeling.

Feelings are real but must be married with fact before decisions are made. Facts are real, but do not suffice alone, they must be married with emotion. This is the world we live in—it is physical and ethereal at the same time. To make a decision based on a partial feeling is what Musashi asks us all to guard against. In the aforementioned boy's case we can easily see why. A good decision is formed from a complete feeling which must have facts and, in many cases time, to let our humanity shape a more circumspect and reasoned choice.

Warrior:

Musashi was primarily concerned with combat, and that meant decisions revolved around life and death. If you are wrong, and someone dies, there is no do over. With stakes this high, you better be certain you are right. A hunch isn't good enough. I think this is what Musashi was getting at with this precept and I agree with him.

This doesn't mean we should ignore our intuition or our gut feelings. We have them for a reason. Gavin DeBecker does an excellent job of describing why we should pay more attention to these feelings in his book *The Gift of Fear*. These feelings can save our lives, so yes, we should definitely pay attention to them.

But I also think Musashi is correct in that we shouldn't depend on partial feelings or incomplete intelligence or information. This is especially true with combat. Information and intelligence is key! Because of a sniper's training in advanced field craft, he could also be tasked to be the eyes and ears of his commander, providing critical information that no one else could supply. This is one of the reasons we trained so hard in stalking and field craft

23

and carried recording devices and cameras with us. Some sniping missions were reconnaissance (military observation of a region to locate an enemy or ascertain strategic features) and information gathering rather than engaging targets of opportunity or providing over watch for troops.

So, while at times we must make decisions without complete information, and sometimes we just have to depend on partial feelings because that's all we have, in general Musashi's advice is sound to seek out confirmation and accurate information before depending on anything.

I entered the U.S. Army during the summer of 1985. My Commander-in-Chief was President Ronald Reagan. It's not often that a soldier gets to meet his Commander-in-Chief, but a few years after I got out of the Army, while a student at the University of Montana, I had the opportunity and honor to spend thirty minutes with former President Reagan alone in his office in California. It was an incredible visit, and one that had a big impact on me. The importance here is that I studied a lot about President Reagan and this precept reminds me of one of the sayings he was known for, "Trust but Verify." It's a saying that recommends that while a source of information might be reliable, it is important to conduct additional research to verify your intelligence and information is accurate and reliable.

Suzanne Massie, a writer on Russia, taught President Reagan the Russian proverb, "Doveryai no proveryai (trust, but verify)." She advised him that the Russians liked to talk in proverbs. This proverb was then adopted as a signature phrase by Reagan, and you can now purchase "Trust but Verify" marble paperweights, coffee mugs, pens, leather bookmarks, and key rings from the Ronald Reagan Presidential Foundation and Library.

I believe Musashi, the originator of the Russian proverb, and President Reagan were all coming from the same place. It's important to ensure you have accurate and reliable information to base your actions, and it is always preferable to have that information before you act.

Teacher:

The old saying goes, "Knowledge is power." Feelings are not power. Feelings are those tender little things that get hurt and cause people to act in ways that a rational person would not.

For me, I would take this line a step further. Instead of "Do not, under any circumstances depend on a partial feeling," I would go with, "Do not, under any circumstances depend on feelings."

The argument could be made that this would cause people to ignore wiser instincts. But if I were to give this advice in modern times, then I would scrap Musashi's line in favor of the one I just offered. Feelings are something that come and go. They change, often quite rapidly. Feelings tie to emotions, and emotion-based decision making is the first step to making a mistake.

I see the Musashi line as being bad advice because of the way that people in our time seem to spend most of their time in a highly charged emotional state. This is evidenced in the all too true joke about "every action having an equal and opposite reaction, and a social media *overreaction*." People will take a bus to a different city and loot and kill over baseless lies told on the internet. None of them are acting on a partial feeling; they are acting on complete feeling... without one bit of rational thinking being done. If this precept from Musashi were to be taught today, it would be a disaster in the justification people would find in some of their asinine behavior.

Looking into context, there is a need for certainty when taking action in a life-or-death situation. You have to be sure what you are reacting to and you had better have the right information. But again, this is not going to be something based on emotion so much as instinct. It is something that takes place in the survival centers of the brain. In the self-defense industry we call this part of the brain the *lizard brain*.

Have you ever known a lizard to get emotional?

Me neither.

Hence the term...

The survival centers of the brain act with the knowledge and experience they have. Make no mistake, the lizard brain *can* and *does* get it wrong and people can and do *die from these mistakes*. But this part of the brain is *without* emotion. The monkey is the part of the brain that acts on the impulse of emotion, not the lizard.

Emotion and feelings cloud judgment, and that is bad in a life-or-death situation. It isn't even good in lesser circumstances. How many times have you watched a friend throw away their reputation, career, or family because of a decision based purely on emotion?

In short, I disagree with this advice in favor of urging people, whenever circumstances allow, to *think* before taking any action or making any big decisions. Humans survived because of our brain and it is a shame to our species that we do not make better use of this wonderful gift. If you have time, think things through… Set emotion aside and think. You will be better off for it.

Insurance Executive:

True, and don't depend on a complete feeling, either, unless you don't have time to evaluate further.

I learned in Vegas to not trust a feeling—Oooo, I got a good feeling about this slot machine—because it rarely pans out. In fact, Vegas is the best place in the world to realize how "I got a feeling…" is meaningless. Of course, ever so often that based-on-a-feeling inserted dollar pays back ten and your trust is reinforced so you're back in the vicious cycle.

That's the problem, and Vegas knows it. When you lose a buck in ten machines that you absolutely "knew" were going to pay, but all you got on each pull was an apple, a lemon, and a peach, you complain you got ripped off because the machines were calibrated too tightly (whatever that means), and Vegas isn't like it used to be. But when the machine shows three apples, you shout, "Oh yeah, I knew this one was a winner. How'd I know? I got a feeling, that's how."

Listen to your feelings, even the partial ones, but don't solely depend on them. The word "depend" means to "lean on," "count on," and "bank on." "Count on" can be a risky decision when it comes to business dealings, social dealings, and matters of personal safety.

Especially in police work.

My husband was in law enforcement for 29 years where there are two rules every officer quickly learns. Rule 1: Everyone lies. Rule 2: See Rule 1. But even veterans get fooled.

When he had about 25 years on the police department, my husband interviewed a Southeast Asia man that another officer felt had gang ties. My husband instantly liked the young man and sympathized with his incredible story of escaping communist Vietnam, and surviving the high seas in a leaky and overloaded boat. "He was a gentle soul," my husband said, "and we chatted for a long while. When we parted, I wished him luck and we shook hands. Then came the next day when I learned the man didn't come to the US via a leaky boat but had flown here. He lived in great splendor in Los Angles where he was the leader of one of the most notorious and deadly street gangs in California. My 'I got a feeling' failed me even as a veteran officer."

For over 30 years in the insurance business I have had countless people lie to me to get benefits. Dealing with clients day in and day out, I long ago developed a feeling as to whether a worker is legitimate or pulling a con. Bruce Lee said there is no sixth sense but rather a sharpening of the five. To be successful in my business, the five senses must be ultra-sharp indeed. So I approach every new case with all of them turned up high, and listen to my initial feelings about the circumstances in general and the individuals involved. But can I always depend on my instincts, no matter how experienced they are? No.

Both workers and employers can be dishonest, as well as doctors and lawyers. If, say, my feelings are suspicious about what I'm hearing, I will continue to investigate the situation, clarify certain pieces of fuzzy information and discrepancies in the stories, and compare the information each person tells me. More often than not while at first the information felt suspicious, further investigation disclosed all the information was accurate, and I conclude the information was valid after all. If I had reacted to and acted out on my initial feelings, partial as they were, I would have set a bad tone, embarrassed myself, angered the people involved, and made my company look bad.

Are there times when it might be advisable to listen to a partial feeling if it only affects me? Sure. Say I need to stop at a 7-11. As I pull onto the lot, I spot three young men loitering near the door dressed in clothes typical of street toughs. I see them check out a customer walking in and then look my way as I guide my car toward a parking space. My partial feelings are conflicted. While they could simply be young men dressed to display a particular style, my sense is they are up to no good. Maybe they will say something to me or maybe they will block my path. Maybe they are about to rob the store. Maybe, maybe, maybe…

My partial feeling, the bad vibes I'm getting, are winning out. I don't have to go to this store; there are others nearby. So I don't pull into the slot and instead head out the other end of the lot. When there are other options, I'll listen to my partial feelings and act accordingly.

As is the case so often, there are no absolutes when it comes to letting your feelings guide you. Listen to them, partial or complete, but don't solely depend on them. Consider your feelings as part of the input you used to guide your path. However, when it's a situation such as the 7-11 scenario, it's better to be safe than sorry.

Businessman:

I see this precept as a warning to embrace important things wholeheartedly. In business, as in life, we often face an all-or-nothing equation, one where if we're going to do something we need to devote all our time and resources until it's done in order to make sure it is successful. Anything less dooms us to failure. That's not to say that we cannot multitask at times, but rather that in certain circumstances that tactic will drive a suboptimal result. For example, all too often in large corporations or government institutions projects are understaffed, underfunded, or under-supported, we take our eye off the prize, and then for some strange reason we wonder why we were ultimately unsuccessful. In the end the project cost too much, delivers too little, takes too long, or ultimately never gets done satisfactorily if at all.

At any given time we are pulled in multiple directions, various projects and programs competing for our attention. This means that we need to prioritize in order to be able to focus and finish on the most important items to avoid those aforementioned unsatisfactory results. Once we complete our top priorities then we can then move on to the next ones and the ones after that. In business parlance this is called portfolio management, that is the application of a systematic oversight and prioritization process that scrutinizes investments, projects, and activities across the enterprise and then assigns resources to them so that the most important ones get done first. We calculate things like ROI (Return on Investment), IRR (Internal Rate of Return), NPV (Net Present Value), TCO (Total Cost of Ownership), and EP (Economic Profit) in order to identify which ventures will generate the best returns for our investments, but the challenge is that numbers alone, no matter how many of them we study, do not tell the whole story. They are not enough. This is where feelings, honed from intuition and experience, play a vital role.

Remember the Ford Pinto debacle of the 1970s? The short version is that failure on Ford's part to invest in a low value part that would have made their cars safer led to the recall of 1.5 million automobiles, massive lawsuits, and a criminal indictment. One of the tools that Ford used to make decisions in those days was a cost-benefit analysis, a very common tool in business. According to the company's estimates their unsafe fuel tanks were projected to cause 180 burn deaths, 180 serious injuries, and the destruction of 2,100 vehicles per year. They calculated that the company would have to pay $200,000 per death, $67,000 per injury, and $700 per vehicle, which made for a total of $49.5 million. This was compared against the cost of $11.00 per vehicle to implement the fix which calculated out to $137 million per year, roughly three times the cost of doing nothing. Clearly it was cheaper for Ford to let their vehicles and their customers burn to a crisp, but was that the right thing to do? Obviously not, but that's the decision they made anyway. Why? In part because nobody was willing to look beyond the economics and talk about right and wrong; they let the bean-counters prevail and suffered mightily for it in the end.

Countless other disastrous decisions are made based on partial data and/or partial feelings. Would you embrace a decision to kill or cripple a few of your customers if it makes a few extra bucks, or would you listen to your gut feeling, determine that it's wrong no matter what the numbers say, and do the right thing? To be clear, not everyone would. Drug dealers know what their products do to their clientele but they justify their actions anyway, thinking something along the lines of, "If not from me they'd just buy it from somebody else, so I might as well get mine..." Even certain legitimate businesses act callously despite knowing better. Undoubtedly somebody in Enron (fraud, misrepresentation), Arthur Anderson (accounting fraud, obstruction of justice), Tyco (securities fraud, grand larceny), Galleon (insider trading), WorldCom (insider training, securities fraud), Hollinger International (fraud, tax evasion, racketeering), and Barings Bank (rogue trading) must have had an inkling that what they were about to do wasn't on the up and up, hence could have acted differently if they'd only had the courage to do so. Instead, most of them are languishing in federal prison.

So, if we have doubts, if we cannot embrace a decision or action wholeheartedly, we are in all likelihood setting ourselves up for failure. Or worse... We must examine our misgivings, our suspicions and fears, and determine why we are feeling them. Uncertainty is okay, it's a normal aspect of business, but it is imperative to listen to our gut and engage in a little introspection before doing anything rash.

PRECEPT 4

Think lightly of yourself and deeply of the world

"There is a huge amount of freedom that comes to you when you take nothing personally."

— Miguel Ruiz

Monk:

On the BBC Television show *Time Team*, a group of archeologists go around the United Kingdom digging up history. A short while ago I saw an episode about the Salisbury Cathedral, a place where I had recently visited during a trip to England. While I had no Idea that they had been there at that point, I walked where the cameramen had walked, where the archeologists had excavated. They were digging up a small personal chapel that Bishop Beauchamp had built adjacent to the larger cathedral. The little chapel, now gone, had been built by Beauchamp and he and a few of his close friends had been buried there. Even though I'd stood at the site I had no idea that the chapel had even existed until I saw the TV show, but here's the really interesting part: While the archeologists were trying to locate the bishop's friend's bodies, they serendipitously uncovered a building foundation that predated not only the Bishop's chapel but also the cathedral itself. Underneath that they discovered an older burial ground that no one suspected was there.

To tease this out; I stood on a lawn, which once held a private chapel I didn't know existed for a prominent Bishop I had never heard of. The private chapel was built on an older foundation from a project that was lost to time. Further, bones were discovered of people who were buried in the chapel that had no documentation. One might make a calculated guess of who they once were, but all records had been lost to antiquity. That's nothing new. Let's face it, history runs deep; and it has no need for your name. The world does not think of you, or me, or any of us truly. You may think of the world, but there is no reciprocity. In fact I'd go so far as to say that thinking deeply of yourself is a waste of time. Eventually, no matter how rich, famous, or important we are in life, we all move from being remembered to being forgotten in death.

Thinking deeply of yourself not only wastes your time, it also makes your ego hard to be around. Everybody has an ego, of course, and that ego is needed to survive. If you didn't have an ego you would die simply because you would take no action to sustain yourself. On the other end of the spectrum is the ego that enters the room twenty minutes before the person arrives. Neither of these egos is very successful over time. Putting your focus on the world, on the other hand, is a way to engage creation in a manner that is far more productive.

We've all heard the phrase, "If it bleeds it leads." When we listen to the nightly news, the focus is about manipulating our emotions the majority of the time. News agencies often have entertaining products because they focus on ratings, since that's how they sell their advertising to fund their operations, but the news becomes valuable to us directly when it speaks to a true threat or opportunity, often a natural disaster, election, or local issue that we need to know about personally. The rest of the time, most of the time really, the news becomes little more than an ego stroke. With these new broadcasts emotions are elicited—simple, direct, easy-to-understand emotions that grab and keep a viewer's attention. This combination allows for a quick validation of our emotions, and the emotions are further validated by jumping to swift conclusions about what we've seen and heard. We think, "That is bad," or we reflect "That was really nice." We have seen something, judged it, and are validated emotionally in the clarity of our choice. A simple, direct formula.

The challenge in all this is that watching and coming to a conclusion based on an emotional response can, more often than not, result in failure. In sports it would be called "losing your head." The emotions have taken over; they are in control which means that you are not. This is what happens when you think too much of yourself. Whether it is the news validating your emotional decision, or the (often) ill-conceived advice from a fellow sports enthusiast, or simply the day to day-to-day emotions that come with your family or occupation, losing your head is not a good thing. The root cause of most of this dysfunction comes from thinking too much of yourself while not taking the world seriously enough. The world you and I all too often live in is constructed around the wrong object, our ego.

The caution that we should think lightly of ourselves is actually very close to what many religions teach in that we should place others' needs ahead of our own. It's a tried and true axiom that comes not only from religions, but also from a master swordsman. Interesting, huh? When you get such divergent origins of the same idea, it is worth review and study. Ultimately, you and I will not be remembered just like that anonymous skeleton buried under a chapel that no longer exists in an island country on a river delta. But, seeing the world deeply and your life lightly is a formula that brings clear insight and a unique beauty to the dance while we are here. That's what this precept is about.

Warrior:

From the Fred Neff and Bruce Tegner books I studied as a kid in the 70s, to my Judo competitions, military years, karate, *taekwondo*, and finally settling with *Hapkido* as my primary martial art, I physically trained and also devoured every text about warriors I could find. Through this training and study, I've come to believe that character is the most important element of living as a warrior, more important than the physical skills, more important than weapon skills, and more important than determined discipline.

It's taken many years of study to realize this. When younger, I was most interested in the physical skills. I wanted to be able to place a bullet down range with precise marksmanship; I wanted to physically defeat those I faced in competition or in those ugly circumstances in barrooms and parking lots; I wanted to be able to use gun, knife, stick, or empty hands to defend myself; I wanted the determined discipline to win at all costs. Fortunately, through all the training, another message seeped through and permeated my consciousness and became a central focus of my warrior training. Not to the neglect of my physical training, but as an integral part of my complete warrior training. I've come to realize, as many have before me, that character training must accompany the physical training or you only create thugs, scoundrels, and unscrupulous denizens with fighting ability, not warriors.

When Musashi wrote "Think lightly of yourself and deeply of the world," I believe he too, as he aged, came to realize that there were things more important to the warrior than the physical skills he worked so hard in his youth to hone and master. In this precept we see benevolence and the true core of honorable character; selflessness and compassion toward the world.

The precept reminds me of the writings of Kumazawa Banzan (1619 – 1691). Kumazawa was around 26 years old at the time of Musashi's death, and I have no idea if Musashi's writings were ever read by Kumazawa, as his beliefs seem to come from his study of Confucianism, Shinto mythology, and his experiences in public service. Kumazawa believed in a concept of social service as the foundation of warrior culture, and among his writings, he stated, "A good warrior is always courageous and deeply devoted to the way of the warrior and martial arts; he takes care not to stumble no matter what happens, respects his ruler, pities everyone from his wife and children to the old and young all over the world, and prefers peace in the world from a humane and loving heart."

I believe both men came to realize what most warriors realize as they age, and that is that selflessness and benevolence surpass might and force when one considers those things that are truly important in life. When your world revolves around service and the death of others and the possibility of your own death, you realize your own insignificance. You look for the greater good. This allows you to think lightly of yourself and more deeply of the world.

Unfortunately, it is a precept that I believe will be lost with youth and only appreciated and learned by those with a number of years behind them. I especially fear this when I witness the constant bombardment of selfish materialism through every media imaginable. Despite the current narcissistic selfie-stick popular culture, every once in a while I witness a young student following the path of his or her elderly warrior instructor, and I have hope.

Teacher:

I often comment to people that they need not take me seriously. I am not a serious person. In the words of Alan Watts, "I am often quite sincere, but only rarely serious." And here I am reminded of the line from G. K. Chesterton who said, "The angels fly because they take themselves lightly."

This is true for me.

Not calling myself an angel, such irony would be too much for me to take. But I do find it easier to get along with other people when I do not take myself too seriously. There are times when I find myself thinking that I know a lot, and at these times I go and look at some of the greats in my field of study and am quickly and justifiably humbled. Not taking myself seriously allows me to learn more from everyone, to hear an insult without taking it personally. When a student insults me, mocks me, or lies to me, or a peer lectures me on a subject he or she knows very little about, I do not see the action as something personal. This prevents my emotions from hijacking the entire event and also allows me to stay more peaceful and keep my blood pressure under control.

This precept is one I can get 100% behind and say that it ranks among the best advice that can be given. In our modern society, so much could be cured so quickly if people understood the importance of thinking lightly of themselves and deeply of the world.

On February 14, 1990, the Voyager I space probe was about four *billion* miles from Earth, just past Neptune. The team of scientists turned the cameras on the probe back toward Earth to get a look at our world from the edge of the solar system. The image captured has been named, "The pale blue dot." It is a tiny dot, little more than a pixel. Dr. Carl Sagan noted that from there earth didn't look like much; but every human who ever lived, lived out their entire life on that dot and called it, "A mote of dust, suspended in a sunbeam."

This thought is humbling if we are the type to allow ourselves a dose of humility from time to time. If people could take themselves lightly, they might be able to think more deeply of the world. People commit horrible atrocities on one another. People kill over religious doctrines, country borderlines, natural resources, pride, and emotions in part because we have forgotten how tiny we are. We puff up with pride and self-importance. We think too much about how *we* look and how *we think* we are judged by others, but we forget that *everyone* has problems and struggles. We lose sight of the fact that our problems are the biggest in the world to us, but that every person feels the same about their own problems.

Worst of all, we hate others for doing the same things that we do.

Setting aside self-importance is a good thing. Seeing the struggles of others helps, but understanding how we are all stuck in this together would go a long way toward getting to a better place. If we were to understand that we are in this together, just maybe we might start to help each other instead of hating and killing each other over what are usually differences in opinion or perspective.

If one looks rationally at the social issues that are thrown at us by the news, they will see that both sides have their valid points and that none of the issues have a simple resolution. Our emotions are what tell us that there are simple answers, but our emotions also tell us that anyone who disagrees with us is our enemy. Rational thought, on the other hand, is our friend.

An attitude of understanding that we are all in this together would allow us to look at solutions of compromise, you know, that thing that grownups do.

Insurance Executive:

America is an individualistic society while the Japanese are group-oriented. The latter prefer not to be alone and not do things differently from others. They typically eat meals together, work together, and travel in groups. While Americans might perceive being part of a group as confining and restrictive, the Japanese believe togetherness gives them a certain degree of being untroubled and, as one Japanese woman said, cheery.

The reasons for this are complex but in short much of it is a result of their geography (their isolation from other countries), history (Japan was closed to the world for over 200 years), and their culture (it's said Japanese are embarrassed or ashamed to do something different from others), which together has created a so-called group-oriented Japanese. In other words, it's a society that generally relies on being harmonious in order to be a unified power to progress.

This might or might not be a good thing but judging it is irrelevant for this discussion. But it does lend light on where Musashi was likely coming from when writing this precept.

America in no way resembles the Japanese culture. In fact, in many ways it might be the exact opposite. America in the 1980s was called the "me generation" and the "greed generation." College graduates in their 20s and 30s were entering the workforce seeking positions of respect and admiration, and spending their money on luxury items. The times are different today (thank heavens the padded shoulders and big hairstyles are long gone), though one could argue the concept of "me, me, me" is back and perhaps bigger than ever. Today it's represented by the selfie, a too often crude byproduct of modern technology. Hold your cell phone just right and take a picture of yourself. Not just one, lots and lots and post every last one of them, even the blurry and crooked ones, on social media.

The self-centered trend has grown to such an ugly place that people now take selfies in front of burning homes, fatal traffic accidents, violent police actions, and in front of open coffins in funeral homes. The subject of the selfie is almost always smiling or making the so-called "duckface," in which the lips are puckered and the cheeks are hollowed. If people aren't taking selfies of themselves at horrific events they do anything and everything to capture the bloody moment on their cells to, you guessed it, post on their Facebook pages. So instead of coming to the aid of people being victimized or in some way hurt, these self-centered people are interested only in capturing the moment on their phones to show their friends.

While these uncaring and egocentric people garner the attention they so desperately desire, it's important to keep in mind there are caring and compassionate people out there. Wherever there is a mob stretching their arms up high to film someone being beaten, robbed, or bleeding out at the scene of an accident, there are (generally) people in the front of them trying to help the victims.

As one lone person, I can't do much to affect the world when it comes to the ugliness of social and technological change, but I can take personal responsibility for my actions. For example, I can resist the temptation to think only of myself to the extent of ignoring others; I can be mindful of compassion and caring for others in need; and I can be willing to step forward, even when the crowd is focused on capturing someone else's suffering on their cells. After all, we're all in this difficult journey together. If we could all step aside from ourselves to respect another person's suffering and to help whenever possible, how much better our small space in the world would be, and how much happier we would be.

Buddha said, "Thousands of candles can be lighted from a single candle, and the life of the candle will not be shortened."

Nothing is hurt but much is gained by thinking of others.

Businessman:

Business often gets slammed as being beholden solely to their shareholders, chasing after the almighty dollar without giving a good damn about their employees or their impact on their community or the world. May Day rioters, free trade protestors, and the like may be misguided in their approach, but in some ways that do have a point... While we are in business to make money, we must do it in a moral and ethical manner.

It is vital to understand that businesses are not faceless conglomerates; they are collections of people who make personal decisions and take individual actions at all levels throughout the organization on any given day. Added together these individual choices drive the way in which the business performs its work, manages its employee base, governs its supply chain, and interacts with the larger community. That means that this is personal. It's not somebody at the top's problem. It's not our boss's problem. It's not our coworker's problem. It is our problem, yours and mine... And our solution. Every day the decisions we make, however big or small, impact the operations of our business and thereby the larger community as a whole.

Thinking deeply on the world in this context, therefore, means at minimum being certain to treat one's suppliers, customers, and employees right. This is not only the ethical thing to do but also a strategy that can pay off over the long run. Studies consistently demonstrate that consumers would rather spend their hard earned money at establishments that act in a socially responsible way as opposed to buying from ones that do not. This includes companies that won't work with foreign suppliers who violate child labor laws, those that embrace "green" manufacturing, those that acquire Fair Trade certifications, and those that only source sustainable products or buy local ingredients, among other factors... In fact, putting their money where their morals are, many folks are willing to pay a premium for products or services that are produced in an ethical and responsible way.*

---

* For example, Nielsen's 2014 global survey of 30,000 consumers in 60 countries on Corporate Social Responsibility shows that 55 percent of consumers are willing to pay more for products and services that come from companies that are committed to positive social and environmental impact. The Asia-Pacific region led with 64 percent followed by Latin America (63 percent) and Middle East/Africa (63 percent) while North America and Europe come in at 42 and 40 percent, respectively.

By taking the larger view we not only do the right things we also grow our businesses in the process. That's all goodness, but the concepts of right and wrong in business oftentimes get muddled through ignorance, politics, or short-term thinking. For example, consider the issue of "outsourcing," something that has come up in the last few national elections in the United States. Politicians and pundits assume that the term outsourcing means sending US jobs overseas, but they are incorrect. Outsourcing simply means buying products or services that we cannot or will not make ourselves from somebody else. The supplier could be anywhere. Since nobody can do everything, businesses buy stuff all the time, things like office supplies, computers, software, building maintenance, vehicles, tools, equipment, cafeteria services, raw materials, precious metals, and the like. Offshoring is actually the term they're thinking of; it means acquiring work from another country.

More important than terminology, however, we need to take a step back and ask ourselves, "What's wrong with this picture?" Is hiring somebody in another country to provide products or services for us inherently a bad thing? Are we entitled to certain jobs simply because we were born in the United States (or wherever we happen to live), even if others can do it better, faster, cheaper, or more innovatively? Establishing a supply chain in an underdeveloped foreign country can mean helping to establish and grow an infrastructure there that leads to clean water, education, and opportunities for folks who could never expect a better life on their own. What's so bad about that? In most instances there are plenty of other activities that can or must be done in house by our employees on our premises, so in growing our business we can help provide jobs for everyone who is willing to work, not just in our home country but all around the world (assuming we're big enough, of course).

Nike, for example, is a paragon of sustainable manufacturing. While their headquarters is in Beaverton, Oregon they have more than 780 factories that employee over a million people around the world who build more than 500,000 different products for them. This is in addition to approximately 48,000 direct-hire employees. To keep tabs on their supply chain they rate every supplier using a Sourcing & Manufacturing Sustainability Index (SMSI) that evaluates labor conditions, health and safety, energy usage, carbon footprint, lean manufacturing capabilities, and environmental sustainability to achieve a score of red, yellow, bronze, silver, or gold (from worst to best along the continuum). According to their code of conduct, Nike only acquires products from factories that are able achieve a minimum bronze standard SMSI on that scale. This means among other things that labor is voluntary, nondiscriminatory, and that subcontractor employees are all at least sixteen years of age, compensation is paid timely, facilities are safe and healthy, and the environmental impact of operations is minimized.

So, we truly do need to think lightly on ourselves and deeply on the world. How can we make our businesses grow by doing a good thing? How can we make a lot of money for ourselves and our stakeholders in a morally and ethically appropriate way? And, how do we define "good" in the global context? In this fashion Musashi's fourth precept should be a beacon for businesspeople everywhere, one that shows us the way to a better future for both ourselves and the rest of humanity.

PRECEPT 5

Be detached from desire your whole life

> "Man is the only animal whose desires increase as they are fed; the only animal that is never satisfied."
>
> — Henry George

Monk:

Over the centuries countless sages have advocated detachment from desire in an attempt to raise humanity above our baser instincts. For example, the Desert Fathers were the earliest recorded Christian monastic order. Living in the Egyptian desert around 270 AD, their goal was to separate themselves from worldly yearnings so as to focus more clearly on the divine. This, of course, conjures up the images of gray-bearded holy men living in caves or on mountaintops disassociated from the world. In reality that sort of thing doesn't happen very much. These early monastics may have set themselves apart from desire as much as possible, but they still had a community. The Desert Fathers did spend large amounts of time in solitude but they also spent time visiting one another, counseling each another and, of course, celebrating communal worship. Their existence was solitary, but far from lonely.

As you can see there is a distinction here. Being detached from desires is clearly a good thing, but being detached from the community of your fellow man is not. That mistake should never be made. Being hard to read or emotionally inaccessible is not a detachment from desire, it is a weak man or woman's imitation of detachment. The idea of being the loner, one who walks a solitary path, is inaccessible, has no relationships, and sports an unbreakable exterior shell is anathema. Humans are social animals, so self-selected outcasts aren't strong; they simply wear masks that hide their internal weaknesses.

Being a loner may be an immature way of expressing yourself, but it is a popular one. Many songs targeted at teenagers, especially young men, have the "I walk alone" teen angst theme. It sells a lot of records, but this is true of far more than music. The icon of the lone warrior has been made pervasive in movies and books as well. Inigo Montoya, Lone Wolf McQuade, The Man with No Name, The Bride (Beatrix Kiddo from Kill Bill), all legends of cinema. The singular man or woman, the avenger, the bringer of justice, the outsider who is smart, strong, and in control, this is an idea that has gone viral in the vernacular of today's youth. Nevertheless, these men and women are all cartoons. They are symbols and should not be mistaken for complete, well-rounded, or real individuals. To have very few desires is a characteristic of personal control few people ever experience. However, in attempting to express that ideal we must be wary of cutting ourselves off from humanity. The human experience is a communal one, it always has been, and always will be one of grouping and self-selection.

That covers the detachment part of Musashi's precept, but let's focus on the desire half of the equation too for bit. The word desire is almost always used with a sexual undertone in the west. The word denotes juiciness, an emotion that if given half a chance would break its lease, just simmering under the topic. Listen to these two statements: (1) "I really want this job," and (2) "I really desire this job." One statement is of the gut, while the other one is of the loins. Musashi is admonishing us to control both and I must say that I agree with his sentiment.

Musashi himself clearly had agendas, most of which were self-serving. He must have had wants and desires too. But, the discipline that he demonstrated early on and carried throughout his life showed that he had a great deal of control over his wants and desires. In fact, Musashi was almost machine-like in his endeavors, fighting, and killing for whatever side happened to suit his needs at the time with no discernible allegiance to faith, family, or friends. Nevertheless, Musashi distinguished himself from the aforementioned icons of the dangerous loner, the wild-west gunslinger, or masterless *ronin* who wandered the land needing little in the way of possessions. Musashi's human contact was utilitarian. In real life Musashi gathered disciples and passed on his fighting style, his artwork, and his writings. In fact, he did just what the Desert Fathers did, but in a different way.

We would do well to follow this example. By controlling our desires we escape the random path, more easily chart the course of our life to meet whatever destiny we have in mind. It's a great precept, and of course, a challenging one.

Warrior:

To be detached from desire, or any strong feelings of wanting to have something or wishing for something to happen, aligns with the philosophic approach of stoicism that Musashi seemed to embrace and definitely encouraged others to follow. It's not surprising, as many self-made men on the battlefield had to confront obstacles and struggle to overcome them, leading to a more stoic philosophy for living. Marcus Aurelius (121 – 180 AD), the Roman Emperor who is considered one of the most important stoic philosophers, had similar beliefs on desire. In his opinion, to desire was to be permanently disappointed and disturbed, since everything we desire in this world is empty, corrupt, and paltry. Aurelius believed death was desirable because it would mark and end to all desires. Both men seemed to believe in stoic ideas revolving around the denial of emotion.

I'm not certain that I agree with being detached from desire as much as I believe in the importance of controlling one's emotions. I'm not totally convinced that all desire is negative and leads to a permanent state of disappointment, but I do believe that desire has led many down the wrong path with disappointing results when not controlled. For the warrior, controlling emotions, especially those such as fear and panic, is extremely important. Fear can cause a person to freeze and be unable to act, resulting in death for themselves or members of their team. When people panic, they make mistakes, also often resulting in death. I understand that this is not what Musashi was writing about with the above precept on desire, but I feel it is a much more important concept that he should have addressed.

The warrior trains so that he or she won't freeze and be affected by panic in the time of emergency. Through scenario training, we find that stress inoculation reduces response time and freezing when faced with life and death situations. To survive, the warrior learns to keep emotions in check and remain calm and steadfast regardless of circumstances. It's not that the warrior doesn't feel fear, but rather that the warrior controls it and does what is required in the face of fear. No matter how much external events fluctuate, no matter what the threat or emergency, the warrior controls his or her emotions so that the situation at hand can be dealt with appropriately.

This is obviously the ideal and not something that is always attained by everyone who draws a sword or carries a gun.* I wonder if Musashi's advice to be detached from desire your whole life is a way to train to control all emotions. Maybe being detached from desire is Musashi's way of controlling emotions hence controlling oneself. Maybe it was a precursor to controlling fear and panic. And maybe I'm just reaching for something that wasn't really there in Musashi's original thoughts and writing. I don't know for sure…

What I do know is this. Controlling emotions, especially those of fear and panic, is a crucial skill for the warrior. Training can help one develop this, and being detached from desire may be a mental discipline and form of training to assist with the development of this skill. So while I don't necessarily agree that all desire is negative, I do believe that regularly detaching yourself from desire is a mental training that helps with discipline and may help with the controlling of other emotions. This control is a worthy goal for any warrior.

Teacher:

In the West, people tend to think only of things of a sexual nature when the word *desire* is used, however Musashi was a Buddhist. However devout he was or was not I cannot say, but he was raised in that culture and as such was undoubtedly influenced by the Buddhist tenets. In Buddhism, desire is more-or-less a want of *anything*, not just sex. The basic idea is that desire leads to suffering when we start to feel sorry for ourselves over what *we do not have*. In this sense, the suffering is the product of our own desire for things we are unable to attain, and as such, it is *our own action* of desire that brought about our suffering. There is also the factor of the way we can seem to be owned by the things that we are attached to.

That said, I still have to disagree with this precept.

It was a desire for flight that brought about the airplane. If everyone were content with what *is*, then the airplane would not

---

* Of course, not all who draw a sword or carry a gun are warriors.

have come to be. Automobiles, same thing. You name it: internet, smartphones, satellite televisions, home computers, videogames, touch-screens, typewriters, mechanical pencils, toothbrushes with those little tongue-scraper thingies on the back, the Hubble Space Telescope, microwave ovens, microwave popcorn, toaster ovens, fire extinguishers, sliced bread, pressure cookers, MP3 players—everything you see around you is the result of the desire someone or some group of people had to make it happen.

Additionally, in the martial arts, a person has to *want*. That is, they have to *desire* to reach that next rank, or learn that *kata*, perform the next technique, or they will never be successful. I tell students all of the time that I can teach them applications until I fall over dead, but they have to supply the *heart*. They have to have that will, that desire, that inner spark that *drives* them to be the *best* that they can be.

The people who lack desire tend to be a lot less successful in the things that they attempt. Those who have that desire are very often the leaders of their field. You don't have to wonder if they are successful, because even people outside of their chosen field know the names of these people. You do not have to be a fan of boxing to have heard of Muhammad Ali, or a fan of martial arts or action movies to know who Chuck Norris is. It isn't necessary to follow basketball to know of Michael Jordan. Without anything above a superficial knowledge of their field, I bet you know about Bill Gates, Steve Jobs, and Mark Zuckerberg.

These people are seen as *specially gifted*. But in reality they had two things that set them apart in each case—work ethic and a desire to be the best. They *wanted* to do what they did, but they were also willing to put in more time and to work harder to be better than their competition.

Desire is that spark that sets these people apart.

Uncontrolled *lust*, sure, that is a bad thing. But desire, properly defined, is not. In the proper sense, desire is the very motivation that drives successful people to do what they do.

And even though it seems that only a few are gifted with this, the truth is that anyone can do what these people have done. We tell ourselves we cannot, and that becomes a limitation. It is self-imposed, but it is a limitation nonetheless. We also let others tell us that we are not good enough, not smart enough, not good-looking enough, and we start to believe it.

But if we shut out the negative voices, we can start to see progress and move ahead toward what we desire. And if we are being honest here, no one really wants to be mediocre. It is quite natural for people to want to be the best at whatever it is that they do. It is rather uncommon that they follow through on this want, but the desire still exists, waiting to be used.

When desire is understood to be more than something sexual, and when it is understood to be the very *spark* that ignites the fire of ingenuity and innovation, it can be seen as a very good thing and something that we really depend on.

Insurance Executive:

There is desire and there is desire so overwhelming, so all-consuming, so over-attached to the thing on which it's focused, it becomes physically, mentally, and spiritually dangerous to the one desiring.

There is nothing wrong with desire. It could be argued that wanting and wishing are powerful motives to help us do the very best for our family, our friends, and ourselves. I desire to be promoted at work because it would provide me with fresh stimulation, better my family's financial situation, and enable me to contribute to more of the causes I believe in. I desire to pass my next martial arts belt exam because it will show me that I'm on the right track, encourage me to continue do my best, and allow me to train with advanced students who will challenge me. I desire to be the best partner to my husband because I want our marriage to continue to be the joy that it is. Lastly, I desire to give my best to my fitness, intellectual and creative pursuits, and my spiritual life. I believe these kinds of desires are healthy and beneficial.

But to be over attached to any of them can be ruinous. For example, if my desire to be promoted at work drives me to backstab, claim credit for work or ideas that aren't mine, or in any other way falsify myself to that end, I risk losing the employee I want to be. Likewise, if my desire to earn the next belt in the martial arts leads me to "kiss up" to my instructor, ridicule other students, claim credit for work around the school I didn't do, or falsify whatever else I deem necessary to make myself recognized, I risk losing the very martial artist I want to be. If in my desire to be the best partner to my husband, I purposely demean his efforts to do the same for me, or I compete on some level to make it appear I'm the only one putting in the effort for our marriage, I risk losing my partner in life and I risk losing the person I want to be for him. Lastly, if in my effort to be the best I can be, I falsify my achievements to others, I risk lying to myself and ultimately living a life based on falsehood.

When desire becomes all-encompassing and I hurt others in my mindless zeal to achieve these things, I lose my compassion, honesty, integrity, and my power. What is my power? It's a combination of my self-control, dignity, love for others, restraint, and sense of civility. These powerful qualities can be lost when a desire is so demanding it destroys everything I want to achieve and the reasons I wanted to achieve them—the betterment of my family, my friends, and myself.

To be overly attached is to live in fear that what I desire will never happen. Then fear only makes me desire it more. In other words, by fearing I won't attain what I want, I will want it more, only to fear not attaining it.

The solution? Follow the middle path. Musashi's disciplined life and spiritual path were set in a culture and time vastly remote from ours today, so detachment from desire might have been possible then, though I have my doubts. Or, might he have written the precept as a goal one should strive for; its value being in the struggle. Perhaps he saw this striving to follow the precept the same way that people who meditate strive to continually bring their wandering minds back to the present.

Businessman:

Being detached from desire might be admirable in those who seek an ascetic lifestyle, but for most of us the world simply doesn't work that way. Think about it. What motivates us to get out of bed every morning, navigate rush hour traffic, show up at work on time, and devote our time and energies toward our career? Even if we work for a non-profit institution or charitable foundation, there must be something self-serving in what we do. Otherwise, why do it?

Is your job merely a way to pay the bills or is there something more? Do you derive a sense of accomplishment or self-worth from what you do? Are you trying to change the world, perhaps succeeding? Are you in it to build your personal brand, for the acclaim, the promotions? Does international travel, a corner office, or a healthy per diem check turn your crank? Or, are you more of a people-person, someone who thrives in a group setting? Do you find that mentoring and coaching others gives you a sense of fulfillment far greater than anything you could accomplish by yourself? Ask a million people and we will likely get a million different reasons, such things are deeply personal, but everybody has one of them… Whatever drives us, it's a pretty safe bet that were it not for some sense of desire we wouldn't show up at the office every morning, especially if we're not the owner or chief executive officer of the company and maybe not even then. After all, they call it work because it takes effort. It's not always fun…

So, why do we do stuff if it's not pleasurable then? There's a fundamental hypothesis that underlies modern economic theory, the supposition that people tend to act in their own enlightened self-interest.* Perhaps not all people behave that way at all times, drug addicts and those on a weekend bender come to mind by way of example, but this assumption tends to hold true for the preponderance of people in the world. In a free market this collection of individual desires translates into collective benefit for all, as those who want to buy are able to acquire goods or services from those who want to sell in a mutually beneficial trade that brings value to both parties. But, what if nobody wanted to make anything to sell? What if there was no marketplace in which to buy? Without desire, there's no drive. Without drive there's no accomplishment.

One of the key reasons that communism failed in the old Soviet Union was that people lost the will to work. They might have shown up at the factory or office place, but they didn't get much done while there were there. After all, going the extra mile (kilometer) wasn't rewarded; it paid the same to sit around and gossip or play cards as it did to work your fingers to the bone. Clearly there were many other factors that played important roles, such as budget-busting Cold War military spending, but

---

* This concept originated with economist Adam Smith when he wrote in his book *The Wealth of Nations*, "It is not from the benevolence of the butcher, the brewer, or the baker, that we expect our dinner, but from their regard to their own self-interest… He intends only his own gain, and he is in this, as in many other cases, led by an invisible hand to promote an end which was no part of his intention. By pursuing his own interest he frequently promotes that of the society more effectually (sic) than when he intends to promote it."

unfulfilled desire had to have been significant since productivity in the USSR was far, far less than that achieved anywhere in the West.*

I'm not condoning greed, corruption, or meaningless personal aggrandizement by any means, but rather asserting that desire matters. Desire to do good work, to earn respect, to take pride in our work… Desire to build a better life for ourselves and our loved ones by starting our own business or securing a better job… Without desire nothing gets done. Without desire most businesses simply could not run.

I'm afraid I have to strongly disagree with Musashi on this precept as written, but there's a corollary that is not only sound but prudent when conducting business, "Business isn't personal; don't hold a grudge." Sadly we all too often make decisions that give too much weight toward emotions over sound logic. This dynamic can be seen in famous corporate grudge matches such as General Motors vs. Ford, Duracell vs. Energizer, Boeing vs. Airbus, Nike vs. Reebok, McDonald's vs. Burger King, Marvel vs. DC, or Nikon vs. Canon to name a few. Competition can be good, of course. It often drives innovation and brings vibrant new products and services to the marketplace. But, blind hatred is, well… dysfunctional to say the least.

Consider, for example, Coke vs. Pepsi. Historically there's been no love lost between the two soft drink giants. For years Coca Cola executives called their rival, "The Imitator," "The Enemy," or "The Competition," refusing to even acknowledge their name. In fact, they were so busy battling each other for market share that they entirely missed the emergence of a promising new segment, energy drinks. Latecomers to the game, they both lost out to Red Bull and have been playing catch-up ever since. It doesn't always have to end this way, however. Think Apple and Microsoft. Despite previous bad blood between founders Bill Gates and Steve Jobs, the two tech giants have developed a much more cordial relationship over time. Apple's current CEO Tim Cook offers an enlightened approach, "Apple and Microsoft can partner on more things than they can compete on. I'm not a believer in holding grudges. Life is short. You're going to die soon. It's better to have friends." Amen to that.

---

* Productivity is defined as the real value of output produced by a unit of labor during a certain period of time. From 1950 through 1987 the US significantly outperformed the USSR every year using this measure. Post-Soviet Russia only caught up with and surpassed the United States in 2009.

PRECEPT 6

Do not regret what you have done

"Accept the pain, cherish the joys, resolve the regrets; then can come the best of benedictions—'If I had my life to live over, I'd do it all the same.'"

— Joan McIntosh

Monk:

Musashi says straight out, "Do not regret what you have done." That is a very broad, all-encompassing statement. He doesn't say, "Think long and hard about what you are about to do," or "Spend some time in thought over how your actions might affect others." Nope, nothing of the kind. Musashi is not addressing the process that leads to action, but simply advocating that we choose, act, and move on. There is value in living in the moment, at least in certain aspects of one's life, and I don't know how much more you can be in the moment than by following this protocol. Nevertheless, we cannot spend our entire existence in that state since we don't learn from the past or plan for the future.

So, let's talk about the past for a moment. There is a powerful aspect of life that doesn't live in the past. The old saying is, "I don't live in the past, but I can visit." This is a fine and healthy statement. Musashi is not suggesting that we not revisit past actions but rather he is telling us to not attach emotion to what we have done. Regret is an emotion and in Musashi's world an unchecked emotion could easily cost a warrior his life. Regret is a backward emotion, it allows us to revisit and though slow reflection make a thorough examination of each moment in time. As a learning experience it can be powerful, but as an obsession living in the past is clearly dysfunctional.

Musashi's utilitarianism and stoicism rise strongly in his statement of how to handle regret. Do you think Musashi would be upset if his house burned down? I suspect not. Do you think Musashi would give two thoughts to the fact that he inadvertently burned down a neighbor's home while mistaking it for a rival's? I suspect neither would move him much emotionally; he couldn't afford the luxury... Or, is what I just called "luxury" an essential aspect of humanness?

In the Abrahamic religious traditions, having regret for what you have done is healthy and wise. Regret makes us ponder our actions, how those actions affected others, and what it means for our relationship with the divine. This thought pattern is communal in nature, whereas Musashi's thought pattern is exactly the opposite. In fact, he turned his back to the gods of his ancestors. He had no ties of social responsibility from any domain, secular or religious. There was nothing to regret, let alone any emotion of regret to work through.

This may have worked well for the feudal warrior, but if everyone were to adopt that attitude society would devolve into chaos and anarchy since there would be no strings that tie us all together. This is where living in the moment fails. Apology and forgiveness are not possible without regret.

These two elements, sincere apology and requesting forgiveness, are critical elements found in virtually every major world religion. Musashi glides unencumbered past these two elements of social and religious action like a man's shadow rolling over an uneven stone wall on an afternoon walk. Without regret it is very hard for society to function as disputes amongst individuals turn to into fights, fights become feuds as friends and relatives take up arms seeking revenge, and the circle of destruction rolls on and on gaining velocity, scope, and scale.

To be clear, Musashi never says, "Don't review what you have done," just "Don't regret what you've done." Healthy observation allows for review of mistakes and errors, how a person might have achieved a more favorable outcome to a situation if he or she had acted differently. Observation allows for audit. Musashi never excludes that idea of learning from what you have done, but he clearly says don't spend time apologizing for your actions or asking forgiveness. Honestly that's pretty extreme... I'm afraid that he has gone full on sociopath here. It reminds me of the criminal who is not sorry for the crime, just upset that he or she got caught.

Observation of an action and regret for taking the action are two different items. Observation is an intellectual act while regret is an emotional one. One is of the head, the other of the heart. To act only from the head, only on information is not being truly human. Acting only on the emotions of the heart is not sustainable either, there must be a balance. This interplay between the head and the heart is necessary for a complete human experience. Musashi may have held no regrets but on a deeper plane he missed many great human experiences that make this life a vibrant tapestry. I cannot condone this precept.

Warrior:

I like to look at this precept in two different ways. The first is to take it at face value. It seems clear enough the way Musashi wrote it, "Do not regret what you have done." Regret, or the feeling of sadness, repentance, or disappointment over something that has happened or been done, has little or no use to the person of action, which is a hallmark of the warrior. In *Go Rin No Sho* as translated by Victor Harris, Musashi wrote, "Do nothing which is of no use." Or translated slightly differently by William Scott Wilson, "Do not involve yourself with the impractical."

It seems clear, and I agree with Musashi that you shouldn't regret what you have done, as it is impractical and is of no use. You cannot change what you have done, so feeling sad or disappointed because of something that has happened serves no purpose unless it is the stimulus to correct past actions. But even then, the correcting of something you have done should be due to it being the right thing, not because of a feeling of regret. Which brings us back to not regretting what we have done in the first place.

I can think of no positive outcomes that wallowing in regret will serve, but can think of numerous negative consequences from such feelings. Musashi believed the Way of swordsmanship was to fight with your opponent and win. Victory was paramount. And when you are dealing with life or death, this belief is absolutely necessary. When defeat most likely means death, victory at all costs becomes much more important and forefront in a warrior's mindset. The impracticality and uselessness of regret has no place in the warrior's mind, when practicing martial arts should be done with their entire being as Musashi taught.

I agree with Musashi on the impracticality and uselessness of the feeling of regret, and that a warrior should not regret what he or she has done because it will reduce the effectiveness of one's abilities. However, I also look at this precept in a second manner. I do believe that those who take up arms, the warrior class, must be guided by a set of morals to keep their power in check. This precept can help define one's future actions by adhering to a code that doesn't allow one to act in a way that would cause the feeling of regret.

I may be stretching Musashi's original intentions when he wrote this down, but I don't have a problem with that if it is useful. And I find it useful to rewrite this precept as, "Do nothing that will cause you to regret what you have done."

In this more forward thinking manner, we are not just refusing to regret what we have done because of impracticality, but rather direct our actions so there will be nothing to cause regret in the first place. I find this to be not only a positive way of thinking, but a powerful way of living. With this rewritten precept in mind, one will not act in a manner that causes harm, loss, or anything else that would result in feelings of sadness or disappointment for having done so. And maybe even more importantly, one will act on those opportunities that arise to prevent the regret of inaction. Wishing you had done something in a past situation is as impractical and useless as wishing you hadn't done something.

I like and agree with Musashi's precept when it comes to the past, but I also like my reworking of his precept when it comes to acting now and in the future.

Teacher:

Everyone has done something in their life that they wish they had not done.

Many people have wished for a "do-over" after certain less-than-pleasant moments in their life. There are some people who seem to have no ability whatsoever to get past a mistake in their life and there are others who seem to have no regard at all for the issues they cause others or the lives they destroy. These are two extreme examples of the reaction of experiencing regret.

So how is it that we call the person who wrecks people's lives through calloused disregard for them and a complete lack of empathy or regret an evil bastard, but when someone says, as

Musashi does here, "Do not regret what you have done," we call them a tough person and admire them?

Regret is a funny thing.

Obviously, regret is uncomfortable. No one likes to experience it. It is not fun to sit and think about the fact that we have done something we wish we had not done. But is there an upside to this powerful negative feeling? Is it possible to turn this negative feeling into something positive?

We do something, we wish we had not, and that is not a good feeling. This is especially so in the light of understanding that we cannot *undo* what is already done, especially if we have hurt someone we truly love. This action may have hurt us personally, or those we love, or those who were depending on us. We wish we had not done whatever it is that we have done. We would give *anything* to go back in time and make that mistake not happen. So regret feels like a very bad thing, and those who want to put on a tough attitude toward the world will say, *do not regret what you have done*. What is in the past is in the past, what is done is done and cannot be changed, so why waste your energy?

There is something very important missing in this tough guy attitude. Something incredibly important, and if we miss it we will have a huge hole in our life-experience. Not every experience that we learn from is fun or pleasant. In truth, we learn the most from mistakes and suffering the result of our poor decisions. In other words, regret is an uncomfortable feeling, but it is also a very powerful learning tool for those who have the strength of character to use it properly.

How so?

Perhaps in a moment of shortsightedness you make a decision and take an action that ends up being a very big mistake. I am using an extreme example, but all feelings of regret offer these same opportunities to grow as a person, in greater or lesser degrees. Maybe this mistake cost you dearly in relationships or damaged your career or reputation, or in some cases all of the above.

Regret is that tool that will make you wiser should the circumstances ever return to where you have an opportunity to make a similar bad choice. The powerful feeling of wishing that you had not done something that you have already done and cannot change *just might be* the very thing that keeps you from making that same mistake again. The poor saps who refuse to allow themselves to feel regret have no such opportunity for growth. And as human beings, all we can do in our short time is to try to grow as people and leave this world a little better than it was when we got here.

Is there a problem with regret? Sure! There is a big problem for some people who go to extremes in their emotions. Some people lose sight of the fact that emotions are to be experienced, felt, and then we move on. The big problem with regret is for the people who dwell on it.

When you make a mistake, you can and should regret what you did wrong. But in no way should it haunt your every waking thought for the rest of your life. Strengthen your resolve to not make that mistake, and then move forward. You may have lost the trust or even the very relationship with people who are important to you. The world keeps turning and we live out our lives. Those people who dwell on their feeling of regret are not learning from their mistakes, they are denying themselves the opportunity to *grow* from the mistake. This is every bit as much true for them as for the people who refuse to feel regret. The person who refuses to feel regret is to be pitied every bit as much as the person who cannot learn and grow from the experience to emerge as a better person. Both are trapped.

There are people who argue that regret is useless because what is done is done. I believe the exact opposite. If we do not learn from our mistakes then we will more than likely repeat them. The result will be the same as the first time we made the mistake and we will have shown clearly that we have not learned anything in the time between the mistakes.

So to me, regret is a good thing when used in moderation, just like garlic! Too much and you ruin everything; not enough and there is something missing from the experience. The good news is that we can learn and grow from what is typically considered to be a negative emotion. We need to be open to the experience and willing to take the lessons offered therein. But it can be done.

Insurance Executive:

"Regrets, I've had a few...," sang Frank Sinatra. "But then again, too few to mention." He goes on to sing how he did it his way. I would venture to say that he didn't look hard enough at his life if he could only come up with regrets that are "too few to mention."

I'm also guessing those words were chosen to make a rhyme, as opposed to being truthful about ol' Blue Eyes and his hard drinking ways.

Writing about another precept here, I talk about the concept of practice. The fact doctors call what they do "a practice" makes me a little nervous, though it's a proper word to describe what I do on a daily basis in my effort to live a righteous life, one in which I strive to be the best person I can be not only for myself but to those with whom I come into contact. Do I have anything to be regretful about in my past? Oooo yeah... I can think of large and small ones in virtually every aspect of my life. Some were people I hurt, paths I shouldn't have taken, and opportunities I missed. Do I dwell on them? No, at least I practice not to.

Making mistakes is part of the human condition. Learning from them is key; acknowledging them to those I've harmed as well as to myself is an absolute. A sincere apology comes with your admission and regret that you did something wrong, and a promise to try to never let it happen again. When done sincerely, the person harmed feels the legitimacy of the apology and it helps both of you move forward and out of the past.

I feel proud when I have the courage to admit my wrongdoing. I feel good about being a fair person and my sense of self-respect gets a boost. The simple act of apologizing—simple but admittedly sometimes difficult—lessens and possibly negates any sense of regret and shame that I was feeling.

Now that I've reached the ripe old age of... forget about it, I'm not telling. Let's just say, now that I've been around for a while, I sometimes wonder how my life would be different right now if I'd taken that other job I was offered; if I'd stuck with my first martial arts school instead of switching; if I hadn't met my husband; if I'd rescued a different dog, and so on. Fun to think about occasionally, but never to feel regret over. If some of my decisions didn't pan out, or I hurt someone, or caused suffering, I try to learn from those things. I also try to learn from the good decisions, because they have much to teach too.

It's clear by the title of this precept that Musashi understood Buddha's teaching—in this case, his guidance on living in this very moment. I believe the great warrior understood that the past is past, the future is in the distance, and what is left is right here, right now.

I say acknowledge your past, including your errors, but don't allow yourself to suffer from what you have done. What does it accomplish other than to make your present self miserable? Apologize to those you can, honor those you should apologize to but have lost contact with, and strive to never repeat your error.

Case in point: On one occasion, the great Buddhism teacher the Dalai Lama was teaching others about rebirth. One student took it to heart and committed suicide so he could be born again into a better life. When the Dalai Lama found about it, he was devastated because he felt responsible. Today whenever he is asked if his feelings about it are still with him, he says, "Yes, still there." They are there because they are part of him. But it's clear that he doesn't dwell on them.

Reflect on errors you have made and work on ways to never do them again. Besides, do you really want past bad decisions to bump into the ones you will inevitably make tomorrow and the next day? No. Guilt and regret are pointless; they are excess baggage that serves only to cause you suffering. The past is gone and cannot be changed.

Musashi undeniably knew that the Buddha taught all human beings should move forward, never backward. To that end, be kind and be compassionate right here, right now. Let that fill your time, not regret for something that can never be changed.

Businessman:

Due to revolutionary new technologies, a global economy, workforce demographics, a patchwork of international, national, state, and local rules and regulations, and ever evolving consumer preferences, the speed of business is unprecedentedly fast, far quicker today than it's ever been at any time since the beginning of the Industrial Revolution. Product lifecycles are continuously growing shorter too, hence the need for unremitting innovation in product and service offerings that can keep up with ever changing demand. In order to remain relevant and profitable through all this churn, agility is paramount. Businesses that cannot keep up eventually fall by the wayside.

While rapid change is part and parcel of startups, for more established companies this can be highly problematic. For example, while filmmaker Kodak has been around for 127 years, the company was forced into Chapter 11 Bankruptcy restructuring in 2013 in large part because they missed out on the digital photography revolution. Today they are a fraction of the size they used to be. Tens of thousands of employees lost their jobs while stockholders took a beating on their investments. They simply couldn't react as fast as they needed to in order to remain relevant and the results were disastrous.

This velocity imperative affects everyone in the marketplace, and it creates a tremendous strain on business leaders. Decisions must be made faster and faster, oftentimes without adequate data or evaluation time. While we must learn from the past and plan for the future, the focus in business oftentimes must be on the now, the things that are urgent and imperative at the present moment or that we believe will be in the very near term. We need to be able to make decisions quickly, oftentimes without the benefit of full information, and move on. In many instances if we were wrong we can course-correct afterwards, but not always, and rarely without cost. Nevertheless, even if we know we'll be able to get things back on track it's hard to "fire and forget," knowing that we may be harming our business and/or our careers in the process.

We can never know for certain ahead of time what decisions will prove benign and which ones may blow back to haunt us. For example, when former Reddit CEO Ellen Pao fired Victoria Taylor, a popular moderator of the company's "Ask Me Anything" section of their website, the user base immediately revolted, ultimately costing Pao her job. In trying to reign in internet trolls Pao wound up in the crosshairs of hundreds of thousands of them and buckled under the pressure. This isn't just a management thing, however, it affects everybody. Even folks on the lower rungs of the corporate ladder can materially impact a business as well as its employees, suppliers, and customers by the manner in which they make decisions every day. For example, while a bad strategy, failure to innovate, or poor product design decision at the executive level may sink a company, something as seemingly insignificant as a rude response to a customer inquiry or complaint by an entry-level call center employee can do much the same thing, costing millions of dollars in lost revenue or adverse publicity.

Nobody's perfect. We all make mistakes from time to time; inadvertently reaching suboptimal or ill-thought-out conclusions hence making poor decisions that with benefit of perfect hindsight we wish we could go back and reconsider. Overly focusing on or handwringing about past failures makes us fearful, however. Rather than leveraging previous errors to grow in wisdom and up our game to take on the next challenge, this often leads to analysis paralysis, where we timidly over-study and underperform. While it's great to have data, to analyze markets, build business cases, and put together a holistic and comprehensive plan before acting, business simply moves too fast for that nowadays. We need to learn to trust ourselves and our team, make the hard choices quickly without the benefit of full information, and not regret what we've done.

This is not easy, but oftentimes it helps to put things into perspective. One mistake is a learning experience. It's only if we make the same mistake twice that we should consider it a failure. In other words, the more we are willing to take measured risks and do the best we can with the information and time available, the better we can become at rapid decision-making under pressure. If we truly want to keep up with the pace of business these days it's vital to be willing to forgive ourselves, our bosses, and our subordinates when seemingly well-thought-out but ultimately ill-conceived decisions are made so long as we're willing to learn from them and move forward. This is not to say that callous, unethical, or foolhardy choices should be tolerated, but rather that well-intentioned actions of goodhearted people should not be penalized.

More often than not it's not the mistake that kills us, it's the way we handle the aftermath. The cover-up is worse than the crime so to speak. The first step in recovering from a mistake is to own up to it, take responsibility, and apologize. The next step is to make things right. This not only means making amends and fixing the problem, but also putting steps in place to proactively safeguard against a reoccurrence. This may require changes in process or procedures, but it should also include documenting the lessons we learned and communicating them to others who can benefit from our experience because they will likely find themselves in the same boat someday. In this fashion we turn the error into an event that adds value for both ourselves and our company.

In business what gets measured gets done. If we want our organizations to embody the kind of dynamic culture that can defeat the competition it is vital to value measured risk-taking and assure that everyone is able to develop the business acumen and experience necessary to do it well. Aflac Insurance has repeatedly been honored at or near the top of *Fortune* magazine's "Most Admired Companies," *Forbes* magazine's "America's Best Managed

Companies," and *Etisphere* magazine's "World's most Ethical Companies." Their CEO Dan Amos wholeheartedly embraces this philosophy, saying in a 2010 interview with reporter Jerry Grillo of *GeorgiaTrend* magazine, "If you're not making a few mistakes, you aren't taking enough chances. You want to make decisions that push the envelope a little bit. If everything you do is right, then maybe you're in too safe a territory. Lot of times, people are scared to make a mistake, worried that they'll be punished. Around here we don't have that attitude. What gets you into trouble around here is if the mistake is there and you don't correct it."

Like Aflac, we must all put in place a structure that rewards those who further the goals of the company and supports them when hard choices must be made. After all, if heads roll at the first mistake (metaphorically speaking, of course) no one will stick their neck out to take chances, even really good ones. Ultimately this will turn even the most dynamic enterprise into a hidebound relic of itself. Conversely, if we set folks up for success, prudent risk taking will become part of the organization's DNA and we will not have to regret what we've done

That's the ultimate interpretation of this precept for business.

PRECEPT 7

Never be jealous

"O' beware, my lord, of jealousy! It is the green-eyed
monster which doth mock the meat it feeds on."

— William Shakespeare

Monk:

Being born with great eyesight is a blessing. I have never known
the gift of good eyesight and many of you as fellow eyeglass or
contacts wearers understand how tough that can be. That fact,
being born with less than perfect, uncorrected eyesight precludes
many of us from many things in life, among them the possibility
of ever flying on a military jet for a living let alone commanding
that aircraft. Getting at least 1,000 hours pilot-in-command time
in a jet aircraft is a necessary prerequisite if you wish to become
an astronaut in the United States. If you are over six-foot and one-
quarter inches tall, you can't be an astronaut either. That's too tall.
A college degree in the hard sciences is also necessary along with
an advanced degree. Further, you need to pass a very demanding
physical fitness test. As you can see, if you want to be an astronaut
you need to win the genetic lottery first, then combine that
fortune with a discipline of mind and body. It's an elite profession
by every definition of the word.

Having been handed a pass on the genetic lottery, and
through diligent hard work achieving all the necessary education
and training, Lisa Nowak became an astronaut. What a high
achievement, earning one of the rarest of high profile jobs on the
face of the Earth, and yet she tossed it all away. Over jealousy.
In 2007, astronaut Lisa Nowak found herself under arrest and
charged with a series of crimes including attempted kidnapping,
burglary, and battery.

You see, by all accounts Nowak was jealous of another woman who was in a relationship with the man of her affections. Nowak drove from Houston, Texas to Orlando, Florida to get revenge. Inside her car investigators found a trench coat, wig, BB gun, garbage bags, pepper spray, and a knife. Even though Nowak used the pepper spray on the other woman, her intended victim managed to escape the attack, saving herself from Nowak's clutches. Who knows what else was in store for her, but it doesn't take much imagination to believe that it would not be a good thing. After all, Nowak was so single-minded in her pursuit that she wore adult diapers during her commute so as not to have to add any time to her already long drive by taking restroom break.

The sixth-century Orthodox monk Isaac of Syria once said, "Passions are like dogs accustomed to lick the blood in the butcher's shop. When they are not given their usual meal they stand and bark." The barking passion of jealousy destroyed Nowak's life despite the fact that she ultimately managed to escape a legal conviction and was allowed to retire from the Navy. Nevertheless, a panel of three US Navy admirals recommended that Nowak be discharged, her rank reduced from Captain to Commander, and that her separation from service be classified as "other than honorable." This not only affected her reputation, but no doubt also impacted her retirement pay and benefits too.

The emotion of jealousy will lie to you, it will whisper in your ear that what you are doing makes sense; it feels good, it is just and correct, and yet jealously is always deceitful. It has to be, because without the lie jealously cannot not exist. Jealousy tears you off of your path and places your feet firmly on a crooked, distorted journey. This distortion does not come from the fact that the other path is bad necessarily, or even that it is poorly constructed, but rather it comes from the fact that it is not your path. You are trying to walk in somebody else's shoes and not in a good way. Their shoes do not fit you. Sadly your desire is so high that you will suffer pain to make the path work for you, or perhaps you will attempt to change the other's path through force like Nowak chose to do. Either way there is no good resolution to the situation.

Jealousy is destructive and like a virus it either maims or kills its host. Musashi, I believe, recognized this essential fact of jealousy and by never engaging in it assured that it cannot exist. It is like a reflection in a mirror; you must stand in front of the mirror in order to see your reflection. If you do not stand in front of the mirror, your reflection does not exist. If you do not engage in jealousy it does not exist.

In three short words, Musashi saves us from one of the greatest failures of the human existence. Never be jealous. Wise words aptly said.

Warrior:

Despite the Aristotle quote, "Jealousy is both reasonable and belongs to reasonable men, while envy is base and belongs to the base, for the one makes himself get good things by jealousy, while the other does not allow his neighbor to have them through envy," I agree with Musashi's precept, "Never be jealous." Maybe it is because I agree with one of my favorite science fiction authors, Robert A. Heinlein (1907 – 1988), who said, "A competent and self-confident person is incapable of jealousy in anything. Jealousy is invariably a symptom of neurotic insecurity."

Okay, maybe Heinlein was off when he said it was a symptom of neurotic insecurity, but I do believe that jealousy is never useful, and therefore "never be jealous" falls within the same rules Musashi wrote about in *Go Rin No Sho* that I mentioned in the last precept, "Do not regret what you have done." I'll remind you that, depending on how it's translated Musashi wrote, "Do nothing which is of no use," or "Do not involve yourself with the impractical." I agree with Musashi's "Do nothing which is of no use," and therefore agree with him when he wrote, "Never be jealous."

Some feelings and emotions can be used. A warrior learns to use pain. It allows us to know we have trained hard, or it tells us something is wrong. Warriors feel fear and use it to keep themselves sharp, and as a reminder use caution at times. The courageous warrior isn't one who doesn't feel fear, but rather one who feels it and acts anyway. But, unlike other emotions jealousy never helps. It is never useful.

To enter battle, a warrior must be secure with him or herself, as well as those he or she is entering battle alongside. When you are comfortable with yourself and have high self-esteem, you don't feel jealous of other's circumstances or relationships. This is one of the primary reasons I agree with Musashi. If you are jealous, you are not secure with yourself. Jealousy indicates insecurity, and insecurity will lessen the competency and effectiveness of the warrior.*

Theodore Roosevelt (1858 – 1919), certainly a warrior, once said, "Comparison is the thief of joy." When you focus on comparisons, and feel there is something else that's better, jealousy ensues. Therefore, the warrior shouldn't focus on comparisons, but rather should focus on his or her own positives and endeavors at self-betterment. Yes, curbing the emotion of jealousy may be difficult, but it is necessary for the warrior to move forward. Whenever feelings of jealousy start to arise, one must immediately shift their focus to their strengths and unique qualities to avoid the irrational thinking that comes with the feeling of being jealous. With practice, this shift become easier, and with an increased self-worth and self-esteem, it becomes less necessary.

Jealousy may be inherent in every human being. It might be natural for people to feel jealous when others do better than them. However, it is a feeling of insecurity and lack of confidence in oneself. Because a warrior can't afford the feelings of insecurity or lack confidence, the warrior must focus on him or herself and never be jealous.

Teacher:

To my knowledge, jealousy is regarded as a sin in every religious tradition. This begs the question of why. Why is jealousy regarded as being sinful? What harm can this feeling possibly cause?

Jealousy causes a lot of harm in that it is a very powerful emotion. Jealousy is a negative emotion too. It speaks directly to our base feelings and the reactions which follow are very deeply scripted in our brains.

People will kill other people over wishing they had what the other person has. In the cases of teens who rob other people of their shoes, it started as a feeling of jealousy over what the person in question did not have. In the cases where people will ransack and loot stores, it often starts as a feeling of jealousy over the perceived privilege that another group is seen as having over the group that is acting out in violence. People will murder over jealousy, as in cases where someone finds out that their spouse is having an affair. They will rob, loot, destroy, and murder over this strange emotion.

---

* Hmm, we are getting back to Heinlein, aren't we?

Never be jealous is an admirable bit of advice. It is harder to put into practice because of the way it seems, for all intents and purposes, to be woven into our DNA. So, where would one begin if they were going to put this into practice? The beginning of not being jealous is going to start, like everything else, within ourselves. We first have to gain control of the impulse to see what others have that we do *not* have, and look instead at what we have.

If you are reading this book, I am going to assume that you have been the beneficiary of at least some education. More than likely, you have had the benefit of a considerable amount of education, but we will just stick with the assumption of, at the very least, *some* formal training in the art of reading. If you spent your own money to purchase this book, I will further assume that your needs for food and shelter are also being satisfactorily met. While I will admit that in the past I have bought books when I *really* needed the money for other things, such as food, I am going to assume that I am the exception that tests the rule. If your needs for sustenance and shelter are being met, I will further assume that you are employed. It may or may not be your ideal job, or you might feel that it is not your *calling*, but you are probably working. You do have an income of some sort.

Here's the deal: If you survived gestation, birth, and childhood, became educated enough to read, have reliable food and shelter, and an income that at least minimally meets your needs, *you are better off than most of the people on the planet.*

Right here we have a good basis to begin to appreciate what we have.

As a youngster who was heavily influenced by anything and everything martial arts related, I was in front of the TV every Saturday around lunchtime for the reruns of the *Kung Fu* television series. A line stuck with me for many years from an episode where someone asked Caine about not wanting to be rich. His reply was something like, "I have work to do, a place to sleep, food to eat, and friends. I am already rich."

I grew up impoverished. I am not joking when I say that we were not poor, we were broke, and had the *hope* to one day become poor. Poor would have meant that we did not have enough money. Broke meant we had none. But I was able to find contentment in what we did have anyway.

When we had baking powder biscuits for dinner, I was *happy*—especially when we had gravy to go with them. The times we had pancakes for dinner, I felt *lucky* because I knew that my school friends would be jealous to know that I was eating pancakes while they were eating meatloaf or pork chops. I grew up in a mobile home in a trailer park in central Texas. We had no air conditioning. As a child, it was hard for me to understand how other kids did not notice the seasons changing sooner than they did. I knew the season was changing for more than a week before my AC-trained classmates. I knew when it was not really spring yet and I knew when winter was really over. They did not. It made me feel smarter than them, which was a rare thing in my life!

When you are able to reach a level of contentment where you are confident that other people would trade places with you, it is easy to not be jealous of what they have. So, this precept is great advice, and while it is challenging to put into practice, the payoff for the hard work of putting it into practice is an incredible peace of mind and a powerful contentment and appreciation of what and who you have in your life. It is well worth the effort.

Insurance Executive:

I probably have moments of jealousy but I like to think not many. I'll tell someone, "Oh, I'm so jealous you're going to Hawaii" or "I'm so jealous you're going to dine at the fabulous new restaurant," but in reality I'm not in the least. I've been to Hawaii and I've eaten in nice restaurants so to be jealous of someone for doing what I've done doesn't really compute in my mind. What I'm really saying to them is this: "I could use a trip to Hawaii right now," and "I have to make plans to eat at that restaurant in the near future." But jealous? Envious? No.

In my experience the thing being envied is often distorted in one's mind. Let's say, Alice, an out of shape woman, looks at a fit woman at the supermarket, and thinks longingly, "If only I had her figure my world would be so much better." Then when Alice watches the coveted woman get into a shiny new Lexus, she thinks, "If only I had that car in my world my life would be so much better." If Alice isn't careful, she will fall into a trap that has caught so many others: To envy to such an extreme there can be no personal satisfaction.

Too often our minds exaggerate the value or significance of a person, place, or thing until it becomes a distortion. Left unchecked, we can slip into an "I've got to have that," or "I've got to be like that person," or "I've got to take that exotic trip." Such thinking can convince us that if we could only have what another person has, life will be grander, happier, and—the biggie—people will envy us. Once acquired, the reality never lives up to the exaggeration-based jealously that so dominated the mind. This is why we must tread lightly so as not to covet things and people to the extent they become amplified into something grandiose, far greater than what they really are. When this does happen, the amplification can create a monumental jealousy that consumes every waking moment.

Consider this thought. Might it be that to feel jealous of another person based on social status, wealth, looks, or skill of some desired trait, is admitting the other's superiority? I strive to look at another person that has achieved much or been blessed with much, and think to myself, "Good for her." In fact, I can't honestly recall any time in recent memory when I've felt even a modicum of jealousy of such a person. Maybe this is because I constantly strive to improve myself, to push to new heights of expertise in the things I'm interested in—work, art, martial arts, and fitness. By thinking in this fashion, I find joy in competing against myself and achieving goals, rather than wasting time coveting what someone else has.

I'm not certain, but perhaps it's been the martial arts that have helped me not to be jealous of other people. I've always seen my training as a method to not only learn self-defense, but also to learn about striving, seeking, and pushing myself. Myself. So if I see another woman that is better at sparring, kicking, or forms, so be it... I have never driven myself mad being envious of another person's achievements in the martial arts or any other endeavor. Again, in my mind, I want to develop myself in all ways, not waste time being envious.

I believe I'm unique. I value the gifts I have been given and the many skills I've developed through my own efforts. I feel good about myself as to the ways I have tried to help others. And I'm very happy with the love I get from family and friends, and the love I give back. All of these things endow me with a powerful sense of self-worth.

Life is simply too short and too valuable to spend it feeling insecure, angry, anxious, and resentful of what others are doing on their life's path.

Businessman:

Jealousy is a vile emotion, one that's destructive to both the individual and the organization in virtually every way imaginable, but also one that for many individuals is extremely hard to overcome. Those who are intrinsically driven have a far easier time avoiding jealousy's clutches than for those who are extrinsically motivated. This is because their behavior that is driven by internal rewards. In other words, they do things because they are self-fulfilling, which makes it easier to ignore what other folks think, say, or do. This contrasts with extrinsic motivation, which involves engaging in a behavior in order to earn rewards or avoid punishments from others.

Here's an example: When I used to compete in tournaments I never minded losing to someone who was a superior athlete or better martial artist. I didn't *like* losing, of course—who does—but I did not get upset about it whenever I found myself outmatched. Win or lose, the only time I really got angry was when I defeated myself, did anything less than my absolute best. In other words, in my mind the competition was all about pushing myself, the other guy was just a yardstick against which to measure progress. Similarly, the awards were nothing more than mementos of what took place. If I earned a trophy that was great, but if I didn't come away with any hardware yet learned something new hence was able to improve my game it wasn't a bad day. In fact, the medal I'm most proud of is silver, not because I took pride in second place but rather because it was from the event where I finally figured out how to beat someone who had stymied me for years in large part because I was afraid of him. Those victories (we fought twice that day and I won both times) were a breakthrough in my development as a martial artist and as a competitor. The guy I lost to in the final was better than both myself and my former nemesis put together, so there was no dishonor in getting my butt kicked by him.

The same thing holds true in business. I really don't feel like I'm competing with my coworkers on a day-to-day basis, even though to some degree I must be since opportunities for advancement are limited, but so long as I am engaged in meaningful work, fairly compensated, and pushing myself to excel I'm happy. It's all about hard work, preparation, and flawless execution rather than titles or acclaim. Most successful businesspeople feel this way to large degree. When they show up at the office and perform their best every day eventually good things are bound to happen due to what they have accomplished over time. Clearly invisible accomplishments don't count so we do need to make others aware of what he have done, but those who self-aggrandize, chase the titles, play politics of destruction, or selfishly put their career interests ahead of everything and everyone else may do okay for a while but ultimately lose out in the long run. People figure them out, discover their true character, and act accordingly.

So, we must all think about how we see the world? In our minds are winners lucky or skillful? We should never discount all the hard work and sacrifice that others must have made to get to where they are today, to earn the acclaim that they have received. Perhaps they lucked into it, but likely not. Over the long term success is almost always earned. Consequently, why should somebody else's achievement be a problem for us? Logically it shouldn't be, despite any emotional reaction we might be feeling.

Think of it this way: It's a significant honor to earn a spot on a country's Olympic team, but despite being ranked with and competing against the best athletes on the planet only three competitors walk away with medals at the end of the day. Does that mean that the rest of the folks on the field were worthless? Does it undo all their hard work and dedication to their chosen endeavor? Or, does it inspire them to do even more, to work even harder for next time?

One of the great things about mentoring others in the business world is that it's a win-win. If our disciples go on to do great things we know that we had a role in their success. And, we've made the individual and the organization better. If we go on to do great things it's in part because we set a good example and led the way. High water floats all boats so to speak... Surrounding ourselves with folks who are smarter, savvier, or more educated than ourselves helps assure success for the business, which in turn creates more opportunities for us to achieve our individual dreams.

So, how do you react if it's the other guy who gets the promotion, the big raise, or the corner office? How do you feel if you miss out on an award or acknowledgment that you feel you deserve more than the person who earned it? In other words, if somebody is better at the job than you are does it spur you to action or drive you into jealously? We all know that our response should be the former not the latter, but in the heat of the moment that can be challenging, especially if we disagree with our boss's decisions about rewarding or remunerating others in our workgroup. While we may not be able to control our instinctive reaction to what we see and hear, we absolutely can and should control our response.

One of the mind hacks I've learned for controlling my emotions is saying out loud, "I'm having an emotional reaction to this." It forces me into a *thinking* state of mind, helping logic override *feelings*. It's much easier to respond rather than react that way. Sure, I might need to take a break, step away for a while in order to get back in control of my emotions if there's something really extreme going on, but that's a more sensible and reasoned response than the alternative. Emotional displays at work are unprofessional.

Don't give in to jealousy. It's a petty and pitiful emotion, one that has no place in business.

PRECEPT 8

Never let yourself be saddened by a separation

"Do not judge men by mere appearances; for the light laughter that bubbles on the lip often mantles over the depths of sadness, and the serious look may be the sober veil that covers a divine peace and joy."

— Edward Chapin

Monk:

"Never let yourself be saddened by separation" is an easy statement for a man who had no meaningful relationships in his life to utter. Throughout his life the few associations that Musashi did have with others were completely one-way, based entirely in what he could get out of the relationship. More often than not he was the boss and everybody else was servile. Musashi had disciples and he was their teacher, this is not a relationship of equals but rather one of subservience and dominance. Musashi's version of the relationship was on his terms and his terms only. Relationship as we know the word today was not in his lexicon. So when Musashi says have no emotion about leaving or being left, it is on his terms. Even when it appears to not be on Musashi's terms, he internally reframes the moment by not attaching emotion to the event.

The ability to act in such a manner, in my opinion, has the makings of a very scary person. It appears that prior to writing down this piece of wisdom he had lived his life this way, even in his youth. An example is the fact that he left the family of his birth, never to return. This ability to walk away is not an act of training, something that Musashi set out to learn, this is systemic to who he was as a person, a loner by birth.

Death is the ultimate separation and Musashi was certainly awash in the validation of both the temporary and permanent variety of separation. Nevertheless his world was very different from our world, especially when it came to death and love. For example, it wasn't until recent history that a long life and a loving relationship with a spouse were considered to be the norm. For most of history there was an assumption that most folks would meet an abrupt end, via accident, illness, violence, or childbirth. Death from old age was the realm of the aristocracy, and even then disease could still slip through the cracks of the castle wall and take the nobility right along with the lower classes. Nevertheless, for most of society throughout much of history dying of what we nowadays consider old age was rare.

Today, almost all of life's separations are against our will. We are simple creatures when it comes to associations. More often than not our associations are formed because we see a value in the grouping and will keep those associations unless forced to separate. For example, marriage was historically more often than not a resource-based decision, one made for reasons other than love. Even today that holds true in many parts of the world.

Now there are many dynamics that went into the historical and modern marriage and not all fit this mold of resource-based survival, but the outcomes without exception are social. This is because with few exceptions human beings are social animals; all of history shows this human need for interdependence. An association can be grounded in many reasons. These can be as basic as providing needed resources or exchanging skills, to something complex and rooted in a deep emotion as love or desire. As social animals we share not only resources, but also emotions. And, we can inoculate or infect each other with emotions depending on the dosage. That's one of the reasons why our Constitutional freedom of speech doesn't extend to shouting "fire" in a crowded movie theater when there's no legitimate danger. This is because a panicked crowd too easily devolves into a dangerous and unruly mob.

Separation from others can create loneliness, and loneliness is a slow, tough distorter of the human experience. There are few people who can be alone and not become twisted in a bad way by a solitary life. We as humans desire each other, and for that balanced life we need each other. Musashi, however, was different. He chose his associations like the rest of us, but he also chose his separations too. And he had many of them. He had the ability to walk away from a situation, such as his family, and he also had the ability to make new relationships whenever it suited his needs. Consequently he used separation as a tool. His actions lacked much, if any, emotion; they were carefully thought out and strategic.

In the end, it is easy of Musashi to say, "Never let yourself be saddened by a separation," because that's who he was, how he interacted with the world. Nevertheless, Musashi's admonishment is a distortion of the human experience and I believe that this idea should be rejected. To listen to what he has to say and integrate this idea, to never be sad because you are separated from something or somebody, tears at the very fiber of what it is to be human. Living a life that does not know the pain of separation is a life that misses a color from the palate of the world.

Warrior:

This is another of Musashi's precepts that presents the way of the warrior as that of an emotionless stoic that shuns many of the most basic human feelings. It's one that I would rewrite as, "Don't let the sadness of a separation prevent you from accomplishing your task at hand." Why the difference? Because I believe that being saddened by a separation is one of the most basic human feelings. Just because one is a warrior doesn't mean these feelings should be ignored or that the warrior should refrain from feeling them.

I can understand why Musashi would write this, especially from a practical stand point. The warrior can't afford to be weakened by sadness. And sadness can be extremely weakening; just look at the cases where people have been paralyzed with grief, unable to do anything, and even so distraught over separation that they take their own lives. The fact is warriors will experience much separation.

The warrior will be separated from friends and family when he or she leaves for war. This separation will be enhanced if spouses and lovers find solace in the arms of another in the warrior's absence. And the warrior will face the greatest separation when his brothers and comrades in arms fall, and he must continue the fight with only their memories and ghosts to keep him company.

The bond formed between warriors during training and combat is unique to only those who experience it, and it only makes sense that if that bond is strained or broken from separation through distance or death, that the warrior will feel sadness. I'd even go as far as saying that if the warrior didn't feel sad when thinking of a fallen comrade, he wouldn't be honoring the dead as he should.

I know veterans who, at times, remember those they lost and experience a rush of emotions that include guilt, loss, shame, and sadness. These feelings are natural, even though sometimes they are almost unbearable. And there are many warriors who raise a glass, with sadness in their heart, each anniversary for someone they lost and are now separated from. This ritual, along with the feelings that come with it, is cleansing for those living. It honors those who are gone. To suggest one should never feel this, that one should never be saddened by separation, especially when that separation is through death, is not only nearly impossible to achieve, but something I wouldn't want to achieve in the first place.

It is only when the feelings prevent the warrior from carrying on his or her duties that there is a problem. The tragedy is when the saddened veteran takes his or her own life over the ghosts that haunt him or her. The dishonor is the unbecoming behavior of the soldier who receives the "Dear John" letter. And the infraction is when the soldier fails to continue fighting after the loss of a fellow soldier. The warrior must still live, and the warrior must still fight, even when those he greatly cares for are gone. That is why I suggest we rewrite the precept as, "Don't let the sadness of a separation prevent you from accomplishing your task at hand."

Teacher:

People often come to the mistaken conclusion that we are *always* supposed to be happy and *never* sad. At all, ever… But, our brains simply do not work that way. The idea of only being happy is as ludicrous as thinking you can only swing forward. When you push a child on a swing there is forward motion, but once that reaches an extreme end of the arc the child will begin to swing backward. Ocean tides come and go. Sound is a vibration, crests and troughs. Everything in life is a vibration of this sort, a pendulum as it were.

Emotions are not really different from all of these. Joy is felt, but after a time we will lull back into our normal resting state. In exactly the same way, when a healthy person is sad, they will be sad for a time and eventually return to their normal resting state.

We may *want* to only feel joy and never be sad, but this is not going to be possible for any of us. Even the most positive person you know has bad days and times when they are sad. It is just a fact of life.

We feel sadness during a loss or separation, it happens. When we try to deny it, we create an even bigger problem. What are the common ways people try to cover up unpleasant emotions? Booze or sex or food or drugs.

The emptiness is still going to be there, whether it was caused by separation or loss or anxiety. You are going to have to face that emptiness at some point, and when it is dealt with there is going to be sadness. It does not go away until it is faced and felt. This is why the ways listed above which are used by people to avoid their feeling always fail in the end. Once you sober up or wake up or crash, the sadness is still there waiting for you. These emotions are how our brain deals with things like separation and loss. If we are going to be healthy, we will have to allow ourselves to deal with these things the way our brain knows how. It is in denying the feeling of sadness that people eventually become overwhelmed by it. This can and does quite often lead to depression.

And what happens when someone is diagnosed with depression? The doctor prescribes happy pills! These medications typically block the receptors in the brain that allow a person to feel sad, or otherwise the pills change the very chemistry of the patient's brain.

This is the exact opposite of what should be done in a great many cases.

If you are sad, feel sad. If you are happy, feel happy. Make no excuses for either state of mind. Emotions are not permanent states. They are part of the experience of living. Carried to extremes, most emotions turn harmful. In the same way that sadness turns into depression, so too a feeling of love can turn into an obsession. Love is good and healthy, obsession most certainly is not.

Of course all of this is assuming the person in question has healthy brain chemistry in the first place. There are a great number of people walking around who have chemical imbalances, and it takes a qualified person to diagnose these things.

In the style of Chinese Martial Arts that I practice, *Hung Gar*, the highest and most treasured form is called the *Iron Thread* form (*Tit Sin Kyun*). This form is very complex in that you have many different things going on at once, five elements, animals, sounds, etc. But for this subject, I will refer to the five emotions that are expressed in the form: (1) happiness, (2) anger, (3) worry, (4) sadness, and (5) fear. Throughout the form we transition from the expression of one emotion to the next and to the next and so on... These emotions are expressed through sound and movement.

For a time in my late teens, I was embarrassed by some of the parts of this form. As I grew up, I wanted to find the significance and gain an understanding of why these features and actions were in the form. When I searched for the significance of this, it always came back to the fact that emotions are like ocean waves, they come and go. You cannot hold onto them. They are experienced and then they are gone. If you can take that lesson to heart, then you do not need to fear feeling sadness over separation.

Insurance Executive:

This is one of those "it depends" precepts. If I'm permanently separated from my arm, I'm going to have a sad face. Similarly if I'm eternally separated from my husband, dogs, job, and a number of other things profoundly close to me. Some of these things time will dull the ache but others I can't imagine not being saddened by the loss, ever.

Even temporary separations of some things sadden me, at least a little. For example, I hate it when we have to board our dogs and cat when we take a trip. I trust where we board them but it saddens me to think our animals are frightened they won't see us again, and they are confused because their routines have been disrupted. (Yikes, I've become one of *those* pet owners).

There is another kind of separation that has taken me until just the last few years to understand. There have been many times when I've met someone, say, at work, in my martial arts training, or in a class of some kind, and we have clicked, as the saying goes. We shared the same ideas about things, likes and dislikes, and interests. But the new relationship was not to last, as one of us had to move out of the city, one of us resigned or retired, or one of us changed martial arts schools. While the end of such a relationship is at first sad, in time it becomes clear we met for a purpose. For example, one or both of us found an answer to something from the other; one helped the other grow in some way; one helped with a problem, and so on. Fate, the stars, God, or some other force brought us together so one or both of us gained. While there is still sadness in the separation, it's made better by the understanding there was a purpose for us meeting.

On the flip side of that, sometimes it seems someone is brought into our lives for the sole purpose of making us miserable. The trick is to figure out some way to make it positive. Either way, it's unlikely there will be sadness with that separation.

One other type of separation-induced sadness is a bit of a strange one. I'm referring to that hint of sadness that sometimes comes at the end of a bad or difficult experience. Here are three examples where I have experienced this:

1) A complicated and difficult case file that painfully occupied my time at work for two or three years finally came to an end.
2) After studying martial arts for several years and after training with incredible intensity for several months in preparation for my black belt test, the day finally came, and I passed.
3) I was given a clean bill of health after a lengthy period healing from an illness.

While these experiences were mentally and physically exhausting, and I was enormously elated to be through with them, they did occupy a significant amount of time in my life. Besides my loved ones, time and my life are the most valuable things I have. While I would prefer to have my precious time filled with pleasurable moments 24 hours a day, it's unrealistic to think that will happen.

Therefore, it's incumbent on me to find value in those periods of my life when things were not pleasurable, even miserable. What did I learn from these awful experiences? What did I gain? How did I grow? How am I better now than before I experienced that miserable chunk of time? Looking at it that way, I see such events as positive. Seeing them as positive, I am saddened a little by the separation of a piece of my life.

Businessman:

Most work is done in teams nowadays, particularly in larger organizations. Multifunctional groups of people come together to create a product, craft a proposal, resolve a problem, or respond to whatever the business imperative of the moment happens to be. They complete the job and then they move on to the next project on the list, oftentimes meeting with different folks from different areas of the company for each assignment. It might be months or years before they wind up working together again, assuming they haven't moved to new organizations or positions as folks often do. Nevertheless, while people may come and go, relationships can transcend the transitory nature of the work. Frankly in most cases they have to because relationships matter. A lot. It's virtually impossible to get anything meaningful done in a large corporation, agency, or institution all by ourselves.

While it is important to differentiate between personal and business relationships, and to keep things on a professional level that might adversely affect our jobs, we are all going to have a lot of relationships throughout our careers, interactions with people who come and go. Some will be more meaningful than others, of course, but thankfully the world today is very different than it was in Musashi's time when it comes to interacting with others. With social media, emails, texts, and videoconferencing it's actually pretty hard to lose touch with those we care about if we don't get so wrapped up in events that we forget to reach out to them occasionally. For instance, using Facebook for friends and LinkedIn for business partners we can keep tabs on and reconnect with virtually anyone anywhere at any time.

Nevertheless, certain things do not go as planned, some relationships ultimately end, and much as we'd like to we won't be able to keep in close contact with everyone. This means a parting of the ways. There is undoubtedly a certain amount of sadness that comes with separation from someone we have grown close to, but work relationships aren't the same as personal ones. Losing touch with a coworker, client, or customer should not have the same emotional impact as a divorce or death in the family. Nevertheless, it often affects us in much the same way, albeit to lesser degree. Consequently we can expect feelings of sadness, confusion, anger, frustration, or exhaustion. That's perfectly normal, but these emotions ought to be relatively low in intensity and short in duration.

For example my boss, one of our most inspirational and effective leaders, recently quit... well retired technically even though she is far younger than most who reach that point in their career. Her announcement came as a surprise to everyone in the organization, but it turns out that she had been in a financial position where working was no longer a requirement for quite some time and the daily grind had lost much of its appeal. When she announced that she was leaving most of us went through denial, anger, grief, bargaining, and depression, all the usual stages of grief, before moving on to acceptance. For some it only took a day or two to run the cycle, but for most it was a crushing blow, something that took them several weeks to overcome. She truly was that good of a leader. Nevertheless, despite the fact that she was gone and wouldn't be replaced for a couple of months the imperatives of business continued uninterrupted. We had to focus on the work, share the extra burden of her absence, and get things done.

Everyone will face a similar situation at some point in their career. If we find ourselves feeling down, a great pick-me-up is to spend time with folks who support and value us, people who can help us work through our feelings and look toward the future. If we're not making progress quickly enough, however, we may need to work with a professional counselor or religious authority that can help us resolve our issues. Don't wait overlong to reach out for help when it's needed, business can't go into a holding pattern and neither should we. And, many enterprises have employee assistance or insurance programs that foot the bill, so there's really no excuse not to reach out when help is needed. Regardless of how well we are able cope on our own, however, we should never forget that even when some of the folks we care a lot about do fall out of our lives, we can still create meaningful connections with new people. That's the upside of the transitory nature of work.

People aren't interchangeable, we all know that everyone is unique and special in a multitude of ways, yet business rarely grinds to a halt over the loss of any single individual no matter how likeable, productive, or critical to the operations they may have been. Apple got over the loss of Steve Jobs, memorialized him, and moved on. Yahoo survived after firing Jerry Yang, Etsy moved past Rob Kalin, JetBlue made due without David Neeleman, and Microsoft made it past the retirements of Paul Allen and Bill Gates. You get the idea… Organizations are comprised of teams of individuals, so when I say that the business moved on in reality it was the people who moved on. They mourned, or in some instances celebrated no doubt, and then they got over it. We can and should too.

It's unlikely that most folks today will face separation with the stoicism of Musashi or his disciples, but while we may be saddened by separation we cannot allow ourselves to be paralyzed by it. That's unproductive and unprofessional.

PRECEPT 9

Resentment and complaint are appropriate neither for oneself nor others

"Beware of the man who works hard to learn something, learns it, and finds himself no wiser than before... He is full of murderous resentment of people who are ignorant without having come by their ignorance the hard way."

— Kurt Vonnegut

Monk:

Rarely do I buy a cup of coffee from a big corporation. I do love my coffee, but it is rare I will shell out the amount of money they require for a cup of coffee when I remember it costing a quarter and still value it at that price today. Nevertheless, the other weekend morning I got up and went down to the *dojo* to clean and do preparation for the coming week. Along the way I decided to treat myself to a cup of coffee from a big, worldwide vendor. In the early morning I was the only person at the store and the staff didn't seem to be all that awake either. I ordered a triple shot cup of coffee (they call it an Americano). That's right, three shots of espresso and some hot water. Paid, thanks exchanged, and on my way... Forty minutes later it became evident that I had been given decaf coffee when I had ordered regular.

I believe that it's rare for anyone to accept the world the way that it is. There's always, couldas, shouldas, and wouldas attached. It would have been easy for me to react like that when I discovered the decaf, let's face it while I like coffee I rarely get what I would consider the perfect cup. So, rather than railing against the injustice of it all—early morning and decaf—I decided that the cup of coffee I had been given was the one that I needed and wanted that day. That cup of coffee became the perfect cup of coffee for me to be drinking at that time.

Doesn't seem logical? Consider this: Was the decaf a nefarious plot executed on me by my barista or was it more than likely just a simple mistake? Was it possible, however unlikely, the three shots of espresso didn't work on my tired mind and body? Had someone switched cups while I wasn't looking? It really didn't matter so I shrugged and moved on. No resentment, no complaint. In fact, it tasted just fine despite the lack of caffeine. Going back to that coffee shop to complain seemed ridiculous to me then as it still does today. I will eventually go back to them to buy another cup as well because they get it right most of the time and they are conveniently located for the half dozen times a year I decide splurge.

Most cultures have a phrase for, "What are you going to do?" For the French it is *"C'est la vie,"* which translates as, "That's life." For the Japanese it is, *"Shouganai,"* which means, "There is no way of doing/going.*"* It's the same everywhere because the mature mind, the one that Musashi sought, understands the moment and moves on. Baggage need not be brought with you into the future. That's the mature way of things, but there's an opposite side too. Proclaiming oneself a victim and railing loudly and to everyone who will listen the litany of all the evils that have befallen you has become a fashionable pastime in popular culture. Nevertheless, gaining or attempting to gain power by thinking of yourself as a victim is a profound act of hubris.

Being a victim is the farthest thing from accepting things as they are. To be angry at the world for what it does gives us a feeling of frustration or anger and those emotions validate the lower consciousness. It's like the body shouting, "I feel therefore I am!" Learning how to accept the world for what it is, on the other hand, makes your thoughts shift away from the realm of victimhood. There are real victims in the world, without question, but the power lies in the understanding of what is real and what is not rather than in finding validation from your troubles from your peers. Once reality is acknowledged, it can be dealt with.

Sometimes reality is incomprehensibly cruel, stomach-turning brutal, and utterly horrific, but it's still reality. Here's an example:

---

* *Shouganai* is actually a shortened or slang way of saying *shiyou ga nai*. Directly translated it means, "There is no way of doing/going," and presents the idea of "it can't be helped" or "nothing can be done."

Gary Ridgeway, the infamous "Green River Killer," was convicted of murdering 48 women in Washington State. He confessed to killing even more and even admitted to fornicating with some of the corpses. Ridgeway agreed to a plea bargain when the DNA evidence presented at his trial was conclusively nailed down proving his guilt. In doing so he saved his life, though he will be locked in prison for the rest of his existence without any possibility of parole. His negotiation for the life sentence was made possible because he agreed to help authorities find the bodies of those young women still missing who in all likelihood would never be found without his assistance as part of his plea bargain.

Ridgeway remained essentially emotionless during his entire trial. At the sentencing that took place after his plea bargain the judge allowed his victim's family members to address Ridgeway in the courtroom. That moment was awful. One after another the families came forward and told Ridgeway about their losses, about the pain and devastation that he had brought on them. They told him about their daughters, sisters, and mothers who were gone forever, taken in the most violent and horrible manner. They put humanity to the women who Ridgeway had seen as objects. The killer sat silently, taking in every bit of vitriol that was thrown at him. He listened to people angrily wishing the worst for him, long painful suffering, and more.

Then one man stepped forward. He stood in front of the murderer who had killed his loved one and said, "Mr. Ridgeway. There are people here who hate you. I am not one of them. You have made it difficult to live up to what I believe, what God says to do… and that is to forgive. You are forgiven sir."

Ridgeway cried.

The man who forgave a serial killer now carries no resentment. Resentment and complaint are easy. But stepping into the realm of forgiveness over a murdered child, an almost incompressible act, makes the waving off of a bad cup of coffee pale in comparison. From the perspective where I stand, this is the only way, sometimes hard, sometimes minor. So again I agree with Musashi. And, again I agree for different reasons. I believe Musashi comes from a position of utilitarianism, I from a spiritual one, yet we both appear to arrive at the same place.

Carry no resentment. Forgive.

Warrior:

This precept is similar to the advice given by Daidoji Yuzan (1639 – 1730) in the *Budoshoshinshu*, a collection of essays he wrote before his death that attempted to address the true meaning of what it meant to be a member of the warrior class and the paradox of that class' existence during times of peace. In William Scott Wilson's translation, *Budoshoshinshu: The Warrior's Primer of Daidoji Yuzan*, he titled the forty-second essay, "Even If One's Stipend Is Diminished He Should Make No Complaint." This section begins, "There will likely be a time when the lord whom a warrior is serving may incur a large expense which causes problems for the clan's financial administration and disrupts normal operations. The lord may wish to borrow a certain sum from the stipends ordinarily accorded to the clan's retainers for a few years. Regardless of how much the amount may be, one should humbly comply and never let even a hint of complaint slip out in his conversations with wife and children, much less in front of others. To do otherwise is not the basic intention of a warrior, and is something to be avoided at all costs."

This is a precept that I definitely agree with, as resentment and complaint bring nothing positive. They are merely a waste of time. Not that I haven't complained now and then, but looking back, it's never been a productive use of my energy. Pondering this, I couldn't help but think of Carlos Hathcock, the famous United States Marine Corps Scout Sniper.* Sitting here, I can look over at my copy of *Marine Sniper: 93 Confirmed Kills* by Charles Henderson. My copy is signed, not by Henderson, but by Gunny Sergeant Hathcock himself. I think about the Christmas cards from him and his wife Jo that are tucked away in a keepsake box; and I remember the conversations we had over the phone, including the last time I talked with Jo when Carlos couldn't come to the phone any longer.**

I think about him because he was a man I greatly admired, and who had many reasons to resent and complain about what

---

* Carlos Hathcock (1942 – 1999) was a US Marine Corps Gunnery Sergeant who served as a sniper in the Vietnam War. With 93 confirmed kills, he was the 4th most effective sniper in American history, trailing behind Adelbert F Waldron (109), Charles Mawhinney (103), and Eric R England (98). After the Vietnam War, Hathcock helped establish a scout and sniper school at the Marine base in Quantico, Virginia.

** That was about 5 months before he passed away after a long struggle with multiple sclerosis in February of 1999.

happened to him, but he didn't. Gunny Hathcock was a legend in the sniping community. Even though I went through the 2nd Infantry Division Scout Sniper School with the U.S. Army, we still knew of the Marine Corps legend. The Viet Cong nicknamed Hathcock "*Long Trang*," which means "White Feather," because of the white feather he kept in a band on his bush hat. After a platoon of Vietnamese snipers was sent to hunt him down, many of his fellow Marines donned similar white feathers in order to deceive the enemy. Knowing the impact that Hathcock's death would have to morale, they took it upon themselves to become targets in order to confuse enemy counter-snipers. I was honored to share correspondences with him and have the conversations we had.

Gunny Hathcock sustained severe burns and combat injuries while selflessly saving seven other Marines from a burning amtrac (amphibious tractor). On top of this, multiple sclerosis attacked his legs and body leaving him wheelchair-bound during his last years. And during his last few years he was also diagnosed with Parkinson's disease. Despite his infirmities, Carlos carried on with dignity and courage and always had time for others. Again, I'm honored to be among those others.

I remember one of our conversations when I mentioned how I really respected how he continued to teach and help others, especially in the military and law enforcement communities. His reply, "Well, you can't sit around and be a slug." I remember his encouraging words when I shared that someone close to me was diagnosed with MS too. But most of all, I remember a man who had every right to resent what happened to him, and who could have complained about any of the numerous obstacles he had to face, but instead remained positive and did everything he could within his restricted physical limitations to help others.

Gunny Sergeant Hathcock was a warrior and a hero.* Not only for his sniping exploits during the Vietnam War, which were extraordinary, nor only for heroically saving those seven Marines at great expense to himself. Carlos was a warrior for those acts

---

* At his retirement ceremony, Gunny Hathcock was given a plaque with a bronzed Marine campaign cover mounted above a brass plate that reads, "There have been many Marines. There have been many marksmen. But there has only been one sniper—Gunnery Sergeant Carlos N. Hathcock. One Shot. One Kill." You can read more about his remarkable life at www. modernamericanheroes.com/2010/07/13/the-story-of-legendary-sniper-carlos-hathcock/

and everything he did after the war right up until he passed away at the too young age of 57. His dedication and service to others without resentment or complaint lead me to believe that he would agree wholeheartedly with Miyamoto Musashi's precept 9. And, I agree with both of these men. *Semper Fi* Gunny!

Teacher:

Resentment and complaint are pretty useless. Resentment goes back to feelings in that you are angry over being treated unfairly. Life is not fair, and thinking that you will always be treated fairly is simply a delusion. Most people are going to be nice to you when they think you are useful to them, and they will set you aside once they feel that you will be of no further use. You can be resentful about this or you can press ahead. One of these choices is a passive, nonproductive state, and the other is an active and productive state. The choice is yours.

The treatment that upsets you may have been from an individual, such as in the case of a romance turned sour, or it could be professional, like when a coworker is found to be a backstabber, or a boss promotes someone other than you. It can also be societal, where a group of people who feel that their socioeconomic group has been ignored or taken advantage of. Sitting around being angry is going to solve nothing. Going out and beating the offender with a bat will only serve to get you sent to prison as well as confirm in the other person's mind what they felt about you beforehand.

Right or wrong, being treated unfairly is another fact of life that must be handled appropriately. And resentment is simply not going to solve a thing.

The better action would be to open a dialogue with the person or people that you feel insulted by, and try to find out (A) if your suspicions are well founded and (B) what is the best way for you *and* them to move forward in some kind of cooperative way. People generally are not good at sitting and talking to each other anymore, but only because we do not do it often enough to be well practiced at it. Everyone has to start where they are, so this is sound advice.

Next we come to complaint. Complaint is really an act of self-pity. It is a person whining about what they do not like. My Father never wanted to hear us complain about anything. He was okay with us telling him about a problem, provided we had the start of a solution to follow up with our initial issue. I have tried my best to live this way. I have had many coworkers refer to me as an *idea person*, because I don't look for problems, I identify problems and then set about looking for a solution. Or at least a bandage until someone smarter arrives with a suitable resolution...

This precept is great advice, particularly in our modern time when people are so quick to resent anyone and complain about anything. If this were taught in schools, there would be a slow but steady change in direction for society, one that could benefit us all.

Insurance Executive:

Resentment is a powerful mindset that most often has very little effect on its target, although it does chew and gnaw on the person holding the feeling. Let's say I resent a friend because her husband makes more money than mine, or because she looks better in the same blouse I own, or because she gets the best assignments where we work. Holding on to anger and bitterness accomplishes nothing. My resentment alone isn't going to change the circumstances and it's not going to give my friend a bad case of the flu no matter how much I will it to happen. These toxic feelings will, however, cause me stress, indigestion, sleeplessness, and harden my personality, especially toward her, someone who might or might not have any control over the things for which I'm resentful.

How ridiculous to be bitter at someone because their spouse has a better paying job. After all, everything is relative. Her husband earns a larger paycheck than my husband but mine makes more money than someone else's husband, and so on and so on. Does she look better in her duplicate blouse because she has skin coloring that better connects with the color of the blouse? Or does she have better genes or is she is in better physical condition? If her skin tone accentuates the blouse better than mine does, why am I feeling anger and bitterness about something I have no control over and, in fact, she has no control over? On the other hand, if she fills it out better because she is in better shape, then I'm stressing over something I can do something about.

A feeling of resentment is often a matter of low self-esteem. Conversely, the more confidant you are and the happier you are with yourself and all that you have, the less chance resentment will rear its ugly head to disrupt your life and your mental and physical health. While I like to think of myself as not holding resentment for anything (anything I can think of right now, anyway) I do have to admit that I'm a bit of a complainer. My husband says I would complain if I were lynched with a new rope.

I do feel that complaining is a form of release. I remember a coworker telling me once about a terrible duty station he had when he was in the Marines. Everyone complained about the lack of sleep, lousy food, terrible heat, awful leadership, and so on. Complaints filled the air from dawn to lights out and it nearly drove him mad because he wasn't a complainer. He agreed with what the others were saying but whining about what he couldn't change wasn't part of his personality. At about six weeks in, he said it began to dawn on him that during those times when the men weren't complaining, they were joking, laughing, and having a good time in their misery. But not my friend; he never laughed and joked. He determined that because he didn't complain and because he held everything inside without ever giving it release, it made him constantly grim, bitter, and angry.

So what is the solution? As I've discussed elsewhere in the precepts, it's always best to take the middle path. In this case, complain a little and then proceed to see what can be done about the issue. In some cases, if you took just a little of the energy you put into complaining about something and applied it to fixing things, you might surprise yourself at how well things turn out. If, on the other hand, you learn there is nothing to be done about an issue, then you've got to live with it. When you have no other choice but to live with it, you do your best to change the way you think about it.

Remember this scientific fact about complaining: 20 percent of the people you complain to don't care and the remaining 80 percent are glad you're miserable.

Businessman:

This precept is a lot like precept 7, jealousy and resentment go together, but this time the focus will not be on ourselves so much as on those around us, other members of our team. Virtually everyone socializes on the job. Friendly banter is fine, most folks want to talk about the weather, their family, their favorite sports team, a new movie release, or their favorite television show, but there's a world of difference between affable conversations and hurtful rumors that are designed to undermine or injure others. Some topics such as religion or politics generally ought to be off-limits in the office, as they stem from core values so disagreements can easily lead to unproductive and vitriolic arguments, but few things are more distractive and disruptive than gossip-mongering in the workplace.

Oftentimes gossip stems from resentment. We may fear others who are smarter, wiser, better connected, or more productive than ourselves and want to knock them down a peg or two. Not only does that sort of thing distract us from performing productive work, but ultimately we all know that we cannot trust those who speak out of turn. When we see someone backstab a coworker, subordinate, or manager we know that at some point he or she will try to throw us under the proverbial bus too. In business where inappropriate disclosure of trade secrets, proprietary processes, and confidential information can be extraordinarily detrimental, lack of trust is a very serious problem.

Do not abide chronic complainers, people who incessantly whine, nitpick, and criticize others. This admonishment does not refer to people who make dreary jokes or cheerless comments from time-to-time, but rather to pessimists who habitually see everything around them in a negative light. There is a world of difference between folks whose negativity inhibits the productivity of others and those who occasionally have a bad day. Further, we should embrace those who uncover flaws in the system, bring them to light, and then go on to make positive changes in the workplace that eliminate the problems they encountered. They aren't whiners; they are positive agents for change. That sounds like a winner in my book.

One way to spot the difference in a person's intent is in the language that they choose to use. Is it a problem or a challenge, a predicament or an opportunity? Downbeat tones of voice and terminology may be innocuous, but often such things are indicators of deeper issues. Eons ago when I worked in finance I had a coworker we nicknamed "Eeyore" because he was such a downer*. At first people ignored him, but after a while they began

---

* A character in *Winnie-the-Pooh* by A. A. Milne, Eeyore was a grey, stuffed donkey with a pessimistic, gloomy, and depressive attitude. He expects the worst in life and rarely if ever takes steps to avoid misfortune.

to sympathize, commiserate, and even chime in. Within a year the group dynamic had changed, we developed a bad reputation, and those who had the option refused to deal with us, turning instead to other teams for help when they needed it. This is never a good thing in an overhead organization where our budget was contingent upon helping line organizations (that produced the products and services we sold) make money for the corporation. Even though he was one of the smartest people in the group, well-educated (he earned his bachelor's, two masters degrees, and a CMA certification*), and productive, Eeyore was the first person let go in the next layoff cycle.

Since negativity tends to be infectious as I discovered while working with Eeyore, we must ruthlessly stamp it out. But, we have to do it intelligently since we don't want to inadvertently reward groupthink or instill a culture of fear. This means that we must make a commitment along with everyone on our team to avoid gossiping, to treat each other with dignity and respect, and to not bring up problems without also suggesting solutions whenever we are able to do so. This attitude can become pervasive, making significant changes in the workplace. That does not mean that no one ever gets upset or says anything derogatory, people are people after all, but rather that the accepted norm is to engage each other in a professional and constructive way.

Once this commitment is put in place we must then hold each other accountable for sticking with it. For example, even if we cannot figure out how to resolve something, we can identify potential paths forward and ask for help where it's needed rather than throwing our hands up in frustration and giving up or making it somebody else's predicament to sort out. A positive attitude can carry us far, personally, professionally, and as an organization… For example, our current CIO earned his position in record time in large part due to his dynamic, upbeat personality.**

---

* Certified Management Accountant, a globally recognized, advanced-level credential for accountants and financial professionals.

** Well, that and being one of the smartest people I've ever met, which in a company that employs a lot of rocket scientists is really saying something. Nevertheless, he was promoted from director to vice president in only a year, and promoted again to CIO about three-and-a-half years after that. That's the quickest I've seen in the 28 years I've worked here. In the process he skipped over many other executives who were equally competent because he was better able to make friends and influence people.

There's an adage in the business world, "Strategy eats culture for lunch." A systemic aversion to antipathy, bitterness, and negativity is a large part of why that saying rings true, as well as why I wholeheartedly agree with Musashi that resentment and complaint are inappropriate for us and for others. In fact, I'd go so far as to say that I'd rather staff my team with folks who have lower skills and better attitudes than with people who are curmudgeonly geniuses like my old coworker Eeyore that nobody can work with.

PRECEPT 10

Do not let yourself be guided by the feeling of lust or love

"To see a man fearless in dangers, untainted with lusts, happy in adversity, composed in a tumult, and laughing at all those things which are generally either coveted or feared, all men must acknowledge that this can be from nothing else but a beam of divinity that influences a mortal body."

— Seneca

Monk:

There are many famous stories of how love and lust have led to poor decisions and bad choices but the lives we have lived are more immediate than any parable. We have all made bad choices when it comes to lust and love. Not knowing the difference between the two, immaturity, or just maybe youthful naiveté, we have all in some moment been under the spell of one, or both of these emotions. Guarding against uncontrolled lust is laudable, but Musashi fails with this precept as he does not differentiate between the results of these two emotions in a person's life. There is a difference between lust and love that is as large as the Pacific Ocean. This lumping together two different emotions into one warning shows a curious lack of understanding in the life philosophy of the famous swordsman.

Lust is an intense desire, and usually attributed to the sexual realm in modern thought, but it can also apply to power, fame, or several other matters too. Lust is also listed as one of the traditional "Seven Deadly Sins" used to educate Christians as to what to avoid in order to live a better life. Being listed as one of the Seven Deadly Sins places lust in the pantheon of serious emotions and traits that can never lead to a good outcome; things that all good and well-intentioned people must all avoid. Nevertheless, lust is timeless and ever-present.

We all know that lust should be controlled, but it's not easy. In Dante's *Purgatorio*, the penitent walks within flames to purge himself of lustful thoughts and feelings. In *Inferno*, un-forgiven souls of the sin of lust are blown about in restless hurricane-like winds symbolic of their own lack of self-control to their lustful passions in earthly life. The challenge is that the only time humans stop having the feeling of lust is when the first spade of dirt is dropped on our graves.

So, managing our lust is really about co-existence. It is about living with the desire, recognizing it, and acting is a manner that is appropriate anyway. Some religions and sages who agree with Musashi offer ways of dealing with lust, some offer prayer, others reconciliation, some counseling. Musashi, however, offers no lecture, no path, no tools, he only says, "Don't."

Mature love, on the other hand, is a choice. The act of love occurs before the emotion. Lust is the opposite; the emotion is set before the action. You can see how the reversal of these two acts and emotions, when switched, are very different animals. Decisions based in lust never seem to work out; they are not sustainable and are a quick path to downfall. On the other hand decisions made out of love are sustainable.

Love is a choice. Love is a verb, not a noun. Love is an action. And love requires that something of one's self must be given freely to others. This is not the world Musashi knew or built around himself. I have no answer, nor do you, but it should be pondered, "Was the swordsman biologically capable of the act of love, would his brain allow such an act?" Some indications, such as his problems at home as a child, his lack of need for human companionship, a few other personality traits and actions give flight to the question of his physiological makeup and socialization.

For whatever reason, whatever pathology, Musashi missed the mark when he recommends that we should stay away from one of the most elemental of all human emotions, love. Love isn't an emotion per say, it is an action, a choice, one that we can and should all make.

Warrior:

I believe Musashi's precept, "Do not let yourself be guided by the feeling of lust or love," comes from a pragmatic stance more than the Puritanical moralism such as may be found within the Christian conservatism in modern America. I believe this because of the pragmatism found within the rest of his writings.

It is interesting that the United States military has specific crimes related to activities guided by lust or love. The first is Adultery. Holding service members to a higher ethical standard than people in civilian life, adultery is a criminal offense under the Uniform Code of Military Justice (UCMJ). The reason the military is strict about adultery is because such conduct is considered prejudicial to good order, to discipline, and could bring embarrassment and discredit to the Armed Forces. This is also why adultery in the military is prosecuted under Article 134, which is known as the "General Article," as it forbids any conduct that brings dishonor upon the armed forces, or conduct which is harmful to good order or discipline.

The military also uses Article 134 to prosecute cases of fraternization and Article 92 which prohibits unprofessional relationships. This again is an attempt to prohibit actions of lust or love that have a reasonable potential to adversely affect the military by eroding morale, good order, discipline, respect for authority, unit cohesion, or by compromising the military mission itself. Notice that the military uses pragmatic reasoning to substantiate these crimes. While Puritans hold strict standards regarding all matters of sexuality based on their interpretation of the Bible and relationship with God, the military's standards are based on good order, discipline, unit cohesion, and the mission. I could easily see Musashi drafting a similar Article if he were to govern a large body of troops.

It doesn't matter if I look at my own past, or read through the history books, to realize that so much of what men do, and I mean men as in the male of the species, because of lust and love. Sure, women act on these emotions too, but men are much more prone to act without thinking due to these feelings. I can think of many instances where I let myself be guided by lust or love when I would have been much better off following Musashi's advice, however I will be the first to acknowledge and admit that there has been much good done because of love. Maybe not lust so much, but indeed love can be a powerful motivator for good. But

I don't believe that is what Musasi was thinking when he wrote this.

Musashi was providing guidance to young men, like myself, who foolishly acted out of the feelings of lust or love. And because I remember the trouble I got myself into, sadly more than a few times, I have to agree with this precept for those kinds of situations and circumstances. Love and lust have turned many men into fools; men that would have been much better off had they refused to be guided by such feelings. Fortunately, most of us who grow older come to the same realization as Musashi, and stop allowing our actions to be guided by these emotions.

Teacher:

Men are very prone to being guided by feelings of lust. This half of the precept, at least to me, seems to be about self-discipline. We have to be in control of our actions. A person without self-control and a sense of duty is going to be a liability. And I don't care which setting you care to place them in, battlefield, classroom, boardroom, marriage—their lack of discipline makes them a walking hazard to those in contact with them. In all four settings, discipline is going to be a key determining factor in the level of success to be attained.

For the second half, not being guided by feelings of love, I have to take issue.

At home, it is love that guides my decisions. Yes, sometimes as a parent one must make an unpopular decision, but this is going to be done out of love and not out of spite. Unless you are a *really* bad parent, of course... In the classroom, a teacher who does not have a love of learning will be very ineffective and, if they are not guided by a parental love for the students, they are going to seem phony to the students hence will be unable to reach or teach most of them.

So if the point of this precept is to recommend self-discipline as a central point, then I am on board with the precept 100%. But if it was intended to remove love from the equation of all decision-making then I have to strongly disagree, at least with the second half of the precept.

The biggest thing that kept me from ever becoming a full on *Taoist* was the lack of teachings about the importance of love. Love will hinder violence, self-interest, greed, lust, neglect, and many of the other ills which plague society throughout the world. Love is also a very powerful motivator. People who love others will often act out of *selflessness*. This is a very rare human capacity; so rare indeed that it could be called a superpower. People are selfish by nature, with the exception of when they are acting out of love for another person.

Absolutely, do not let yourself be guided by lust, there is only trouble waiting on that path. But, you could do a lot worse than to allow love to be a guiding factor in your life.

Insurance Executive:

Many problems are to be had when one allows lust to guide their actions. Actually, the same can be said for love, but I'm guessing that lust—so often wrongly based and fleeting—causes people and kingdoms the most grief. Ask Bill Clinton and Bill Cosby. Let's look at love and lust as it relates to relationships.

One problem with lust is the more one is filled with it and consumed by it, the less the chance of them finding true and romantic love. There is a young man where I work who is hot on the trail of Paris Hilton. It's Paris Hilton this and Paris Hilton that, 24/7. He owns every book and magazine about her, and every poster that depicts her image. He is a nice looking young man but I'm convinced it will be a long while before he finds real love, as everyone he meets cannot possibly compare to Paris and the distorted vision of what he thinks she is.

Lust is usually based on a physical attribute: beautiful eyes, a fantastic figure, and a walk that makes wild horses stampede. But these things are short lived and are often only surface deep. Another man in my office just went through a divorce. "She was a beauty," he said. "But underneath that attractive thin veneer was a terribly ugly and awful person."

It is said that lust can make a person crazy, while love can give them sanity. Was Musashi ever in love? I've never seen it mentioned in all the stories about his exploits. One reference says he was a complex man who never married and never settled down. Other sources mention sons. All the tales of the swordsman say he was unwashed, dirty and smelly. So maybe this was one of the reasons he never found lasting love... Or might it have been his intense drive to be the warrior he became?

In his early years he was intent on perfecting his martial arts and in his later years he focused intensely on his writing, painting, and Buddhism. As someone turned so intently inward, maybe there wasn't time left for love. Or perhaps he was so driven by these things that he truly felt love would only distract him from his pursuits and lead him away from what he felt was his destiny.

Perhaps he was a practical man and as such, love in all its mystery, distraction, mind bending, foolishness producing, and intense focus on someone other than oneself, didn't fit into his internal world and his pursuits therein. Regardless, if he had never experienced it, perhaps he didn't understand that love, in time, wasn't about looking deeply into one another's eyes forever, but rather looking outward together in the same direction. For all his accomplishments, that's something important that he missed.

Businessman:

This is very sound advice for business ventures. To be sure, there really is no place in business for lust or love, save perhaps in the pornography industry, and then only superficially. In order to avoid unnecessary and often career-limiting or lawsuit-inducing complications such as allegations of sexual harassment, favoritism, nepotism, or creating a hostile workplace we all need to separate our work life from our everyday life.

Under state and federal laws, many employers are required to establish and maintain anti-discrimination policies that protect their employees. Even when not specifically mandated by force of law, it is a good idea to put rules in place that prescribe appropriate conduct in the workplace. This generally means assuring that there will be no discrimination in recruitment, employment, working conditions, compensation, advancement, or termination based on a person's race, creed, color, national origin, gender, past or present military service, or sexual orientation. Further, policies should safeguard against harassment of any kind based on any of the aforementioned personal characteristics as well as ban stalking, unwelcome physical contact, or solicitation of sexual favors for continued employment or preferential treatment.

Offensive remarks, obscene gestures, and inappropriate jokes may be proscribed as well, though we must be clear and unambiguous about definitions in such policies or the unintended consequences may create more harm than good. For instance, human resources policies at more than one large corporation stipulate that an employee can be fired for complementing someone on their appearance or attire. That may be well-intended, but it's probably a little over the top... Nevertheless, there must also be a process for reporting, investigating, and adjudicating all allegations of inappropriate behaviors in a fair, objective, and timely manner.

Many corporations, colleges, and government institutions go a step farther and put special rules in place to keep people who are related to or seeing one another romantically from working within the same reporting relationship (e.g., work group, division, or other arrangement where one party has direct or indirect control over what happens to the other in terms of work assignments, advancement opportunities, or pay and benefits). This is not to say that we can never work alongside a parent, child, spouse, or significant other, in some circumstances such as a family-owned business that might be perfectly appropriate, but rather that an ethical firewall should exist between the personal and professional aspects of our lives and due diligence should be undertaken to avoid any appearance of or actual improprieties.

As you can see, the workplace can be fraught with perils if we do not establish and maintain clear expectations around acceptable and unacceptable behaviors. The job, however, often extends beyond our office walls. For example, anyone who has ever attended a tradeshow or symposium will undoubtedly recognize the term "booth babe," a slang that has grown up around the widespread tendency of vendors to highlight their wares by sending beautiful, often scantily-clad, young women to represent them to the public. Gorgeous spokesmodels of both the male and female variety may be fun to look at, but anyone foolish enough to commit millions of dollars of their company's resources simply because a hot chick (or dude) flirted with them for a while on a showroom floor is downright stupid. The same thing goes for accepting kickbacks or bribes, they may be a necessary evil in certain regions of the world, but they're evil nonetheless. Purchasing decisions should always be made based on the merits of the product or service that we are evaluating, and then only after a thorough technical, financial, and contractual review. In other words, it's a business decision. Lust or love should play no part in making it.

On or off the job, anything that impairs our judgment around those we find attractive should be treated cautiously. Dangers can include things like going out for drinks with coworkers and imbibing too much, but certain less obvious behaviors like having an "office spouse" can easily become problematic too.* An office husband or wife is a co-worker with whom we share a special bond. Since many of us spend more time at the office than we do at home, we can become very close to our coworkers. That's not a bad thing per se, but the danger is that creating deep emotional connections similar to those found in intimate physical relationships can often lead to an intimate physical relationship, even when we aren't actively trying to create one.

We may temporarily be caught up in the emotions of the moment, but to the extent possible the prudent businessman or woman must make decisions based on objective evaluations of relevant facts and data. We have a fiduciary responsibility to our employers, our employees, and ourselves, one that must be carried out with all appropriate diligence. In that vein, we categorically must not allow ourselves to be guided by the feelings of lust or love in our decision-making while on the job.

---

* Studies indicate that roughly 1/3 of married office workers in the United States have a trusted confidante (usually a member of the opposite gender) that they consider a "work spouse," someone with whom they share an emotional attachment similar to or greater than that of their actual spouse.

PRECEPT 11

In all things, have no preferences

"As long as we respond predictably to what feels good and what feels bad, it is easy for others to exploit our preferences for their own ends."

— Mihaly Csikszentmihalyi

Monk:

In 1812, Napoleon Bonaparte's massive army invaded Moscow yet after one month of enduring the harsh Russian winter they were forced to retreat. Napoleon's soldiers had a poor diet in the field. Typhus, diarrhea, and dysentery were common. Soon other illnesses and injuries took hold and as the campaign continued and exhaustion set in. Starving, demoralized, and devastated the French army had no choice but to withdraw from battle, retreating in haste.

As they haphazardly made their way west, the degraded army slowly froze and starved to death. This retreat was a disaster of astonishing levels. The troops had no supplies so they had to forage to eat. Some soldiers killed themselves, others simply collapsed and died where they fell from exposure to the cold. There is one recorded instance where Napoleon's men broke into a local doctor's office where they found medical samples of human tissues preserved in formaldehyde... and they ate the medical samples.

When it comes to food, I'm not picky. I learned early in life to eat whatever was put before me and I have carried that mindset with me. I simply am not all that particular. Now I am not suggesting that I will eat the worst of the worst, I mean the mere thought of eating the formaldehyde preserved specimens makes me shudder, but it is all context isn't it? I have choices, thankfully, but starving men have no option of having a preference. Most of us have not known hunger or the desperation of the type that Napoleon's men had to endure that winter in 1812. Having preferences is contextual.

Having preferences when you have control of your environment is a mature act of will. Similarly, having no preference when you have control of your environment is also an act of will. When placed under extraordinary circumstances such as living at the lowest level of Maslow's hierarchy of needs, then fundamental things like air, food, drink, shelter, and warmth become all that matters.

When Musashi admonishes us to no preferences in all things, the preferences part resonates but it is hard to accept the idea of, "All things." I think it is more mature to say, "In most things..."

It is safe to say that Musashi lived on the margins of life at times, a margin that most of us will never experience. The level of needs that Napoleon's army experienced is unlikely to be our lot as well. For our needs, we should look at it in the way my family dinner was presented—some nights it was food I loved, other times less so. My complaints about what was being served fell on deaf ears, so I ate what was set before me anyway. Further, in my ignorance of youth my complaining about the meal disrespected my mother's hard work, but she, like all good mothers, did her best to provide a well-rounded meal and not take insult from my complaints. All the effort my father put into earning the money necessary to buy the food was also dismissed in my arrogance too.

What I learned as I grew up was that being appreciative of whatever is given is a great way to honor the efforts of those that have taken their time and effort to prepare for our needs. This idea, of course, can be extended into other aspects of life too...

In having very few preferences, a person can move through life smoothly and mentally unencumbered. On the outside, the world is no longer about you. The extreme example of Napoleon Bonaparte's men cannibalizing preserved human remains is something that we all hope to never experience. However, what if you approached your next meal with just a dusting of Bonaparte's men? It'd make you more thankful wouldn't it? What if you looked at your car as a tool needed to get from here to there, instead of what your vehicle looked like or any prestige that might be attached to owning it?

Having no preferences at all is extreme, but having some preferences managed and held lightly is a better choice.

Warrior:

I think I might understand where Musashi was coming from when he wrote this precept, but on face value I think it is absurd. Actually, it's worse than that... To say, "In all things, have no preferences" is asinine. A warrior must have preferences, because a warrior must stand for something. It's like the old saying, "If you don't stand for something, you'll fall for anything." I'm not sure who said it first, but it is absolutely correct. If a warrior doesn't know why he or she is doing something, in the face of great personal risk, it will be easier to falter or be derailed. The warrior must stand for something in order to stand fast to the end.

One of my favorite military leaders, General George S. Patton, Jr. (1885 – 1945), certainly understood the concept of standing for something as he was known for telling his troops that it was better to fight for something in life than to die for nothing. In the book *General Patton's Principles for Life and Leadership*, Porter B. Williamson shared part of one of General Patton's talks to the troops:

> "We are in war! We have a chance to fight and die for something. A lot of people never get that chance. Think of all of the poor people you know that have lived and died for nothing. Total lives spent doing nothing but eating, sleeping, and going to work until the retirement watch is received. Nothing to live or die for.
>
> "We are lucky that we are fighting a war that will change the history of the world. If we live, we can put our grandchildren on our knees and tell them how we won the war. If we die, our friends will tell how we died to make life better for them. If you are going to die, might as well die a hero. If you kill enough people before you die, they might name a street after you."

The more I think about this precept, the more I disagree with Musashi and wonder how someone who was so familiar with life and death that he included in these twenty-one precepts, "Do not fear death," that he would also write "Have no preferences." When you face your own mortality, as Musashi did on numerous occasions, you become very clear about what's important and what is not. This clarity should lead one toward preferring certain things over others. This clarity should lead one toward taking a stand.

Once a warrior has a preference and takes a stand, he or she can accept being killed for being true to that purpose and stand. That would be an honorable death, and acceptable in all warrior cultures I can think of. But I'm having difficulty understanding how a warrior can take a stand, one that he or she is willing to die for, without first having preferences. And at the very least, on a general level, the warrior must prefer right over wrong and good over evil.

Teacher:

At the base, this is no different than the precepts against desire and jealousy. When you have a preference, in and of itself, this is not a big deal. But I think what Musashi was getting at here is the way we lean toward demanding that things be *just so*. It is absolutely natural to have a preference. I prefer to have cheese on my fries when I eat a hamburger. I prefer to sit in the front of an airplane. I prefer to have dinner guests *not* blow their nose at the table while I am eating. I prefer that no one speak to me until after my third cup of coffee.

Preferences are really nothing more than *what we want*. I cannot remember the number of times my Parents told me, "It ain't what you *want* that makes you fat, it's what you *eat*."

In my recent experiences though, I think I can see some of what Musashi might have been pointing at here. Just look around at the number of people who prefer to not see or hear anything that offends or upsets them. After being brought up in what amounts to a bubble, there are masses of human adults out there who feel that anything offensive, or anything that reminds them of a bad experience, or anything that makes them *uncomfortable* in any fashion must be hidden away. As long as you stay inside of that bubble, surrounded by people who are willing to cooperate with your preferences, there will be no issues for you.

But, there are many people in the world that will not cooperate. There are some who will use your preferences for how the world *should* tailor itself to your wishes as a way to get to you and destroy you. In this sense your preference becomes a weakness. By using a framework of your own creation as an outline of how the world is supposed to be, you end up limiting your vision of what truly is. By self-imposed weakness, you create an opening for others to take advantage of you and possibly do you great harm.

This is an extreme example, but there are lesser variations.

When we would rather have things be *this* way than the way they really are, we stress. Now, Musashi could not care less if we are stressed about something, but stress *is* a distraction. Stress alters our focus, interferes with our attention, and on and on.

Maybe we are certain that a trusted friend would never steal our idea in order to cement their position within the company where we work so we share this idea with them in the interest of getting the ball rolling on making a needed improvement. Our very thought that people we classify as "good people" would somehow *never* act in a selfish manner is a weakness that will allow another person to steal the idea and take the credit for the concept as well as build their own reputation within the company as an innovator. They can still be a good person, but even the best people are prone to acting selfishly when they think there is a benefit that will outweigh the cost of losing our respect or friendship. To not know this or acknowledge it under the guise of preferring to think that "good people would never do that" is folly. Good people are still *people*, hence will act out of self-interest at any time. Your preferred belief about how people should act means nothing.

Having a preference is natural, but extending your belief in that preference as being *the* way, or the *right* way, or the way *things are* is asinine. It's a fantasy. The real world doesn't work that way.

Insurance Executive:

This depends on the subject.

I prefer not to step onto the freeway during rush hour, or at any time for that matter. I prefer not to go skydiving after Edward Scissorhands has packed the parachute.* But in other things, I try to evaluate the reasons and potential ramifications behind my preferences. Here are some examples:

When there are two apples in a bowl, my preference is for the big juicy one over the one with bruises and wrinkles. But if I take it, it would mean my husband would be left with the sad-looking one. So I take the lesser apple and chomp around the brown spots.

---

* Tim Burton's 1990 movie Edward Scissorhands is about a synthetic boy named Edward (played by Johnny Depp) who is created by an eccentric scientist (Vincent Price). He is human virtually every way but fitted with long, scissor-like extremities instead of fingers on his hands.

While my preference is for the better one, my final choice makes my husband happy and, ultimately by choosing to do something good for him and sacrificing only a little, I feel good about myself too.

In my martial arts class, I prefer to work with Adam because as a long-time student, his movements are fast and strong, his precision is flawless, and his amazing skill brings out my best. But sometimes I choose Sara. Although she has been training for two years, her coordination is quite bad and her control is poor. In this case, my preference is to do what I can to help a student who needs all the help she can get. To be honest, however, there are two rather self-serving reasons I like to train with her. It makes me feel good about myself to see how my teaching method—one of giving lots of positive feedback as opposed to always pointing out errors—makes her excel. I also want to train with her because her awkwardness and the unpredictability of her choices when attacking and countering, keep me on my toes, and ultimately helps me improve me skills too.

Another area where I try to monitor my preferences, or lack thereof, is in my work as a claims adjuster for a major insurance company. I never, and I mean never, prefer one customer over another based on age, race, or sexual orientation. I strive to give every person 100 percent of my best work to make what can be a difficult and red tape-strewn process easier for them. Okay, maybe I do have a preference against one type of customer—one I prefer to give a hard time. I like to give those people who try to defraud the system—i.e., steal money and services by filing false claims—a difficult time with a preferred goal of sending them before a judge.

While I understand that having no preference in things is ideal, I would argue its implementation is next to impossible, which only means I should try harder. My approach is to monitor my preferences and strive to make choices that benefit my loved ones, other people, and me, and try to do it in that order as much as possible. Hard to do? Oh yes…

Like so many of Musashi's precepts, the task of following this one isn't easy but that simply means we must try harder to do the best we can. In the matter of preferences, when our choices favor ourselves, or one group of people over another group, it's simply wrong. Sometimes a preference might not be overt but rather subtle, such as having a preference for one of our children over another, one parent over the other, or even one friend over another. While these feelings might be impossible to avoid, it is imperative that we strive to never, ever, allow them to be apparent.

Businessman:

This is a nice philosophy, it rolls off your tongue in a pleasantly Zen-like way, but as laudable as having no preferences may be it simply isn't practicable. In business we *must* have preferences. Let's begin with the enterprise itself, the reason that we're able to compete to sell our products and services to folks who might want to buy them. No company can be all things to all consumers. For example, when we hear Nordstrom we usually think about unbeatable service whereas when we hear Walmart we tend to think of unmatched low prices, right? Imagine for a moment if Nordstrom wanted to go head-to-head with Walmart to compete on price. Could they be successful in that endeavor or do you think they would they get sideways with the culture they have carefully nourished for over 110 years, and crash and burn in the process?

Clearly all businesses must build a strategy that helps them differentiate themselves from their competitors in order to win market share, and then carefully focus all their efforts toward bringing that strategy to fruition. It's vital to focus on what we're good at. Straying too far from the path tends to end badly. Consider the AOL/Time Warner merger by way of example. Lots of things went wrong, including cultural clashes and lack of synergies between the two heritage company's business models. Ultimately this led to over a hundred billion dollars in lost capital, an unprecedented disaster, before the union between the two companies was finally dissolved.

Undoubtedly a merger between Nordstrom and Walmart, were one to be attempted, would end just as badly. Not only are their business models and cultures totally different, but also the very things that makes one enterprise successful could easily undermine the other. We can all control costs, but to drive the lowest prices in the industry while simultaneously delivering the highest customer service is virtually impossible. It's kind of like the old adage, "You can have it right, you can have it cheap, or you can have it fast... pick two." There are too many trade-offs to accomplish everything all at once.

Similarly, at a macro-level the three main methods of standing out from the competition include focusing primarily on (1) operational excellence, (2) customer intimacy, or (3) product differentiation.* We *might* be able to get two out of three, but no one can have it all. In fact, most companies can only do one of three really well. Here's how they work:

1) Operational excellence is defined as providing customers with reliable products or services at competitive prices that are delivered with minimal inconvenience. To succeed with this strategy an organization must become world class in continuously improving efficiencies in order to drive profit margins since they are primarily competing on price. Companies that excel in this space include Walmart, UPS, and Dell.

2) Customer intimacy is defined as precisely segmenting and targeting markets, then tailoring offerings that exactly match the demands of customers in each niche. To succeed with this strategy an organization must be brilliant at combining detailed customer knowledge with the flexibility to respond quickly to almost any need. Companies that excel in this space include Nordstrom, Kraft, and Home Depot.

3) Product differentiation is defined as offering customers leading-edge products or services that consistently enhance their use of the merchandise. To succeed with this strategy an organization must be exceptional at understanding what their customers value most and then boosting the level they come to expect beyond what any competitors can provide. Companies that excel in this space include Apple, Johnson & Johnson, and Nike.

For long term growth and profitability we must be exceptional at harnessing our organization's strengths while minimizing our weaknesses. This means that we need to be focused like a laser beam on our strategic imperatives. This not only necessitates preferences, but requires near religious devotion to implementing them. In the most successful organizations the company's vision, mission, strategy, and tactics are all aligned to assure that one

---

* For more information about these business models see "Customer Intimacy and Other Value Disciplines" by Michael Treacy and Fred Wiersema, *Harvard Business Review* (January–February, 1993).

of the three aforementioned strategies is communicated and carried out at all levels throughout the enterprise. Where I work, for example, virtually every leader has a print out of the company's management model which summarizes our corporate strategy hanging over his or her desk, in part because our job performance is measured based on adherence to that plan.

Organizations must identify and build up their core business, design a reasonable path forward that makes them grow, and then exercise prudence in straying beyond their carefully charted route. For the most part new products or services need to be extensions of existing ones rather than branching out in an entirely different direction as the AOL/Time Warner merger attempted to do.

Take Honda, for example. At heart they are an engine company. Those engines might run anything from power equipment to motorcycles, cars, or trucks, but everything the do is based on expertise in designing, building, selling, and servicing world-class engines and the vehicles powered by them. Were Honda to venture into building rocket engines or aircraft propulsion that might be a stretch technologically, but at least it would be an understandable one based on their business model. On the other hand, any attempt by them to enter into the entertainment, software, or consumer electronics industry would be a gigantic leap, undoubtedly a highly problematic one. Odds are good that venture would fail because it strays too far beyond their core competencies.

In business we must have preferences. Our companies and our careers depend on them.

PRECEPT 12

Be indifferent to where you live

"A man's homeland is wherever he prospers."

— Aristophanes

Monk:

The truth is that for the most part most people don't put too much thought into where they live. Much of the thought process is built around comfort or pain. If the comfort level is adequate and needed resources are available most people tend to stay where they are. This is nothing new. For most of history tribal identification aided in survival, reinforcing the need to stay together in small communities for comfort and safety. Movement for most of man's time on earth meant risk. For example, hunter gatherers were at more risk than their brethren who made more permanent camps, but their search for food outweighed the risk of starvation, so they moved about but traveled in packs to assure a minimal level of safety.

Lack of vital resources is enough to make most people move, at least those who are able to do so. For example, between the years of 1845 and 1855 the great potato famine in Ireland caused mass starvation. About a million people died, while another 1.5 million took a risk and sought out a new life in America. They were willing to risk a perilous sea journey, disease, and even indigenous prejudice upon arrival because all that peril outweighed the near certainty of death by starvation.

Sometimes opportunity leads folks to move as well. In the middle of the Irish potato famine, during the winter of 1848, United States President James Polk announced that gold had been found in California. Suddenly the California gold rush was on. While famine pushed people from their homeland, the Gold

Rush pulled people on to new lands. This combination caused the non-native population of California to swell to about 100,000 inhabitants, up from a mere 1,000 before the influence of these forces came to play, all in about a year's time.

With this precept Musashi is telling us that it makes no difference where we live. Of course he is not talking about extreme situations like leaving crowded, plague-infested towns for the safety of the countryside during the Black Death or escaping famine in 19th Century Ireland. Supporting life is essential and foundational. Nevertheless, Musashi was saying that he didn't care if he had prestige address, a master bathroom, or a walk-in closet. These 21st Century amenities would have been absurd to his utilitarian worldview.

Let's face it, a bathroom is not a necessity from a comfort standpoint, but it is important from a sanitation standpoint. Even in feudal Japan, placing 20,000 samurai on a field in preparation for battle required proper sanitation to avoid disease, so they dug latrines, assured adequate sanitation, and kept their cookpots clean. Similarly, a Neanderthal's wooden peg driven into the wall kept his furs out of the mud on his cave floor just as well as any walk-in closet keeps our clothes off the floor in modern homes. It's all a matter of degree... In other words, utilitarian sensibility lightens our load in life and frees us to explore other, more meaningful aspects of existence.

This is a time-honored tradition. Looking at all the great religions you will see that their mystics all lived lightly. In secular society most great artists live a Spartan existence too, keeping only what they need for their artwork plus, perhaps, a little extra for comfort and convenience. It is a focus, a clarity that only gets sharpened by the divestment of worldly importance of "things." An address, on the other hand, means little, it is nothing more than a function of the residence. The real question is whether or not the address we have chosen provides access to needed resources, adequate safety, and friends or family. If so, a move is unlikely. Moving is a disturbance, oftentimes a risky and time-consuming one, that's best forgone except to escape danger such as famine or disease or to move toward significant opportunity such as education or employment.

I agree with Musashi. In the end it makes little difference where we live, so long as we can live our lives with the qualities that make for a good life.

Warrior:

I understand this precept and why Musashi included it in his 21 lessons. However, while I agree with some of the sentiment behind this precept, I disagree with taking this on face value and having an indifference to where you live.

First, let's look at the positive aspects of this precept. It reminds me of the old saying, "Home is where you hang your hat." I like the belief that you should not be affected or influenced by your physical environment, and that you are who you are no matter where you are. I also like the belief that you can become all you can be regardless of where you live or grow up. It also aligns well with the romanticized wandering warrior who endures harsh living conditions while traveling forsaken paths to right wrongs and avenge injustices. Additionally, it is a practical precept for the soldier or warrior in combat who must be indifferent to living conditions and focus on the task at hand, namely killing enemies, winning battles, and ultimately becoming victorious in war. So, yes, I get all that. But I still don't agree with being indifferent to where you live as this precept advises…

There are several reasons why I don't agree with Musashi, and the first relates to safety. There is no question that where you live relates to safety issues. When you live alone and are arguably the greatest swordsman in the land, being indifferent to where you live comes a bit easier than it does to most of us mere mortal types, especially when we have families to think about. When selecting a place to live, I don't just disagree with Musashi, I think it would be stupid to be indifferent. I teach people to think about safety when choosing a place to live. This includes a location that is in a safe neighborhood, has safe schools, and an apartment or house that has safety features that not only protect from the criminal element, but also natural disasters that are frequent in that location. I understand that there will be financial and other conditions that come into play, and the levels of security that each individual is comfortable with will vary. But that in no way means people should be indifferent in regards to where they live and safety issues, it just means that it is up to each person to seek the most secure and safe place to live within their means. In this context, indifference really could be the difference between life and death. There is no way I'm going to be indifferent when it comes to my family's safety. You shouldn't either.

The second reason I don't agree with Musashi's precept relates to productivity. Where you live and where you work directly affect your productivity. Yes, I know that some individuals can perform an enormous amount of work with little resources and under less than desirable conditions and locations. But in general, if you create the living and working environment that works best for you, it will increase your productivity and enjoyment of what you are doing. It is very individual and will be determined by your own values, your own likes, dislikes and other personal preferences, not to mention, finances. Where you live can affect your productivity when it comes to your work, training, and everything else you do. You won't maximize your potential if you are indifferent to where you live.

The third and final reason I disagree with this precept that I'll address here is related to enjoying life and living to the fullest. While I don't advocate the extravagant gluttony that some homes of the rich and famous seem to ooze from their seams, I don't believe in living the life of an ascetic either.* There is absolutely nothing wrong with wanting to own a nice home and possess luxurious things. There is nothing wrong with wanting to provide the absolute best for your family. I'll even go so far to say if you are a parent, it is your duty to provide not only love and nurturing, but also the safest and best home to your children that you are able to provide. And you are not going to do this by being indifferent to where you live.

Musashi may have been indifferent to where he lived, and as a warrior I understand the precept for limited conditions. But if you want to furnish a home for yourself and family that provides safety, a place to be productive, and a nicer place to live, you must take an active interest in where you live and work toward making it the best home you can.

Teacher:

I don't know what Musashi was trying to get across with this precept. Could it be a follow up to the previous precept on having no preferences? Is it referring to castles vs. huts or caves? Or is it more about, as he never did in life, settling down. My mind leans toward him advising against settling down in one place.

There are those who view the settled life as a type of prison. When a person settles, they end up with responsibilities toward

---

* Unless that is really your calling and what you choose to do. It's admirable in a way, but not something I would choose.

other people. To some these responsibilities are part of life and in no way present a burden of any kind, but to other people who want to only answer to their own whims settling down can be highly problematic.

We could debate back and forth about which side of that argument is correct, but the person advocating either side of the discussion is going to be arguing from his or her own bias. I would be arguing for the idea that settling down and raising a family is the more rewarding way to live. I would be able to give all kinds of reasons, justifications and evidence as to why my position on the topic is correct. But a person who has chosen to be responsible only to their own self, life, and wishes is going to be able to provide the same strong reasoning for their side of the argument.

It is important to recognize that Musashi was speaking from his own experiences and personal worldview. Personally, I could not endorse this precept if my assumption about his intended meaning is correct, which it may or may not be. Nevertheless, from my perspective there is simply too much good that has come from having my wife and my three wonderful kids in my life. I would not trade them for anything or anyplace in the world.

Settling down or moving about, it's a preference that often changes with one's age and lifestyle too. Perhaps you've grown up in a small town and want to move across the country for college, to be with your significant other, or to find a job. Or, maybe you grew up in a big city and want to give rural culture a try. Perhaps you want to travel around the world, sow your wild oats as it were, and then identify the perfect place to settle down. This is something that each individual must grapple with on his or her own.

Insurance Executive:

Maybe if we still lived in Musashi's time and we could hack to pieces the neighbor on our left that plays his music too loud or hack up the moron on our right that allows his pit bull to run free I'd agree with this precept. But no such luck, err, I mean, thankfully we now live in civilized times with strict laws against such violence.

To be apathetic about where one lives is a whole lot of naïve and potentially dangerous. Let's say you live on the edge of a high seaside cliff that is crumbling away each year. While you might not have as much lawn to mow as you did when you first moved in four years ago, your indifference to where you live might result in your family and your house falling off the edge and dropping into a furiously agitated sea.

While he wrote this precept, one has to wonder how closely he followed it himself. For example, he wasn't indifferent as to where he lived when he wrote at least one of his books. He didn't choose a writing site in a densely populated community or next to a musician who taught young people wind instruments. No, he chose the dark, dank quiet of a cave.

But might this precept be a metaphor, say, a continuation of the great swordsman's philosophy of don't sweat the small stuff? Perhaps he meant it's far more important to spend every waking moment on perfecting the self, in his case his martial arts, writing, sculpting, and painting. Maybe he thought that compared to the mastery of self-defense—let's not forget the violent times he lived in, not to mention all the challenges that came his way—the place he rested his head at night was irrelevant. While the times are certainly different today and our modern culture is remote from the late 1500s and early 1600s Japan, I think Musashi might even today still be indifferent to those things he deemed of less importance than his pursuits.

Some pundits say he was a genius because, by his own words, he was self-taught. He never had a teacher for any of the things he came to master. As we see so often, geniuses—great composers, scientists, actors, and writers—are often so intensely focused on their narrow field of expertise that other parts of their life are found lacking. Put on a pleasant outward appearance? Who needs it? Friends, family, and a spouse? Nah, too distracting... Home and hearth? One more thing to sidetrack from what is really important.

Perhaps the takeaway here is how we should examine our lives to deem what is really important and what we are wasting too much time on. People for example. So often we waste time thinking about people from our past. We still feel hurt by their actions or angry at what they didn't do. Why give them our precious time? After all, there is a reason they didn't make it into our future. When you dwell on such things too much and too long, you make them more important than they really are. Don't waste time on people and things you have lost. They are in the past. Learn from the loss—sometimes you discover it really wasn't much of a loss after all—and focus on your life right here and right now. Live life in the present with an eye on the future, don't live it backwards.

To take this precept literally, I would have to disagree with the great Musashi. It's very important where you live. As a metaphor I can agree with, however, care about the people and things in your life that are important to you and rid yourself of those things that waste your precious time.

Businessman:

Most businesses are hierarchical in nature, with an executive or executive council at the top, various layers of management in the middle, and ordinary employees at the bottom. This structure, which varies considerably with the size and scope of the organization, is designed to balance accountability with the need to make and enact decisions quickly. While there are thousands of entry level positions at the bottom of the pyramid available for those of us who are starting out our careers, the number of job openings diminishes quickly the higher up we go. There are only a handful of executive openings at any given point in time in any given industry. Consequently, to have the most opportunities for career growth we may need to be indifferent to where we live, at least if climbing the corporate ladder as quickly as possible is what we have in mind for success.

Yes, we may need to move around from time to time, but we must do so thoughtfully. All jobs are not created equal. Take the right position at the wrong company and we face a cultural clash that will make us regret it… and force us to quickly move on to other things. For example, former CEO of Continental Airlines Gordon Bethune pulled his ailing airline company out of bankruptcy and made a remarkable turnaround. Under his leadership Continental went from being ranked at the bottom of every measurable performance category to winning more J.D. Power & Associates awards for customer satisfaction than any other airline in the world. At Continental Bethune was a rock star by any measure, but he did not have nearly the same legacy during the six years that he worked at The Boeing Company.

Bethune was responsible for the aerospace giant's Renton factory that produced their "narrow aisle" 737 and 757 airplane models. Despite being a licensed commercial pilot, FAA-certified airframe and power plant mechanic, and airline industry expert, all factors that at face value should have meant a perfect fit, he felt stymied in that position. In fact, he told reporters that he was "tired of the bureaucracy" when asked why he left to take a new job at Continental. We all must heed this lesson. Before accepting any job it is prudent to clearly understand the corporate culture, what we are being asked to do, how success will be measured, and what support we can count on. In this fashion we have a better chance of knowing that the opportunity is a good match for our knowledge, skills, and abilities and that the bureaucracy will allows us to succeed before taking any new job.

Locations matter too. For example, a position that pays $150,000 a year in Charleston, South Carolina has far better remuneration than an identical one with the same salary anywhere in Silicon Valley, the high-tech center located in the southern portion of the San Francisco Bay Area in the state of California. Relative buying power between the two areas couldn't be farther apart. In fact, as of 2013 median salaries were roughly 3.2 times higher in San Francisco than they were in Charleston. Tax rates, buying power, and job opportunities all differ dramatically by where we live. And, let's face it, there's a tremendous difference in culture between the Southern United States and the West Coast, one that not everyone can comfortably adapt or transition to.

Where we live determines who we meet, what we can and cannot do, and a host of other lifestyle factors that merit consideration beyond the job. We may be in the office 10 to 12 hours a day in many cases, but there's more to life than working. For example, I love Anchorage, Alaska. I have several relatives who live there and it's one of my favorite places in the world to visit. Despite a multitude of creatures that might want to gore or eat me, the fishing, hunting, boating, and outdoor life simply cannot be beat... for about two thirds of the year. The rest of the time it's dark, cold, and nasty. Folks who live there may not get their vehicles started without a block heater and simply driving to the store for a carton of milk can be hazardous to their health since they're often doing it in the dark in the middle of a snowstorm while traversing sheets of compact snow and ice. If you can't handle several months at a time with virtually no daylight and frigid temperatures, Anchorage in wintertime is not a very good place to be.

So, should we be indifferent to where we live as Musashi instructs? That really depends on our priorities. If career success tops the list and we find the perfect opportunity then we must be willing to move around despite any discomfort with the geography, weather, or culture we encounter in the new location. However, if other factors are important to us then we may need to hurt our heads a bit more before deciding whether or not to take the job.

Some factors to consider should include the relative cost of living, stability of employment at the new company/location, alternate employers in the area in case we get it wrong, the price of comparable housing, reimbursement for moving expenses, traffic and commute times, accessibility to friends and family, availability of quality healthcare, recreational opportunities, and weather conditions to name a few. If we have young children then availability of reputable daycare, the quality of nearby schools, and the impact on our family will likely play a significant role in our decision too. And, of course, there's the inconvenience and aggravation packing up all our stuff, getting out of our lease or selling our home, and moving to contend with too. Carefully consider these and other meaningful factors and balance them against the opportunity costs of not making the move. It's a cost/benefit analysis tempered by the aforementioned intangibles that should ultimately determine our decision.

Personally I am by no means indifferent to where I live. That's both a luxury and a hardship, but one I'm more than willing to endure.

PRECEPT 13

Do not pursue the taste of good food

"You don't have to cook fancy or complicated masterpieces—just good food from fresh ingredients."
— Julia Child

Monk:

As a young man working construction, the hours were often long and the work was always hard. When I say construction I don't mean that I worked on a steel girder supervising others, I mean I was on the ground with a shovel in my hand more often than not. Some days if I was deemed "on my game" I earned the privilege to go ahead and run the Bobcat, a small front-loader. We were paid every two weeks, but it didn't really cover the bills. The money was always short by the end of week two. That summer the best meals that I ate were the ones that I made in my apartment's small kitchen. I had a bag of frozen vegetables, a bag of rice, and two fresh trout that my father gave me. I metered out the rice, the two fish, and the vegetables. That day was Tuesday and I had to make it all last until Friday.

Those evenings I found myself eating my meager meals and not being horribly particular about them; I was happy enough just to have had the food. In fact I remember sitting in the hot apartment on a used couch rolling the skin of the fish around little balls of rice I had formed and eating the skin so as not to miss any food. In other words, I was just eating what I had so that I wouldn't starve—nothing close to pursuing the taste of good food. Heck, it was the only food I had.

Sustenance is core to human existence, so food is something that's addressed by a variety of different sources, both secular and religious. For example, St. Benedict (480 – 543 AD) wrote

73 conventions for his monastic brothers to follow. These rules, called "The Holy Rule of St. Benedict," cover subjects as diverse as when a brother should or should not speak to an admonition not to strike each other (unless of course the abbot has given the brother authority to strike another member of the order). Like Musashi, Benedict had a word or two on food:

> "Above all things, however, over-indulgence must be avoided and a monk must never be overtaken by indigestion; for there is nothing so opposed to the Christian character as over-indulgence according to Our Lord's words, 'See to it that your hearts be not burdened with over-indulgence' (Luke 21:34). Young boys shall not receive the same amount of food as their elders, but less; and frugality shall be observed in all circumstances. Except for the sick who are very weak, let all abstain entirely from eating the flesh of four-footed animals."

Two men from different cultures, backgrounds, and times who clearly never crossed paths came to similar conclusions. Interesting, huh? When this commonality of thought arises from such divergent sources, it requires a review, an audit as to why and how these similar recommendations were made. Now Musashi was far pithier than Benedict (whose quote runs far, far longer than the excerpt I listed above, 231 words to Musashi's 8), and what is said is often as important as what is not said, however, when it comes to the heart of the matter it is clear that these two men saw food in a similar light. They both believed that food was sustenance. It was to be utilized as nourishment, not sought after solely for enjoyment. I am quite confident that these men took small pleasure in whatever came their way whenever skillfully prepared food was available, such as during liturgical feasts in Benedict's time, but they didn't go out of their way to search for it. Both men were honed by hunger. Musashi lived for a few years in a cave and so did Benedict. Both men scavenged, accepted charity, and maybe indulged in other ways of getting food as well.

For those who have lived a Spartan existence, hunger gives a new appreciation to food. Having food is far different than not having food; only oxygen and water rate higher on the needs list of human existence. And although it appears obvious, this concept is rarely thought about or addressed. Hunger re-contextualizes a person's relationship to food, as food is suddenly about survival and not just enjoyment. And, it does so for the rest of the person's life. Musashi and Benedict want you to keep food in perspective.

Don't get focused on food for food's sake, but rather enjoy what you have. Make the most of the food you have, and then use that food for the bigger things in life.

Warrior:

I'm going to come right out and say I don't agree with Musashi on this precept. However, it does appear that Bruce Lee at least read these precepts a time or two. In the book *The Art of Expressing The Human Body*, compiled and edited by John Little, it states, "Lee made the following annotations about consuming only the calories your body actually needs, rather than simply indulging yourself in the culinary pleasures: 'when you are a martial artist, you are a nut; you go to extremes to improve yourself as a martial artist. And one way is to eat only what your body requires and not get carried away with sensual [eating] pleasures.' Lee also noted: 'When you are a martial artist, you only eat what you require and don't get carried away with foods that don't benefit you as a martial artist.'"

While Lee believed in staying away from foods with empty caloric content and little nutritive value, according to Little, he didn't actually give the subject of nutrition more than a cursory investigation. And according to Lee's wife, Lee enjoyed Chinese food over Western food as he felt the latter was rather monotonous, even though he was fond of Western steak and even ate at McDonald's from time to time. And note that Lee didn't say not to pursue the taste of good food; he just said not to get carried away with sensual eating pleasures. There's a big difference in the two.

I'll be the first to say that we shouldn't take the gluttonous path of over indulging in high fat, high sugar, non-nutritious junk that has contributed to what the media calls an obesity epidemic. However, I think we should pursue the taste of "good" food where good is defined as healthy and nutritious; and I don't believe we have to completely omit the pursuit of good food where good is defined as tasting great even if not quite so good for you. Maybe on this topic we should listen to the founder of Aikido, Morihei Ueshiba (1883 – 1969), who wrote in *The Secret Teachings of Aikido*, "Food is a gift from the universe. No, in a sense food is the universe."

When we take this as meaning to pursue the taste of good food, as in food that is healthy and nutritious, it is easy to agree with me and disagree with Musashi. We want to eat foods that nourish and energize us, while avoiding those meals that make us feel tired and sluggish. We also know that conditions like hypertension, heart disease, certain cancers, diabetes, osteoporosis, and osteoarthritis can be attributed to diet. It only makes sense for a warrior to consume foods that will keep him or her as healthy, fit and strong as possible. And when I was in the Army, this meant large quantities of any food I could obtain. And you can bet that all of us preferred and pursued better tasting food than the MREs we had to eat in the field whenever we could.*

But, what about the interpretation of this precept that we shouldn't be pursuing foods that taste good but are not healthy for us? One could agree with this and say that it is good advice to follow. Nevertheless, I'm still going to disagree. I know that M&Ms, milkshakes, French fries, the skin of fried chicken, biscuits and gravy, ice cream, and mashed potatoes and gravy are all high calorie foods with minimal nutritional value compared to the calories. I've eaten them in the past and I'm going to continue to eat them in the future. Why? Because they taste good and I like them.

I don't believe a warrior, or anyone else for that matter, must live the life of an ascetic. Just as I stated under precept 12 that there is absolutely nothing wrong with wanting to own a nice home and possess luxurious things, there is nothing wrong with the pursuit of eating fine meals that you enjoy. Yes, the warrior must be disciplined and ensure that he or she maintains a high level of health and fitness, but that does not mean you can't look forward to and indulge in a treat once in a while.

Teacher:

To me this speaks directly to thoughts of moderation. But I have to stop short of saying that this one is a good precept.

Life is short. I have long been an advocate of people spending their money on experiences rather than on things. Food is somewhat unique in that it is both a thing and an experience.

---

* Meals Ready to Eat (MREs) were brought into military use during the 1980s to replace heavy, bulky food supplies, making them easier for soldiers to use in the field on deployment. MREs are self-contained and usually include a heating device. They have a durable packaging that can withstand high drops a shelf-life of about 5 years.

And there is nothing more beneficial to my very being than good food enjoyed with the people I love.

I cringe when I see people eating kale and other horrible tasting cuisine in an effort to be healthy. Food isn't medicine, it is sustenance! The experience of good food is a pleasure almost without equal. Almost…

Like anything else in life, food of any quality must be kept within moderation. As I mentioned earlier, I had my time where food was my life. I overdid it and I now suffer from some medical issues as a result. But this does not lead me to preach that good food is to be avoided. I tell people to exercise discipline in their diet, but any extreme in any aspect of your life is going to be bad for your overall health. Never forget that it is every bit as possible to kill yourself by drinking too much water as it is by eating too much bacon.

Sure, we should not overindulge, but why can we not enjoy the taste of good food? We only get one pass through this life. Enjoy what you can because the ride gets really rocky way too often.

Insurance Executive:

Buddha and Socrates lived roughly 2,500 years ago. While it's doubtful they ran into each other, they shared one philosophy of life that has remains to this day. Socrates said, "Everything in moderation. Nothing in excess." Buddha said, to paraphrase, "We find glory and wonder when we walk the middle way, i.e., moderation."

I'm guessing more people violate this precept than follow it.

Taking the precept "Do not pursue the taste of good food" literally, the words of Socrates and Buddha mean not to overindulge in food, but rather consume enough to satisfy hunger and fuel the body with the nutrients it requires to sustain good health. Sadly, you only have to look around you to see many people in the United States are not following this wisdom.

Keeping with the literal translation of this precept, I would ask, why not pursue it? Eating delicious food is one of the pleasures of life. Good food nourishes the body, nourishes the soul, and when it's shared with friends and family it enhances the joy. Is it possible to enjoy and share the moment and do so with moderation? Yes. Can it be hard? Oh yes. Ignore the middle path and you will suffer gastric discomfort, added weight, and deterioration of health.

It has been said, the author unknown, "A life devoted to seeking pleasure is a life committed to discontent." Moderation is not only important in the quantity of good food consumed but also in the pursuit of it. When you pursue anything to the extent other aspects of life are ignored, it becomes clear there is an unbalance. But when you travel the middle path, life is more in balance and thus more complete and satisfying.

If we take a broader view of the precept, Musashi might have been saying there is danger in focusing on only one thing. For example, there are upwardly mobile people in my field who work 10- and 12-hour days, including one or both weekends. Yes, they might very well climb the corporate ladder but at what expense? It's not uncommon for such narrowly focused people to lose connection with their spouse, children, and friends, all for prestige, wealth, and an expensive house. But of what value is a million dollar abode when there is no one in it waiting for you when you do come home?

If we replace the pursuit of "food" with the relentless pursuit of fame, fortune, prestige in the workplace, mastery of the martial arts, physical perfection, endless sexual conquests, and even advanced degrees in education, it becomes clear the middle path has been lost. When that happens, more times than not, what follows is a disaster. This can take the form of destructive mental stress, physical debilitation, and total loss of those things given up during the all-encompassing pursuit.

So am I saying not to master whatever interests you? No. It's important, however, for the sake of your health and relationships, to tread softly so you stay as close to the middle path as you can. In this way, you maintain balance in your life as you pursue your goals and you will do so without losing other things that are important to you.

Businessman:

Unless we're awful lucky in playing the lottery or some other game of chance, or have inherited great wealth and fortune, we're going to need a job to pay the bills. Work is, well… work. We all know that we must take work seriously while at the office, but we also know that it's unhealthy to live for work alone. Sometimes a simple reward, a good meal or an excellent drink shared with a close friend, lover, or even a professional colleague, is exactly the right thing to make our day a little brighter. We certainly don't want to be consumed by it, obsession is never a good thing when it comes to dining or drinking, but pursuing the taste of good food from time-to-time is not at all bad. In fact, it can be an important part of conducting commerce too.

Here's the deal, business meals matter, especially in certain parts of the world, so we need to be educated in the etiquette of dining appropriately. There are obvious things such as validating the reservation, arriving a little early, following the lead of our host, not ordering the most expensive item on the menu, not consuming or at least not overindulging in alcohol, turning off smartphones, being courteous to those around us, not talking with our mouths full, and the like, but it can go deeper than that. There's a plethora of protocols to consider. For instance, understanding which fork to use with each course of the meal, knowing how to sniff the cork and test the wine prior to accepting it from the sommelier, and similar nuances of dining decorum can make us come across as sophisticated and worldly or crude and naïve. These impressions matter, particularly when these business meetings are with folks who work for other companies such as during protracted contract negotiations where off-hours get-togethers are part of the "dance." The same thing holds true for less pretentious things such as interviewing for a new job or impressing a skill team or advancement committee to earn a promotion.

For example, when the Nordstrom family was directly involved in hiring executives back in the 80s through the mid-90s, they would routinely take leading candidates to lunch or dinner as part of the interview process. If the prospective executive put salt or pepper on his or her food prior to tasting it that person was not hired under the assumption that they made decisions by force of habit rather than after prudently investigating the situation, whereas someone who tasted their food first and then seasoned it had a chance to earn the position. Many other companies include meals in the interview process too, since working lunches, dinner meetings, and the like a normal part of the routine while on the job. In fact, I once had an interview where the search committee had the restaurant's server intentionally bring the wrong thing to observe how I reacted to his error.*

Our approach to food even goes beyond the job, affecting our everyday lives too. According to a recent study published in

---

* Apparently I handled it well since they offered me the job.

the journal *Obesity*, people who eat an eclectic variety of foods, things like *kimchi* (a spicy, fermented Korean side dish made from vegetables), beef tongue, and *seitan* (a Japanese wheat "meat" made from gluten), tend to be more physically active, interested in nutrition, and healthier than their peers who partake in less adventurous diets. Foodies tend to have a lower body mass index, which is virtually always a good thing, and they tend to have a greater love for cooking which implies that they eat a diet that is simultaneously more wholesome and more cost-effective than that consumed by their peers as well. Gluttony is clearly unhealthy, but as this and other studies agree, there's nothing wrong with caring about food, knowing your way around the kitchen, and enjoying a good meal.

I must disagree with Musashi about this precept. Pursuing the taste of good food or drink can be highly rewarding. To give some credence to his admonishment, however, we must not overdo it to the point of obsession or gluttony.

PRECEPT 14

Do not hold on to possessions you no longer need

"There are only two kinds of freedom in the world;
the freedom of the rich and powerful, and the freedom
of the artist and the monk who renounces possessions."

— Anais Nin

Monk:

The woman sat across the desk from me and talked about cleaning out her father's home after his death. Her father had put everything in order, from final instructions to legal paperwork, all the way down to the boxes in the attic that he had neatly stacked and labeled. Nevertheless, it was still hard for her to go through everything as you can well imagine. Up in the attic she came upon her rocking horse. An only child, her parents had kept it in hopes that that she might have a child someday, but she had chosen not to do so. So, now the painted eyes of her childhood toy were staring back at her. A little wooden rocking horse that held the memories of childhood, and quiet hopes for the future.

She threw the rocking horse away.

Reading about this incident our emotions want us to go directly to the rocking horse and her tossing it into the dumpster. We might wonder why she couldn't have given it away to some kid who could have used it instead. After all, it was meaningful enough to her father that he'd kept it for decades. Maybe she had friend or relative with a small child who would similarly cherish the heirloom. Seems heartless doesn't it? A dumpster?! Stop, don't focus on how she chose to get rid of the rocking horse, but why.

When something is no longer useful, it is important to let it go. This can refer to emotions, items, and even memories. All of these three things take effort and energy to hang onto, so it can easily become energy poorly spent if we focus on the wrong things. Repeatedly reliving bad experiences is a waste of energy just like reshuffling old boxes of VHS tapes when we no longer have a player that can be used to view the movies on. Useless emotions, worn out objects and hurtful memories are all rubbish and should be treated that way. This doesn't mean that we can't learn from them, sort of like recycling to keep the analogy, but if anything is no longer useful it ought to be discarded.

And, of course, there's the question of whether or not we truly own anything in the first place? The answer clearly is no, we don't actually own anything we only borrow it for a time. With this simple knowledge we should look at the things in our life and ask the question, "Do I need this?" We must evaluate whether or not we truly need it while being brutally honest with ourselves and our emotions. Musashi lived a life of few possessions except what he considered to be truly important. If he had no use for something it was discarded, or more likely never considered for inclusion in the first place.

Most of us aren't ascetics or hoarders, our lives fall somewhere in-between. But, most of us err on the side of holding on to too much stuff, crowding our lives, our homes, and even our heads with junk. Take some time to do an honest self-audit. How much stuff are you holding onto that you no longer need? Toss the clutter and you'll be far better for having done so.

Warrior:

This precept is one of practicality, and one I agree with completely. However, I do have to admit that it is one I haven't always followed. I too have been caught up in the materialistic habit of keeping stuff.* Allow me a circuitous route to get to why I think Musashi was on point with this precept on not holding on to possessions you no longer need. A fundamental trait of the warrior is that of taking action and getting things done. At its very core, taking action saves lives. The warrior knows he must get off the X. If someone is shooting at you, slashing at you, or throwing a punch at your nose, you must take action. Doing nothing will get

---

* If you haven't ever listened to George Carlin's bit on "stuff," you should go find it on YouTube. Not only is it funny, it's an accurate reflection on our society's obsession with collecting more possessions.

you shot, stabbed, or hit. What you do will be dependent on many variables, but you absolutely must do something. This is true for just about any threatening situation. People have survived plane crashes only to die from smoke inhalation because they failed to immediately get up and get off the aircraft. Survivors actually passed those who later died on the way toward the exits. Taking action saves lives.

Because of the necessity of taking action to survive combat, and the discipline instilled through a warrior's training, warriors are often high producers that get more done. When I teach people warrior principles to help them achieve success in various occupations and endeavors, the principles of discipline and taking action are among the most important. When it comes to taking action and getting more done, few have a stronger and better message that Don Aslett (1935 –). I've had the pleasure of meeting this prolific author from Idaho and have enjoyed many of his books. He said is perfectly in the first book of his I read back in 1996, *How To Have A 48-Hour Day*. He wrote, "The number one, the very first step to become a 'more doer,' a high producer, is to stop accumulating and start eliminating. In other words, dejunk!"

Junk and clutter in and around homes, offices, and lives creates stress and results in an amazing amount of wasted time. There is a lot of time consumed over the ownership of stuff. And many of these possessions are no longer needed and don't add any value to our lives, but they certainly waste our time and create unnecessary problems we'd be better off without. Therefore, if you want to be a top producer, a person of action, a warrior; get rid of anything you don't use or want. It's ridiculous to love what can't love you back, and a warrior will refrain from becoming attached to anything that doesn't serve his or her purpose.

I think Musashi understood this key to efficiency and time management. After all, time spent with possessions you no longer need is time taken away from the most important of activities: training. I think this is one of the most important and practical of Musashi's twenty-one precepts. It's not only important for warriors, but for anyone wanting to increase their personal productivity and efficiency. So, take Musashi's advice and get rid of that stuff you no longer need.

Teacher:

There is something to be said for being practical. As I read it this precept is all about being practical. For a person in Musashi's life and time having too many possessions, especially any unnecessary possessions, would be a real hindrance. And for some people in our own time, this advice will ring true.

It also follows along with Buddhist precepts too, in that when we have possessions we seem in a very real sense to be owned by them rather than owning them. For some people, possessions alter their decisions and attitudes toward people or life changes. For an example, I kept my trophies from martial arts tournaments in my younger days well into my middle age. One was a prized possession to me. It was from a *taekwondo* tournament in 1995, a National Championships Grand Champion trophy. As I aged and my body became less flexible and much more crumbly, that trophy became a more and more powerful reminder of the person I was back then.

Unfortunately I held on to that trophy for too long. I remember almost losing my temper when it was broken when being moved into the garage. Thoughts about how my wife had always hated that trophy because it represented a time when I was the *best* started rolling through my mind. It was much like the father in the movie *A Christmas Story*, when the mother breaks the lamp. I am thankful that rational thought took over before I started actually *saying* the words that were in my head. There could have been a big problem… There was also a strange but powerful sense of shutting a door when I threw the trophies in the trash when we sold that house and were leaving for the final time. I was no longer going to have to find a place to keep my sacred objects. Never again would there be a moment of losing my temper over things that were no longer needed.

This is just one small example of the way that our possessions start to change our thinking. In my case it served as a reminder of past triumph. In most cases it is merely a reminder that the past *really* happened. For many people, the past seems too much of a dream to have been real, and we need those reminders that certain things actually occurred.

We place a higher than needed importance on the past, and often we do so at the cost of the present. This also falls back onto the Buddhist philosophy of "living in the now." But we do need to remember, regardless of our personal religious beliefs, that the now is all that is real. It is all that we have and all that we can influence.

Insurance Executive:

Someone said an object in possession seldom retains the same charm it had in pursuit. It's fine to value your possessions but some people find themselves continuously seeking more and more for no other reason than to acquire. Those rare few that are able to stop the madness—usually with the help of a therapist or the sudden realization of some kind—and look at themselves and their possessions objectively, realize they don't need most of it.

My husband claims his only bad habit is he buys a new car every two years. He knows it's a waste of money but he does it anyway for no other reason than he likes to drive a new car. He even admits that while the joy wears off in three or four months, he continues this habitual pattern anyway because at least for the remainder of two-year period, he has a shiny ride with that new car smell. Before I met him he owned a new BMW. He said it was a wonderful car but owning it was extraordinarily stressful. He was constantly worried he was going to get into an accident, someone would bang their car door into it, or it would be stolen. As it turned out, he did back into another car and break a taillight and someone did ding his door with a grocery cart. Topping his worse fears realized were the astronomical cost of repairs. That time he didn't wait the full two years before he got a new car, a Ford pickup.

Is this sick? Crazy? Money wasting? I suppose one could argue it so, but I figure if it's as he says his only fault (yeah, right), it can be overlooked. Plus I get to ride in a new car too.

He teases me that I will soon reach my goal of possessing every perfume in existence. Okay, I might have one or two… hundred, but it's something I enjoy. Sick? Crazy? Again, one could argue it so. For now, I'll stay out of the fray and spray on a little Jasmine Noir.

If acquiring new possessions can be a problem when taken to extremes (collecting perfumes not being one of them; I'm sure of it), holding onto old things no longer needed just might be an issue. Psychologists tell us that possessions have a way of tying us down. When you think of your situation honestly, some of your things really bring you joy, while your remaining possessions clutter your environment and ultimately your mind. A cluttered mind means more stress, and don't you already have enough? Besides the clutter factor, there is also the worry factor: Someone could steal it or damage it… or maybe it'll become obsolete.

I had a friend who was never happy unless he had a new boat, car, or house. The new car he got every year, the new boat every two years, and a different house every five. He kept pictures of them in an ever thickening scrapbook and would page through them wistfully smiling and remembering, just as other people do when looking at their photos of their vacations or family gatherings. He married a woman who was the same way. The marriage would be short-lived, though—just like their possessions.

What I try to do, and it can be difficult and I'm not always successful, is to distinguish between what my husband and I *need* to truly enjoy our daily life, and get rid of the rest. There is great pleasure in freeing up space that was only cluttering our lives.

Might this also relate to toxic people in our lives? Most religions teach us to love one another, have compassion for others, and help our fellow man when we can. After all, we're all doing the best we can in this difficult life. But this doesn't mean we have to like every person we meet on our path, nor does it mean we have to keep him or her in our lives if there are options. It's not always possible, but when it is, it's important to our sanity to clear the clutter of those toxic to us. Easy? No, especially when it's a relative or a long-time friend that no longer is.

The Dalai Lama said, "Happiness is not something readymade. It comes from your own actions." So take action now and begin to get rid of old possessions you no longer need and those people poisonous to your wellbeing.

But leave my perfume alone.

Businessman:

The phrase, "We've always done it that way," is anathema in business. It has been the death knell of all too many enterprises, making them late to embrace needed innovations or new opportunities. They blindly cling to the past while losing market share, customers, capital, and jobs. Remember when Polaroid was synonymous for photograph?* Not so much anymore, huh?

---

* Founded by physicist Edwin Land (1909 – 1991), Polaroid was an early innovator, creating 3-D motion picture cameras and polarized filters for

We must constantly guard against becoming dinosaurs like that at all costs, striving to keep the bureaucracy in check such that we can continuously improve our processes, tools, technology, and talent. In this fashion we will have a real shot at creating products and services that will remain desirable and affordable for our customers. This means being willing to let go of the past to embrace the future. It can be scary, but it's also imperative.

For example, we all know that Thomas Edison invented the first device ever made for recording and playing back the human voice in 1877. His inventions included both the Dictaphone, which was extensively used in business, and the phonograph, which was used by music lovers all around the world. He also founded the world's first record company, Edison Records, an accomplishment that eventually led to the creation of the modern music industry. But, sadly, that invention didn't work out so well for him because Edison Records got left behind... The inflection point came during World War I when the raw materials they needed to manufacture his company's secret wax recipe became scarce. They failed to make the jump from wax cylinders to "needle-cut" records, even though the technology was another Edison Labs invention. This eventually drove them out of business and the company closed its doors in 1929.

Edison Records' experience is by no means unique, oftentimes early inventors lose out to followers because they feel beholden to their discovery and cannot adapt fast enough. If you're old enough you undoubtedly remember Commodore Computers. They were shipping two million units a year during the mid-1980s, a roughly 50% share of the total personal computer market, yet they were bankrupt a decade later. By contrast Apple, one of Commodore's chief competitors from that era, is still going strong today. Why? In large part the company does well because Apple has developed and cultivated a culture of continuous innovation, one that assures that the products and services they offer remain

---

military use during WWII. Their first commercial cameras went on sale in 1948. In the 1970s, a time when cameras used black-and-white film that required harsh chemicals and lengthy post-processing, they introduced a line of automatic, single-lens reflex cameras that produced self-developing color photographs. After Land retired in 1980, the company suffered a steady decline leading to a bankruptcy filing on June 11, 2001, in large part due to their failure to embrace digital technology until well after their competitors. They remained in bankruptcy until 2006, ceased making cameras altogether in 2007, and stopped producing instant film in 2009.

meaningful and relevant to their customer base. And, they've invented some truly out-of-the-box concepts such as iTunes where it's not the music they are selling as much as the delivery channel. In this fashion they make money on other people's hard work as well as on their own. Pretty slick, huh?

Innovation can be challenging, but there's a science to it:

- **Ideate**. At the simplest level the process begins by generating ideas. This can include brainstorming, crowdsourcing, and a host of other methods of coming up with concepts to evaluate. Some ideas may be new things entirely whereas others repurpose old inventions or ideas such as 3M did with its Post-It Notes.*
- **Analyze**. The next step is to open-mindedly vet and analyze the ideas, letting the best ones bubble up to the top. With limited resources we cannot implement everything so we must choose only those that are most likely to pay off in a big way, discarding lesser concepts altogether or saving them for later.
- **Prototype**. Next we create a trial run of the product, service, or process using a "fail fast, fail often" approach as we attempt to develop and refine something we think will be a winner.** Typically this includes leveraging customer input, market research, beta testing, and other factors to help us be certain that we're on the right track and assure that what was envisioned will actually come to fruition.
- **Produce and Support**. Leveraging what we learned with the prototype we finalize the design and put it into production. During the useful life of the product, service, tool, or process there is almost always room for continuous improvement, so we must devote time and resources toward that too.

* Dr. Spencer Silver at 3M was attempting to develop a super-strong adhesive when he accidentally created a low-tack, reusable, pressure-sensitive glue in 1968. He had no use for it until 1974 when a colleague, Art Fry, came up with the idea of using the adhesive to bookmark his hymnal and suddenly the Post-It Note was born. This "fortuitous accident" sells over 50 billion units a year today.

** Fail fast, fail often means that through a process of rapid prototyping we can discover things that won't work with minimal expenditure of resources, set them aside, and move on to the next iteration or idea. It's a way to bring products or services to market faster, cheaper, and with more assurance that they will meet our customer's expectations.

- **Repeat**. Finally, we need to restart the process for our next iteration of invention.

It's not just businesses; careers are killed by blindly clinging to the past too. Continuous learning is vital for keeping ourselves employed and employable. It is a very good idea to obtain a professional certification appropriate for our occupation wherever possible so that we will not only be accredited but also be continuously introduced to thought-leaders and cutting-edge innovations in our industry and vocation. Attending conferences or classes oftentimes lets us rub elbows with pioneering thinkers from other companies whose ideas we can adopt for our own (assuming we obtain permission first, of course). For example, I brought a supplier innovation process into an aerospace company that came from a soft drink manufacturer. While the two industries couldn't be farther apart, we both manage our supply chains similarly so it was a natural fit.

It's not so much unneeded possessions that we need to guard against holding onto in business, but rather outlived ideas, processes, and knowledge. As we evolve, learn, and grow personally and professionally we can discard the things we no longer need.

PRECEPT 15

Do not act following customary beliefs

"One should guard against preaching to young people success in the customary form as the main aim in life. The most important motive for work in school and in life is pleasure in work, pleasure in its result, and the knowledge of the value of the result to the community."

— Albert Einstein

Monk:

Sir Isaac Newton (1642 – 1726) was by all accounts one for the greatest minds that ever strode upon the face of the Earth. For example, he wrote the *Philosophiae Naturalis Principia Mathematica*, the foundational work for the study of mathematics as we know it today. He used prisms to manipulate light and built the first practical reflecting telescope too. He studied sound, motion, cooling, fluids, and much, much more. Newton's scientific studies are transformational, profound, and utterly brilliant even centuries after they were written.

That was all accomplished during his lifetime, however. The majority of his work released posthumously dealt with alchemy, mysticism, and biblical research, dangerously touchy subjects in his day. You see, because the Church and the Crown were one for all intents and purposes during his time, going against any doctrine of the Church was the same as going against the Crown. Even though he disagreed with some of their tenants he wisely held his counsel. Had he pushed the boundaries too far he would have been considered a heretic and punished accordingly, and his vast contributions to science may never have seen the light of day.

Times may be different today, you almost certainly don't risk getting burned at the stake for apostasy, but if you plan to leave the comfort of customary beliefs, attitudes, and ideas you will need to first be prepared to get called out, dismissed, browbeat, and marginalized. This is because every community believes that they are different, they are special and unique, that they are in fact just a little smarter, a little better than the people over in that other town. And why wouldn't somebody think that way? Whether you live where you live by choice or by chance, the odds are good that your residence is in a place where you like the rules and norms that the community has decided to live by. You find enough value, enough reason to stay where you are. It works.

The challenge is that staying in your comfort zone, following the crowd, may serve you well but it simultaneously makes you average. Doing what everybody else does has never been a formula for becoming extraordinary. It's the folks who stray far from the beaten path who make things happen. We all know that Musashi used two swords when everyone else used one. One sword held with two hands on the grip worked well, it won. It was the norm in feudal Japan. This two-hands on one-sword method was refined and perfected until it became truly effective at killing. Musashi rejected this tried and true norm of two-hands on one sword. He went off into the woods alone and came back holding two swords, one in each hand, with which he blazed his bloody path through history. Soon he had grown from bludgeoning a man to death in the street with a wooden stick to perfecting his innovative two-sword method, and even took on disciples whom he felt worthy to learn this new style.

While innovative ideas can set you apart and above the rest, it is important to listen to what is being said about a community. Norms are normal for a reason and we break them at our peril. However, to understand them we must dig deeper. The basic driving forces of life are the same. Everybody wants to be loved, everybody has fear, and everybody has some form of hope or faith. So the customary beliefs are not really customary beliefs, they are affectations of an expression of core human behaviors. You don't necessarily need to break from these values, but rather finding the way that best expresses them uniquely is your challenge.

In other words, if you focus on the affectation, because it is how the community differentiates itself from the rest of the world, then you have lost. Every community, real or virtual, has its rules of membership. Metaphorical dances that must be engaged in and the folks who dance those dances are the mean, the sum of all values divided by the total number of participants. The mean is safe. The mean is comfortable. But, the mean is also conventional.

Look at every great person of history and you will see that he or she not only rejected the norm but more often than not shattered it. Your path to greatness then is to know where the lines are drawn and figure out how far and how fast you can stretch them. You might think outside the box yet keep your counsel like Newton, or boldly challenge the status quo like Musashi, but either way it's vital not to blindly stride along the well-beaten path. Chart your own course in order to leave your mark in life.

Warrior:

As I pondered this precept, I couldn't help but think of one of my favorite Native American warriors, Chief Crazy Horse. This leader of the Lakota has been a favorite of mine ever since visiting the Crazy Horse Memorial in the South Dakota Black Hills a few miles from Mount Rushmore when I was young. Crazy Horse (1840 – 1877) was a leader of the Oglala Lakota (Part of the Sioux Nation) who took up arms against the U.S. Federal government to fight against encroachments on the Lakota territories that included leading a war party to victory against General George Armstrong Custer at the Battle of the Little Bighorn in June 1876.*

The reason this precept reminded me of the great Lakota chief was because of something I read about Crazy Horse in *The Code of The Warrior: In History, Myth, and Everyday Life* by Rick Fields. He wrote, "As Crazy Horse gained experience in fighting the white soldiers, he realized that the Indians would never be able to win if they continued to fight in the old ways. Bravery alone was

---

* Discovery of gold in the Black Hills in 1874 triggered an influx of prospectors into sacred Native American territory which in turn led to retaliatory attacks on the interlopers. In the spring of 1876, the U.S. Army moved against the Lakota and their allies the Cheyenne, who were led by Chiefs Sitting Bull, Crazy Horse, and Gall. On June 25, Custer's scouts spotted an Indian encampment in a valley near the Little Big Horn River. Underestimating the size of the opposing force, the general chose to attack before support could arrive. He and all 225 soldiers under his direct command were slaughtered by the Indians in what has been dubbed "Custer's Last Stand."

not enough against the superior numbers and firepower of the whites, and so Crazy Horse became a skilled strategist."

Even though Crazy Horse wanted nothing to do with the white's civilization and wanted the Lakota to be able to live as their fathers did, and as their forefathers had done, the famed warrior realized that he and those that followed him must fight and engage in battles differently than they customarily had in the past. The ability to adapt and overcome, regardless of the obstacles before him is a trade mark of the warrior throughout centuries. I believe Chief Crazy Horse would understand what Drill Sergeant Hernandez meant when he said during my basic training, "I can roll left, I can roll right, I can low crawl up the middle." Warriors, even those who honor tradition, will shun customary beliefs and methods if there are new and better ways to accomplish the warrior's objectives. The warrior will roll left, roll right, or low crawl up the middle, whichever is necessary to win the battle.

Crazy Horse did whatever he needed to win battles, and he won many, even though he eventually lost the war as the superior numbers of white soldiers were finally too much for the Sioux nation. But while he was fighting, Crazy Horse's strategy contained campaigns that involved using decoys to lead the white soldiers to ambushes, a strategy that didn't always work, but it certainly did against the arrogant and ambitious Lieutenant William J. Fetterman (1833 – 1866). Fetterman had boasted that he could ride through the entire Sioux Nation with eighty men. Against strict orders not to pursue the Indians, Fetterman gave chase to Crazy Horse and his decoys. Fetterman and his eighty two men were wiped out in what became known as the Fetterman Massacre because Chief Crazy Horse learned from past attempts to use decoys and his willingness to look past customary beliefs and act in accordance with what would defeat his enemy.

To use an overused cliché, I believe this precept was Musashi's way of saying, "Think outside the box." One shouldn't just follow customary beliefs for the sake of custom. With each new war, technological and strategic advances are made, and it is critical that the warrior stay ahead of these advances with forward thinking strategy and leadership. Following customary beliefs just won't get you there.

Teacher:

There are several paths that flow from this precept if one were to really take it to heart. These paths can lead to the life of the bold innovator, the rebel without a cause, or the psychopath.

The bold innovator looks at customary beliefs or common knowledge as challenges instead of barriers. The smartphone that is never far away from you is a result of people who looked at the possibilities instead of the difficulties, expense, or customary beliefs regarding what was possible to accomplish. The four-minute mile is another example of a customary belief which fell away after the conviction that a person could not possibly run a mile in four minutes was proven to be wrong in 1954 by Roger Bannister. So, we can see that in one way of looking at this precept there is the possibility of the type of bold innovation which has the potential to really change the way people look at or experience the world. It can be a good thing.

The rebel without a cause is the person we all know in our modern time. These are the people who have dropped all standard or customary beliefs. For instance, their parents were religious so they have decided to *not* be religious. In place of religion many of these folks substitute *causes*, movements such as social justice by way of example. While it sounds good, there is the factor of not examining *why* they are deciding these things that comes into play.

In the case of the modern day "social justice warriors," for instance, most of them do not have the gumption to follow through with their stated beliefs. For example, on the day that the U.S. Supreme Court decided that there was a constitutional right to gay marriage, the social justice warriors were all over social media with a hashtag campaign of *love always wins* (#lovealwayswins). What viscerally demonstrates their true lack of conviction, however, was the fact that on that very same day the terrorist group ISIS executed hundreds of gay men by throwing them from the rooftops of high-rise buildings and posting videos of their atrocities on social media using the exact same hashtag. Despite this, the terrorist's actions were ignored by the social justice crowd.

If they really believed in gay rights this should have been a major problem to them, but it wasn't because they were more interested in the social media aspect of what they were doing. In other words, they were all about making a statement without taking action. Actually taking the fight over *there* would involve work, so nothing was done and the horrific murders were ignored. If these social justice warriors truly cared about gay rights, or women's rights, or freedom of religion, or ending discrimination, or virtually any of the major causes they claim to support then ISIS would be a fruitful target. After all, ISIS terrorists wantonly kill and oppress the very same folks these warriors for justice are ostensibly fighting for. But, there would be hard work involved, as well as the risk of becoming unpopular with ISIS, a group that enjoys killing everyone who disagrees with them.

This lack of action is the end result of wanting to have a cause, needing to stand for something, but not being willing to do any of your own thinking or even honestly caring about the very thing you claim to be fighting for. No terrorist group will ever change their behavior based on some silly hashtag campaign, or a colored overlay on somebody's Facebook profile picture, or anything else for that matter that falls short of extreme force that makes them stop killing people. It would take effort and endanger the lives of those dedicated to the cause in order to stop them. Which, of course, is why the rebels without a cause won't get involved in such things.

Lastly we have the psychopath. The psychopath is going to ignore customary beliefs because these beliefs are for the benefit of the *tribe*, not the individual. Doing what is good for the tribe is in large part what has made our species successful. Sometimes we really need to set our personal pleasures, comforts, and desires aside and do what is best for the group. Our children survive us and we need to ensure that there is a social system still surviving so that *they* may survive. And their children after them... In this fashion we help assure the long-term existence of humanity.

Nevertheless, the psychopath has no way of placing the needs of others above his or her own. What he wants is what matters to him. This is a way out-of-control version of the selfish bastard that we all know. This one is so far out of control, in fact, that not only is he unable to even consider the wants or needs of others he does not even see them as people. They are something else. He has *othered* them. Whatever it is that he classifies himself as being, they are different from that. They are not him, and as such they do not count. Not one iota.

Along with this goes ideas about the general rules we all agree to follow as a group for the common good. The psychopath has no need for these things. If you can imagine, think of something you wanted at some point in your life where literally *nothing* else mattered. This is the mindset of the psychopath. They see what they need or want, and nothing else is there, or at least nothing is there in any degree that would matter. Is there anything that you want so badly that you would do whatever it takes to get it; even if that means that someone would have to die in the process?

For most people, the answer is a quick "no" followed by a qualifying statement. "I could never do that, unless my kid's life was on the line."

See how easy it is go from seeing the thought pattern as being wrong, except when it affects you personally? This is a smaller version of the thought pattern that we are discussing here. Except, where the psychopath is concerned, he does not need a significant other or a child to quantify his statement. His is the more brutal "yes" answer to the original question of *Is there anything that you want so badly that you would do whatever it takes to get it, even if that means that someone would die in the process?*

Customary beliefs are what help us, as a group, to distinguish right from wrong. They help us to understand which actions will be in the interest of all rather than ourselves alone. It is in this way that I have to disagree with this precept.

Insurance Executive:

Clearly Musashi was a free thinker. Although born just a few years after Portuguese trade ships first landed on Japanese shores, Musashi would witness the beginning of a swing in the culture, specifically, the introduction to never-before-seen firearms and Christianity. The cultural change, however brief, wasn't a smooth one. In the Battle of Negashino, for example, the Portuguese employed 2,000 guns to fight an army of sword swinging Samurai (violating the axiom: never bring a knife to a gunfight). Other countries would follow—Netherlands, England, and Spain—bringing with them Christianity as well, in the form of Catholicism.

While a new shogun would expel all foreigners in 1635, the Christian religion remained, along with many European customs. Those Japanese who had converted to Christianity would be persecuted, but no doubt a number of people continued to believe and many of the new customs remained as well, albeit behind closed doors. Musashi lived through many of these turbulent years, especially as an adult in the 1600s. It would seem an easy assumption given the master swordsman's dedication to the samurai way of life, including Buddhist traditions, that he would intensely rebel against customs and beliefs that didn't relate to his thinking as to how Japanese life should be.

I like to think I have always followed my way of thinking and doing things even when they were outside the "custom" at the time. For example, as a teenage girl growing up in my city, it was virtually a tradition to party, meaning drink hard, take drugs, drive dangerously, and do so weekdays and weekends. I didn't go along with the crowd, though, as I decided early on that following the pack and acting out in such a fashion wasn't for me. I didn't believe in it and it didn't fit my personality. So instead of following others, as if I were just another sheep, I stayed away from the herd, and did what I wanted, which was to study business and martial arts. It paid off for me because my skills learned in business classes led me to a career I'm still involved in today. My early martial arts training was sporadic, but when I found the right schools to fit my needs at the time, I jumped in with both feet and have remained actively involved in the fighting arts for many years.

I taught my children to think along the same lines. I taught them when something was popular and in accordance with what they believed was right then they should go ahead and participate. In fact, if a leader was needed, jump in with both feet and lead the pact. Conversely, I said if the popular thing was not in accordance with what they believed to be right—drugs, drinking, stealing from stores, marking walls in graffiti—they should be brave enough to refuse to be involved.

There was a popular poster at the time that depicted a line of girls standing by a balance bar attached along a wall in a ballet school. All the girls were prim and proper in their ballet outfits, standing on the tips of their toes in typical ballet fashion, and extending one graceful arm. Except for one girl; she had hooked her knees over the bar and was hanging upside down, her dress bunched around her head, and her tongue was sticking out at the camera. I told my children, "Be that kid."

There is nothing wrong with following beliefs and customs but only if they fit who you are. If they don't, you should be courageous enough to stand up for what you believe in even when all the sheep are against you.

Businessman:

I see this precept as a call for open-mindedness, a willingness to explore any opportunity no matter how bizarre it might seem at first blush, at least until it's well understood and evaluated. In other words, it's about thinking outside the proverbial box... Few companies do it better than Amazon. After surviving the dot-com bubble which destroyed most internet startups of that era, Amazon has grown up to become what is arguably the world's best business-model innovation organization. While most companies tend to focus on refining what they're already good at, branching out only in narrow ways, Amazon has been able to identify and grasp onto opportunities that virtually no one else saw coming. In the words of their CEO Jeff Bezos, "If you want to continuously revitalize the service that you offer to your customers, you cannot stop at what you are good at. You have to ask what your customers need and want, and then, no matter how hard it is, you better get good at those things."

Sounds simple, but it takes fearlessness, discipline, drive, money, and the willingness to get it wrong from time to time in order to make that happen. To quickly recap their evolution as an enterprise, Amazon originally set out to change the way people bought books. When they found that they had excess capacity they began brokering an online marketplace with other sellers, expanding their core e-retailing model to cover a plethora of products far beyond books. Nowadays it's tough to find anything (legal) that you can't buy on their website. With an extremely efficient supply chain and delivery processes, they can either directly sell or broker everything from consumer electronics to handyman services, clothing, sporting goods, and fresh groceries. Their "Prime" subscription service used to be a way to get free shipping, yet now it leverages their IT investments to come with streaming movies and music, cloud photo storage, and a Kindle sharing library.

Speaking of Kindle, their e-reading platform leverages an application that can be downloaded onto smartphones and computers or used on their inexpensive tablets so that customers can be continuously in touch with their content no matter where they are or on what device they wish to access it with... And, much like Apple's iTunes, Amazon takes a small cut out on every transaction. They even own a publishing house, CreateSpace, to help their user base generate original content such as books and videos. Leveraging the technologies that built their own website and vast IT infrastructure, Amazon Web Services (AWS) has commercialized cloud computing to grow their application hosting service into a multibillion-dollar business too. All these innovations flowed from their core business as it continuously expanded, but they did so in unconventional ways.

Clearly not every business has a culture that can embrace risk-taking or become as entrepreneurial as Amazon. We may not be Amazon, or want to be for that matter, but we certainly can learn from them. We all need to innovate, but not just in products or services. We also need to be able to identify opportunities to create and deploy new business models too. For example, we must ask ourselves how we can utilize excess capacity better in our enterprise; find ways to leverage our resources toward optimal business value much as Amazon used excess IT capacity to build their AWS hosting services. This requires creative thinking.

Everyone has the capacity to be creative, in most cases our imaginations ran wild as kids, but many of us have had the creativity socialized out of us as we grew up. In other words, in school we discovered that there's only one right answer, which by implication means that everything else is wrong. That may be true in mathematics, but in business more often than not that's simply not the case. There really is more than one right way to do everything, yet some are more profitable and less risky than others. This means that we need to do the hard work of innovating, churning through, trying out, and discounting ideas, in order to discover the best ones. Oftentimes this means failing along the way... It's okay to fail from time to time, but it's not okay to give up. For instance, Thomas Edison created nearly 3,000 different ideas for lighting, evaluating each of them for practicality and profitability, before inventing the light bulb that he became famous for. Clearly creativity isn't just throwing out a bunch of ideas to see what sticks, it requires hard work, but the end results are worth it.

A challenge, however, is that creative thinking draws critics in much the same way that fresh manure draws flies. After all, if we come up with something that has not been done before, our innovation challenges the status quo. It's threatening. But, we can prove the naysayers wrong, even when it is our own selves who get in our way. For example, a decade or so ago I published an editorial in *ForeWord Magazine* titled "Romancing the Tome, An

Ode to the printed book." As you can no doubt guess from the title, I wasn't a big fan of e-readers back then, yet today I do virtually all of my recreational reading on a Kindle or via the Kindle app on my smartphone. At the time I wrote the article I meant every word of it, but it turns out that I was mistaken… After evaluating the benefits like cost and convenience I was also willing to admit that I was wrong and embrace the change.

We must all force ourselves to be open-minded in order to be able to adopt valuable new ideas. Albert Einstein once said, "Imagination is more important than knowledge. For knowledge is limited to all we now know and understand, while imagination embraces the entire world, and all there ever will be to know and understand." If we wish to be truly innovative, to break from customary beliefs, we must let our imaginations soar free.

In this precept, Musashi was spot on.

PRECEPT 16

Do not collect weapons or practice with weapons beyond what is useful

"Practical wisdom is only to be learned in the school of experience. Precepts and instruction are useful so far as they go, but, without the discipline of real life, they remain of the nature of theory only."

— Samuel Smiles

Monk:

Often people accept an edict from authority unquestionably. This, of course, happens in religions of all kinds. However, sometimes when one examines these edicts a conflict arises. This is discovered discord. Discovered discord can take many different forms but one of the most common ones is when something that appears to be necessary and essential simply is not. As an example, it is not necessary to say the Nicene Creed to be a Christian.* You could argue the reasons why it is necessary to say the creed, of course, but Christianity is not dependent on that creed. Belief in an omniscient, omnipotent, and omnipresent God who is the creator of everything that exists, and the agent of redemption, Christ, these are at the core of Christianity's tenants. These aspects exist regardless of whether a creed is stated or not.

This same discovered discord can happen in all aspects of our life. While reading Musashi's simple statement, "Do not collect weapons or practice with weapons beyond what is useful," a moment of clarity happened for me. I have a pair of *sai*, Okinawan

---

* The Nicene Creed is a statement of faith used by many Christian churches. It was written in the year 325 at the First Council of Nicaea, in what is modern day Turkey, and is recited daily by worshippers across the world in numerous church services.

weapons that looks like mini handheld pitchforks, which I have owned since the early eighties. While they are very high quality, I rarely use them and they mostly collect dust.

In general, I have little interest in martial arts weapons. Outside of the little boy inside me that likes sticks and swords I have no real use for these *sai*. Oddly however, I have an emotional attachment to them even though they honestly serve no real purpose for me. I handed them to one of my black belts and said, "You like these, go ahead take them home, you can practice more there." These are not useful to me and I have stopped practicing with and teaching them. In fact, I suspect they are going to go the way of the buggy whip; horse-drawn buggies are gone and with that them the once ubiquitous buggy whips used to control the horse. Similarly, the *sai* are on the same path as the buggy whip. If they are not at that point for everyone, they surely have gotten to that place in my mind anyway.

It is evident that I no longer need to hang on to weapons that I no longer need. To that end, the *sai* and *tonfa*, two weapons that have great historic value but are not horribly practical in modern times are no long going to be part of my martial arts effort. I don't practice enough with them to have the level of competency that I require of myself so they have become as Musashi puts it, "Beyond what is useful." I will go even further with Musashi in that in his *Book of Five Rings* he states that I need to, "Be familiar with all weapons." Musashi, with these two writings, has made his opinion clear. Be familiar with what weapons that are out there and how they are used, but practice with your weapon, the one you find most valuable, and get very good at using it.

In my case, my focus is on an empty hand. While karate might have some synergies with weapons forms, it is not dependent on *kobudo*, the practice of traditional Okinawan weapons. This is not a case of me telling others what to do, not in the least. My martial arts are not defined by the collection of forms or weapons, just as the heart of a person is not determined by the presence or absence of a creed. The immense majority of my training is empty hand. I am also familiar with the many *kobudo* weapons; while I'm not highly proficient with them, I know what they can do. So, I am in agreement with Musashi. I will no longer divide my study time between karate and *kobudo*.

Warrior:

I have to disagree with this precept. To do anything but disagree would be hypocritical, as I have a huge weapon collection. Many of them that I practice with are more for preserving the older "arts" they come from and enjoyment in doing so than for anything practical or useful today. Sure, one can fantasize that during the zombie apocalypse the *katana* will be useful again, a la Michonne in *The Walking Dead*,* but in reality it is extremely doubtful I'll ever use my swords outside of training, and the same goes for my *nunchaku*, throwing knives and tomahawks, and other weapons that I've amassed over the years and practiced during my martial art studies.

Except for my knives (tools that can also be used as weapons) and firearms, one could argue that all of the other weapons I possess and train with are beyond useful. And it isn't even that clear cut with the guns and blades as there are numerous magazine articles each month debating the merits of various firearms and cutlery. Rather than go through my entire collection, I'll focus on the *nunchaku*, a staple of martial art schools after Bruce Lee made two sticks joined by a short chain or cord popular in the early 1970s. Legally, I'd be in just as much trouble for beating a person to death with *nunchaku* as I would be for shooting him or her. So, why in the world would I practice swinging and striking with these two sticks when I own a firearm?

The easy answer is that I enjoy learning and passing along knowledge accumulated through the traditions that have been handed down from generation to generation. Without the continued training with such weapons, that tradition would be lost. Training with *nunchaku* and older traditional martial arts weapons preserve the various styles and systems. While I fully understand that the practicality and usefulness of some martial art systems and weapons have been lost to modern advances in not only technology, but in science and training of the human body, I still enjoy practicing these ancient ways, and feel the preservation of art is a worthy goal in itself.

Beyond the preservation of tradition, training with older weapons can help develop coordination skills and the ability to recognize weapons all around us. I think everyday items are more readily identified as improvised weapons by those who have

* It is because of her being a bad ass with that sword that she's my favorite character on the show.

trained with a variety of traditional weapons first. A broom, mop, or pool cue resembles a staff. Scissors or a tactical pen can be used like a dagger. And when you think about farmers using whatever they had available to defend themselves, you start to see how the tools and items you have available can be used in self-defense.

I personally like the fact that training with *nunchaku* helps develop coordination and timing, both important attributes for any combat, modern or ancient. Many martial arts teach that the weapon is an extension of your body, and this means coordination and timing are essential. And hitting yourself in the mouth (I only did it once) is a good way to learn a lesson you won't soon forget.

I could go on and list more reasons why I disagree with Musashi and believe that collecting and training with weapons that may be considered of little or no use by many is a valuable endeavor, but I think one of the most important reasons is that it's fun. So when you go back to the question, why train with *nunchaku*, the easiest answer is because it's enjoyable. It's fun.

Yes, the modern warrior should be proficient with the most up to date weapons available and carry those that are the most useful. But, there is nothing wrong with enjoying the collecting of weapons and the practicing with them for the sake of preserving older traditions and the enjoyment of training in and of itself. There's nothing wrong with having fun with your training. And who knows, you just might find yourself someday needing to defend yourself with nothing but a pair of sticks and a short cord. If that happens, you'll be glad you spent all those hours twirling and striking with an archaic weapon.

Teacher:

Obviously, as a weapon collector, I must disagree with this precept at its base. Nevertheless I do understand the call for practicality, and in that, can somewhat get with this idea.

Back in the mid to late 1990s, I started buying every weapon I could get my hands on. I purchased an authentic chop-your-body-in-half *guan dao* along with a whole lot of useless items too.* Have you ever seen those guitars that are kind of like double guitars?

---

* Sometimes spelled *gwan dao* or *kwan dao*, the *guan dao* is a Chinese pole weapon that is somewhat comparable to a medieval glaive. It has a heavy blade with a spike or notch at the back designed to catch or control an adversary's weapon mounted atop a stout pole.

You know those guitars that have two necks and a double set of strings? Well, back in the 1990s, I bought a knife that was a double knife. It had one handle, but *two* blades. I remember joking that it would be a perfect murder weapon because if you were on the stand and the prosecutor lost his cool and challenged you, "Did you or did you not stab the victim, Joe Blow, twenty four times with a knife?" then you would be able to respond honestly, "No I did not. I would never stab anyone more than twelve times."

Those readers who are interested in swords will no doubt have heard the term "wall-hanger." A wall-hanger is a non-functional but good looking sword which is suitable for nothing more than hanging on a wall. Well I have a number of wall-hanger swords. They are practical in no way, shape, or form. Why? Because they are made of inferior materials and would probably cause the death of the person trying to use them as a sword.

They might look good on the wall, but what are swords actually made for? Killing people, right? They are weapons. So, this precept boils down to advising people to be practical. In that context this precept makes a lot of sense. If one is a soldier whose job is to kill the enemy, then yes, training with impractical weapons is worse than a waste of time, it is a loss for the military.

There is a lot of silliness that goes on in the weapons divisions of modern martial arts tournaments. I cringe as I watch people compete in staff and spear divisions especially. I am often reminded of the scene from the movie *Tombstone* when Doc Holiday and Johnny Ringo meet. There is a bit of discussion, at the end of which Johnny pulls his gun and points it at Doc Holiday's head. Holiday does not even flinch, as one might imagine a person who has a death wish would probably react. Then Johnny Ringo goes into this bit of tricking where he twirls the gun around and around his finger—this way and that way—trying to impress the crowd. At the end of this exhibition, Doc Holiday begins his own tricking, only with a whiskey cup. In real life the insult would be huge. It was a quick and simple point made that guns were not made to be spun around one's finger.

Guns are made to shoot. Spears are made to stab, and staffs are made to pummel without mercy. Twirling weapons of any kind is really pointless and shows nothing of real applicable skill. In that, Musashi has it right. Any form of martial study needs to be practically applicable or it is quite pointless.

Insurance Executive:

This precept appears to be a tweaked Buddhist teaching that suggests you not acquire material things just for the sake of acquiring. I must admit this is a tough one to follow because, according to my husband, I'm "a hardcore shopper." Of course, I refuse this label. I think of myself as an enthusiastic shopper without the word "hardcore" attached to it.

As it relates to weapons in general, Buddhism teaches nonviolence, although depending on the teacher, there are times when it's permitted, such as in war and self-defense. Case in point, on one occasion when the Dalai Lama was asked about self-defense, he answered, "If someone has a gun and is trying to kill you, it would be reasonable to shoot back with your own gun."

Having spent time in *Zendos* and Buddhist temples, and seeing how some people act holier than the Buddha himself, or at least put on airs to, I'm sure this sent a shockwave through their psyches. While I admit I never got to know such types intimately (deliberately so), I will nonetheless hazard a guess and say I doubt they share the same familiarity with violence as does the Dalai Lama. In fact, I've read articles by some of this ilk that say using violence in self-defense is wrong. <Sigh>.

Musashi seems to be saying this: Because weapons give us the ability to defend ourselves and others, they should be used only for this purpose and not as a toy for entertaining ourselves. If so, the assumption would be the great swordsman never ever trained for the sheer pleasure of exercise and fun with a very sharp toy. Well, I don't believe this for a second. Forty plus years as a swordsman is an awfully long time to never pause for a little enjoyment with one's weapon.

Since the precepts were written in the twilight of his years, when he spent his time, perhaps the majority of it, writing, sculpting and painting, it's not a stretch to think he had mellowed a little from his years of travelling the land and challenging people to battle. Similarly, many police officers today retire to never shoot their gun again. A few keep sharp with occasional visits to a shooting range, at least for a few years, while others (arguably most), put their weapon in the bottom of their socks drawer where it collects lint.

The words "beyond what is useful" are curious. Who can say what is useful? Is one gun in your sock drawer enough? Maybe… unless the threat comes in your back door, 60 feet from your bedroom dresser, or a carjacker jumps in your car 25 miles from your sock drawer. My husband and I have weapons—not all of them guns—within a few strides of every entry point in our house. A pacifist might cry that this is extreme and psychotic, that is, until the threat attacks him in his weaponless house as he is eating a bowl of granola.

Perhaps Musashi is telling us to walk the middle path even with our tools of self-defense. Are there people obsessed with weapons? To answer that we would first have to define the word "obsessed" and my guess it's a word few people would agree on. My husband told me he once saw a police reservist at the firing range looking at a 45-caliber semi-automatic he had just bought from a real police officer. He was holding the gun in his palm, completely lost in thought with a dreamy, faraway expression on his face, as he caressed the side of the weapon as if he were petting a kitten. My husband said it caused him great concern and hoped that the young man, who probably worked as a box boy at the local grocery, wouldn't make the evening news for shooting passersby on Main Street.

Collect whatever weapons you like. Think of them in terms of their usefulness in self-defense as well as in whatever way you enjoy them recreationally. Do so being cognizant of every safety practice applicable to each weapon—gun, sword, axe, knife—and think of them as just one other *aspect* of your life, not *all* of your life.

Businessman:

While the infantry soldier might look to a rifle as his primary weapon of war, in business our "weapons" could be considered the tools we use to conduct all the imperatives of running a successful business. Our key processes are automated or augmented with software, that is the plethora of applications we use to develop a strategy and chart the course for our enterprise, manage our human resources, capital, and supply chain, design and produce our products/services, sell and deliver goods to our customers, administer warranty claims, expand our market share, pay our bills, continuously improve our processes and systems, and much, much more. Virtually everything we use from the tools in our factories to our timekeeping and payroll systems requires software of one type or another. There challenge is that there's not only an overabundance of applications, but also that the marketplace of tools is continuously growing, evolving, and changing.

For example, business intelligence can be defined as the process of boosting our company's performance by arming key decision-makers with the insight they need to make good choices. Analytical software used for this purpose ranges from simple spreadsheets (such as Microsoft Excel) to statistical software packages (such as StatSoft Statistica) to sophisticated business intelligence software suites (such as those provided by IBM, Oracle, or SAP). The goal is faster and more informed decisions, yet each choice in how to accomplish that aim has strengths and weaknesses which must be balanced against the cost of purchase, the learning curve for use, and the ongoing expenditures needed for support and maintenance. In some respects this is an advantage that small businesses have over larger ones; they cannot afford to let their software grow out of control so an overabundance of tools is rarely an issue. In major corporations, government agencies, and educational institutions, however, this can become a significant challenge, one that is not easily resolved…

We may have a compelling desire to follow Musashi's admonishment and not collect or employ tools beyond what is useful, but unless we have a centralized command and control structure it is very difficult standardize on singular solutions that can satisfy all the competing demands that can and often will crop up across the enterprise. This means that in order to be successful we must develop and ruthlessly enforce enterprise-wide standards and robust change control measures to control the chaos. Anything new must "buy its way in" to the system, meaning that the business case must be compelling even after we consider the holistic impact of multiple tools to learn, integrate, support, and maintain. Without this centralization we sub-optimize as most major corporations have done today, making certain departments or functions happy while damaging the efficiency and effectiveness of the company as a whole.

For those who have never worked for a Fortune® 100-sized enterprise, hence have not experienced tool bloat, it's likely unfathomable to think that this sort of predicament exists, but believe you me it is far too commonplace to ignore. Look to your phone's app store for a more familiar example. Even basic applications such as those that let us use our phones as flashlights have dozens if not hundreds of competing choices. Now, imagine that you downloaded the top six apps for everything, including audio, games, family, books, business, comics, communication, education, entertainment, finance, fitness, health, libraries, lifestyle, live wallpaper, media, medical, music, news, personalization, photography, productivity, reference, shopping, social media, sports, tools, transportation, travel, video, weather, widgets, and so on. You'd have a lot more stuff, clearly, but would your phone be easier or harder to use? Would you want or need all that functionality? It's a safe bet that if your phone came with all that bloat the first thing you'd do would be to spend a few hours uninstalling all the stuff you didn't want, need, or ever intend to use right? That's what I'd do…

To facilitate the solution to tool bloat there needs to be a single point of accountability, a sort of tool Tsar if you will, to own and control the process. In order to be successful this must be someone who is highly respected and senior enough pull together all the right stakeholders, evaluate their needs and desires, and create a consensus on how to proceed. This person typically leads a group of architects, technologists, and businesspeople who act as a change board to balance competing interests and force everyone along the right path. In this fashion we do not collect or practice with weapons beyond what is useful for optimally running our organization.

All this bureaucracy would likely make Musashi's head explode, but businesspeople should follow his precept nonetheless. Even the most complex corporations can embrace continuous improvement.

PRECEPT 17

Do not fear death

"Too many people are thinking of security instead of opportunity. They seem more afraid of life than death."

— James F. Byrnes

Monk:

Standing at the edge of my grandfather's grave I remember turning to my dad whose father had just received the graveside service and pausing for a moment with a 'what do you say to your dad at this moment' kind of silence. My dad looked at me and with what could only be described as enduring calmness and said, "Dying, we all get to do it." That statement seemed perfect at the time. It was his father's time and we all acknowledged the moment. There was no fear in my father's voice, only an acknowledgment of the natural course of life.

Should a person fear death? No, I don't think so. I think the fear comes from the unknown. If one has a form of belief in the afterlife then death becomes a transition and not a final moment. Of course in my tradition, there is the promise of a life after this one. The afterlife is presented as a wonderful, idyllic new life in the presence of God.

When somebody dies, we often use the euphemisms, "They have gone to their reward." This is fine in perspective, but to be clear actively seeking the afterlife is a disservice to this life that has been granted to us. Any society or ethos that becomes a culture of death eventually passes from the face of the earth via extinction or wholesale change. There is a difference between a short-term commitment to death, such as there was by the Allies in defeating the Axis powers during World War II, versus a long-term systemic culture of death that propagates the idea of giving your life for a cause. The former may be required for a time, but the latter is destined for failure.

If my life is centered on the idea that I can have no greater experience than giving my life for my king or country or cause, soon that value proposition glows like a flare, a dazzling light ready to burn to death any bug that dares approach too closely. When you do not value your own life or have subjugated your life to another person or political movement, you walk a fine line. This is why the military has strict rules of conduct regarding the actions of its soldiers, in particular, rape. In 1945 U.S. Forces executed 29 of their own soldiers for rape in France. To add further impact, some of the soldiers were executed at the scene of their crime. In U.S. General and Supreme Commander of Allied Forces Dwight Eisenhower's mind there were combatants and there were civilians and they had to be treated differently.

The culture of death, on the other hand, was with Musashi and he was also of it, yet he still managed to stand outside of it. With this life comes the responsibility of stewardship. To seek death in the manner that the kamikaze pilots of Japan did during the later months of World War II is contrary to proper stewardship. Understand the difference—fighting to the death with one's back against the wall is distinctly different than actively climbing into an aircraft or strapping on a bomb with intent to kill yourself in the line of duty. Gray area? Maybe. However, that is the line that I draw.

Further the culture of death that the samurai engaged in held that they could kill any lesser person in their caste system if they felt insulted and would be fully justified in that killing. I have never heard a report of Musashi killing anybody but a person who had accepted the terms and conditions of a duel or taken the battlefield for the opposite side to engage in mortal combat against him. This is an interesting contrast that I think requires more thought, the fact that a man who killed for profit and status only killed those who had agreed to the terms of battle. It appears that he never murdered anyone and that speaks volumes to his character. He was a killer, a functional psychopath, but he also stuck to a rigid moral code.

I want to imagine that before a battle Musashi was stoic, confident, and ready to let the cards fall where they may. That is the icon that I have in my mind. He was everything that a strong, resolute warrior was supposed to be, yet I wonder if having seen the randomness of death on the battlefield, knowing that he could be struck down from an unforeseen place or an errant strike that was not meant for him but landed anyway, that there must have been some uncertainty. It seems fantastical that he would never at least consider these things by the campfire the night before a battle. And yet, because of his physiological make-up, the ideas of these random ways of losing one's life may simply not have gained traction in his mind or thought process. After all, he was the hero of his own story and the hero always wins.

Musashi may have lived in a culture of death, but he clearly did not want to die, nor do I wish to do so on any day, but his day eventually came and mine surely will too. I doubt Musashi feared his demise and I doubt that I will either, but we both have different reasons for coming to a similar conclusion. Whether or not it is based in religion every human has faith, it is part of our deep seated psychological makeup as individuals and sociological makeup as a society. That conviction helps carry us through our trails and times of terror.

Warrior:

With this precept, Musashi is aligned with the warrior ethos from history to modern pop culture, and it reminds me of both Yamamoto Tsunetomo (1659 – 1719) and Billy Jack (cult hero in a series of four movies from 1967 to 1977). In the world of the warrior, death has always been paramount. The death of enemies as well as the reflection on one's own death... Before examining the concept of fearing or not fearing death we should look at some similar references.

In the first chapter of Yamamoto Tsunetomo's *Hagakure*, which is often called the *Book of the Samurai* (William Scott Wilson translation), we find, "The Way of the samurai is found in death." Yamamoto continues by advising to set one's heart right every morning and evening, to live as though your body is already dead, in order to gain the freedom in the Way, and thus succeed in your calling.

While not identical, I feel the same sentiment regarding living is found in the courtroom scene from the film *The Trial of Billy Jack* (1974). In this scene, Billy Jack (played by actor/director Tom Laughlin) refers to death as his constant companion, who eats with him, walks with him, and even sleeps with him. Billy Jack then tells the courtroom that each and every one of us has death as a constant companion, and that he sits with each of us every second of our lives but we are too terrified to think about it. Then, one of the most important concepts of the movie is expressed when Billy Jack states, "But once you do (think about death), it will completely change your entire outlook on life." When asked, "how so?" Billy Jack replies, "You ask yourself even in the most serious crisis, 'how important would this really be if I were suddenly told that I just have one more week to live?' So you learn to take nothing too seriously. On the other hand, you ask yourself 'if this were my last act on earth, is this what I really want to do?' So you learn on the one hand to be detached from the temporary things in this world, and on the other hand you learn to appreciate every little thing in it all the more."

Viewing Musashi as a functional psychopath, he likely wouldn't fear death due to his personality disorder, and therefore, it would be quite easy for him to admonish others to not fear death as well. However, that does us little good when trying to apply his precepts to our own lives. It's too flippant for a psychopath to state, "Do not fear death." It is more beneficial for us to acknowledge our fear of death, to understand it, to respect it, and as Billy Jack advised, to think about it. In this way, it can be liberating and we can maybe gain the freedom Yamamoto wrote about.

Understanding, and more importantly accepting, that we will die will allow us to be detached from the temporary things in this world and to appreciate them even more as Billy Jack suggested. But it also enables us to become greater warriors. Not only can we better face combat with the acceptance that we will die, if not in this battle, at another time, thus freeing ourselves to do what is needed to survive and win, but we can become more righteous in those battles we choose to fight. The understanding and acceptance of death, combined with the appreciation of life, enables us to overcome our ego and only enter combat for those reasons honorable and justifiable to our own moral code.

I agree with Musashi that we shouldn't fear death. We should think about it, understand it, respect it and accept it. This might not reflect Musashi's thoughts when he wrote these words, but it's how I think we should read and apply them today.

Teacher:

Even though few of us talk about it, nearly every rational person fears death. This precept is worth trying, yet most people do not even see their own fear of death as a real fear. This is because we push all thoughts of death off into some dark corner in the back of our minds. And why should we not? Most people have colored the idea of what happens when we die with ideas that are quite monstrous! Very often, we do not even allow ourselves to admit just how horrible our concept of what happens at death really is.

Take for example those who believe in reincarnation. You will be reborn into another life where you will receive the rewards or punishments for your actions in this life. It sounds well and good on the surface, but every person reading this knows that they have gotten away with some truly awful stuff. Don't lie, you know you have... Every adult reading this was once a teen and teens take many actions for which they give very little forethought about possible consequences. When these consequences do not turn up, they know that they got away with something. In this sense, the thought of a cosmic reckoning can be a nightmare!

Or, maybe you believe in heaven and hell... This belief contains an understanding that upon your personal death, you will stand before the Supreme Being, God, and you will be judged for your actions in this life. If you were good, you will be allowed to enter heaven, and if you were not, you will be sent to a place where you will be punished forever and always. And once again the understanding that we have gotten away with all but murder in this life sends chills down our spine when we pause to consider the divine judgment that awaits us.

Still others believe that nothing happens at all. We die, we're buried, and our bodies become worm-food. Many people envision that idea as being shut in a box forever and ever, while others might see it akin to falling asleep and never ever waking up. *That* thought gives us the heebie-jeebies.

In this space, it is not my intent to go into which idea is correct, or even which one I subscribe to. I merely wished only to illustrate some of the ideas which give people their fears about death. Clearly there are more than the three I just covered...

Now to address this precept.

Fearing death, to a practical person, is a *waste of energy*.

You are going to die. I am going to die. Everyone you know is going to die. Everyone you hear about on the news is going to die. Your favorite celebrities and favorite people and favorite pets are all going to die. Death is a simple, unpleasant, and undeniable fact that goes with the reality of living. Just as tall and short, up and down, and big and small contrast one another, the same applies to life and death.

Most people get the chance to never really think much about their own mortality. They live their life with the thought of dying as something that they push to the back of their minds, even to the point of forestalling estate planning or avoiding making a will. This allows them to place a greater importance on the trivialities of life. But in many cases it also limits the experiences of life.

Others have had moments where they knew they were about to die, they knew there was no way out, this was the end, and in many of these cases, ended up with a moment of *accepting* their own mortality and ultimate demise without consideration of what might happen after the actual event of death. For these people, should they end up *not* dying in that moment, nothing is ever the same after. They live much more fully and much more happily from that point on. There is that deep and real understanding that all of *this* will end. They understand at their very core that no amount of angst or denial or fear or sheltering will change that. And this understanding changes you at an incredibly deep level.

Once you stare death in the eye, you understand in a way that most other people do not that this life only goes on for a little while and that we waste too much time being afraid and focus too much time on things that do not matter. Unfortunately, nothing that I can say here will impart this deep understanding. This really is one thing that has to be experienced to be understood, and many people will never experience it until it is too late. They get the experience at the very end and so never get a chance to do anything with their newfound knowledge.

Fear of death is a waste of time as well as a waste of a perfectly good life. And I will make one last point. Whether you are afraid of dying, or refuse to admit that you will die, or have no fear of death whatsoever, the end result will be the same. The only difference will be in what happens between now and that final day.

Insurance Executive:

A woman came to the Buddha in great anguish, carrying her dead child pleading him to bring the little one back to life. The

Buddha said, "Bring to me a mustard seed from any household where no-one has ever died and I will fulfill your wish." The woman couldn't find any household in which no one had ever died and it was then that she realized the universality of death.

It's often said the samurai were greatly feared on the battlefield because unlike most people, they didn't fear death. They followed the soldier's paradox: If you fear death, you will die. Might their courage have been fortified a little from alcohol? My husband and I have a large and colorful samurai figurine that depicts a warrior in kimono, holding a sword with one hand and in the other a large bowl. The bowl, if the figure were life sized, would have a diameter of 12 to 15 inches. An expert on samurai told us the bowl would hold an alcoholic beverage the warrior would consume before heading out to the battlefield.

If I knocked back that much, even if it were Bud Light, I would no longer be afraid of spiders.

The highly disciplined samurai valued their traditions, one of which was to drink sake together before they commenced to fight. It would be a time to imbibe and promise each other to either be victorious or die with honor and courage. The tradition was brought back during World War II by the kamikaze. They too would drink before diving their planes and themselves into American ships. After the samurai completed their battle, they drank again, but more so than before the battle. The kamikaze never got to enjoy that part of the custom.

I'm in no way making light of the great samurai. Certainly, their courage is legend. I'm just pointing out that in many instances *sake* helped to calm the warriors' nerves.

Although Buddhism teaches much about death, it teaches more about living a life of peace, compassion, love for each other, and doing good. While living in this fashion certainly doesn't make one want to hurry the inevitable, it does give the Buddhist, and for that matter the Christian, some modicum of comfort that there is something after death: Buddhists will be reincarnated and Christians will go to heaven. Musashi would have known this from the Buddhist perspective.

Experts on the samurai believe they intuitively knew that fear causes the brain to shut down—the result of an accelerated heartbeat, shallow breathing, tunnel vision, and the exclusion of select sounds. The impact of this prevents the warrior from employing any fine-motor skills and having to rely only on broad and crude slashes with his sword. The samurai weren't technically knowledgeable of these fine points but they surely must have experienced them in the early stages of their development. For this reason it was critical they went into battle with a firm grip on their fear of death.

I fear death but I probably fear suffering before my death more. There is nothing I can do about this but accept the inevitable and have some degree of comfort with the acceptance. With this objective, I try, "try" being the significant word here, to accept that my life will end in an hour, tomorrow, or 20 years from now, and accept I might suffer in the process. If I can truly accept this reality, this impermanence—lots of people carry on as if they were going to be the one that death passes by—I believe it will help me to live the best life I can, be the best person I can be, and leave a positive footprint that indicates I was here and I helped smooth the path for others to do the same.

Businessman:

While all businesspeople will eventually die, few things in business are life-or-death struggles outright. Unlike soldiers or law enforcement officers we rarely face the probability of leaving for work and never making it back home because of some inherent danger on the job or jobsite. But, there are a lot of "career-killers" to be concerned about such as failing to understand the culture or navigate the politics where we work, becoming complacent, violating company policies, behaving unprofessionally, or failing to deliver on our commitments.

For us, I think the most relevant perspective about this precept is to take it as an admonishment to do the right thing despite any potential impact to our jobs or careers. For instance, when pressed by looming deadlines it's easy to take shortcuts, to let things slip or look the other way, but we all know that's the wrong thing to do. And, that at times it can lead to serious injury to our customers or our company. When faced with an ethical dilemma we must never let fear of repercussions prevent us from taking a moral, principled stand. There is an ancient quote by Heraclitus of Ephesus that I find apropos:

> "The soul is dyed the color of its thoughts. Think only on those things that are in line with your principles and can bear the light of day. The content of your character is your choice.

Day by day, what you do is who you become. Your integrity is your destiny—it is the light that guides your way."

Truly what we do *is* who we become, it's one of the reasons that businesspeople who over-focus on results without paying attention to means or methods ultimately get themselves into serious trouble. If we give in to temptation once in the name of expediency it becomes easier to take shortcuts a second time, progressively leading us deeper and deeper into a sewer of graft and corruption as we chase after profits or promotions over principles.

This is exactly the sort of thing that has led to Enron and other infamous corporate scandals of the past, and can easily lead to future disgrace. For those who do not remember, Enron started out as a niche natural gas pipeline company, but manipulated markets to quickly grow into the seventh largest publicly-held corporation in the United States. And, those same corrupt business practices that buoyed their growth ultimately destroyed the company in 2001, with 16 former executives landing in prison in the aftermath. As their $90 billion empire shattered it wasn't just the folks in charge who lost out, however, their greed ruined people's lives, displaced thousands of worker's jobs, and flushed retiree's savings down the hole with them.

Everybody works for someone. For example, the buck may stop with the CEO (Chief Executive Officer) of a publicly held corporation yet he or she is ultimately accountable to the Board of Directors who, in turn, are held accountable by the company's stockholders who can vote them out of office. It takes courage to adopt a principled position and stand up in the face of pressure from our superiors, but it is something that we all must be willing to do if or when we find ourselves in the unenviable position of being the only voice of reason in the room. With the right culture, that's not so hard to do. A simple litmus test to demonstrate that an enterprise has created an ethical culture is that even the lowest level employees in the company feel comfortable pushing back on unscrupulous activities, even when it means the situation is personally or professionally awkward.

Take for example the accounting profession. Back in the days before the fallout from Enron and other fraudsters when congress passed new laws such as Sarbanes-Oxley and Frank-Dodd to help keep corporations in line, it was relatively easy for accountants to "cook the books" and misrepresent how well a business was performing. In those days a CPA friend of mine worked as an accounting clerk for a rapidly growing company which was headquartered in the Seattle area. While putting her company's financial reports in order prior to an IPO (Initial Public Offering), a stock sale that if everything went right would make the company's founders millionaires overnight, she discovered a programming error that had been miscalculating their capital equipment depreciation for quite some time. It wasn't a huge deal dollar-wise, just a few hundred thousand dollars that needed to be restated once all the errors were added together since many of them canceled each other out, but since she knew that any accounting irregularity could taint public perception and torpedo the stock deal so she was very concerned about bringing the error to her boss's attention. Nevertheless despite the lousy timing she knew that it was the right thing to do.

Rather than responding angrily or trying to sweep the error under the carpet to protect his reputation, when the CFO (Chief Financial Officer) heard her story he immediately thanked her for her diligence, told her to report the adjustments, and asked her if she needed any help in order to ensure that the mistake wouldn't happen again. It was a risk, but it paid off... Rather than backfiring and hurting their IPO, the company's restatement of their financials actually helped convince potential stockholders that they would be a good investment. My friend wasn't senior enough to get rich at the time, but she was well-compensated for her efforts and rapidly rose through the ranks due to her intelligence, business acumen, and integrity. In this fashion a junior member of the organization not only did the right thing but also received support from her senior leadership in doing so. Together their efforts protected the businesses from scandal while enabling outside investment and rapid growth for the company.

All enterprises should operate this way. Sadly many don't. Have you read about Volkswagen's tribulations recently? Their stock plummeted 30% overnight when it was revealed that they cheated regulators and customers alike by lying about their diesel vehicles' emissions. Imagine how things at VW would have worked out differently if some engineer told his or her manager, "Hey boss. You know this software we've developed to evade emission controls on our diesel vehicles? That's probably not a great idea.

I mean selling millions of cars that violate clean air laws probably won't end well. Beyond that whole illegality thing, most of our customers buy 'clean diesel' cars because they're environmentally conscious…"

Clearly someone on the program must have thought that, but either no one carried that message forward or it was ignored by their superiors. Either way, after a year of obfuscation and sparring with the US Environmental Protection Agency, Volkswagen reluctantly admitted on September 22, 2015 that 11 million of its diesel vehicles contained software that was designed to evade emissions controls, sparking a crisis that cost them more than 24 billion Euros (~ $26 billion) in market value overnight. Two days later CEO Martin Winterkorn was forced to resign in disgrace and the company went full-tilt into damage control mode. An unidentified company source told reporters that the head of the company's U.S. operations (Michael Horn) and top engineers at Volkswagen brands Audi (Ulrich Hackenbergand) and Porsche (Wolfgang Hatz) were about to be fired, regardless of whether or not they knew about the cheating.

"Brands are all about trust and it takes years and years to develop," brand consultant Nigel Currie told the press. "But in the space of 24 hours, Volkswagen has gone from one people could trust to one people don't know what to think of." While VW set aside an initial 6.5 billion Euros (~ $7.3 billion) to cover the fallout and "win back the trust" of its customers, they risk fines of $37,500 per vehicle, which could total more than $18 billion if the full value is assessed. They also face criminal investigations from European, Asian, Russian, and US lawmakers and, of course, lawsuits from the customers they cheated.

As of this writing it's been 14 years since the Enron scandal yet it seems that something like this makes headlines virtually every day. With a little foresight virtually all of it is avoidable. It's not that folks don't know when something is wrong but rather that they don't take action, standing idly by as leaders make uninformed, unethical, or unsound decisions.

Don't let it happen on your watch! If as a businessman or businesswoman you do not fear death, it's easy to do the right thing… even if it may be career limiting. Who knows, in the right corporate culture doing the right thing may even prevent scandal, save your stockholders millions in lost value, and earn you a promotion.

PRECEPT 18

Do not seek to possess either goods or fiefs for your old age

"Make wisdom your provision for the journey from youth to old age, for it is a more certain support than all other possessions."

— Bias of Priene

Monk:

My parents live about four hours away by car. When they come to visit, or I visit them, I often find myself with something in my possession. "This was your great grandma's…," or, "This was Dad's (my Grandfather); I thought that you could use it." My parents are divesting themselves of items—things that they don't want or need, yet still have an emotional value. I have my great grandmother's vase on the shelf in my office next to my grandmother's apple-shaped candy tin. Little items that have sentimental value… I plan to pass them on with some written history attached, but if it doesn't happen, if I never get around to it, that's okay because it is just paraphernalia, stuff that is nice to have and look at, remember, and enjoy, but not a focal point of my life.

Focal points change as we move through life, each time having its distinctive trappings and desire for those trappings. It is easy for a person who is in their seventies like my parents to say, "Here, I don't want this anymore, but I think you will find value in it." When people reach a more mature place in life, where they have more days behind them rather than in front of them, their values change. This is a normal course of life. To behave in a way that is not consistent with the person's place in life is odd. The man with the hair plugs and Botox injections who buys that expensive sports car and hooks up with a 20-something trophy wife at age of seventy looks a little weird to the rest of us. And oftentimes his behavior is chalked up to immaturity. It is as if we intuitively understand how somebody of a certain chronological age should behave.

It is a normal and natural flow for divestment to occur as people get older. Values shift when life is seen through more mature eyes. Parents pass on family heirlooms, businesspeople groom their successors, and kings divide their kingdoms.

It is difficult for a younger person to act in such a way, to not seek let alone divest themselves of what they have. It would be a far tougher charge for a person to follow if Musashi were to say, "Do not seek to possess either goods or fiefs for your youth!" The idea of not building, not owning, and showing prowess via acquisition is not a normal act. In the same way that the older man with the car and hair plugs looks odd, a young man in his twenties wearing a conservative, three-piece suit, and smoking a pipe is just as odd, but on the other end of the spectrum.

Wisdom and experience are valued at a far higher level for the mature person than any vase or candy tin. What Musashi is saying is that you must grow into your role as life moves along. In this particular charge of not seeking material items in your old age, Musashi underscores and brings a normal progression of life into the light for us to observe. It's good advice.

Warrior:

I'm not sure if this precept comes from Musashi's stoic and ascetic philosophy for living or something else, but I rather look at this precept in a way that makes sense for modern day living as I see it through a warrior's lens. First, we should look at the probability of a warrior even reaching old age. In Musashi's time, a cut from a sharp *katana* could be fatal even if it was a minor slice. While it takes cutting off your opponent's head in the *Highlander* movies and television show to kill immortals, in reality the rest of us can easily die from infection from even minor wounds. It's only been in recent years that the advances in medicine have reduced the number of deaths due to sickness. For instance, disease, infections, and gangrene killed way more soldiers during the Civil War than bullets. Musashi certainly saw his share of death by infectious disease and illness and most likely was more acutely aware of mortality than most. And with this in mind, I want to look at the precept in a way to live life more fully in the present.

Most people, if not warriors, seldom think of their own mortality, and in fact often behave as if they will live forever. The reality is that no sunrise promises a sunset. Every single day people wake up, fully expecting to be here tomorrow, but never make it to the end of today. It's for this reason that we must appreciate each day and live in the moment. This doesn't mean to recklessly abandon our plans and goals for the future, but it does mean we shouldn't sacrifice everything in the present for a future that may never arrive.

I may not be aligned with Musashi's thoughts on this one at all, but when thinking of the above, I look at this precept and think about those who waste their lives saving for the future, or trying to amass possessions, wealth, and properties at the expense of enjoying any of them in the present. I believe there needs to be a balance between living for today and planning for the future. A reckless carefree lifestyle can leave a person wanting in the future, and giving up everything now to possess luxuries in the future can backfire if you don't live to enjoy them.

So I try to apply this precept by remembering to enjoy the journey, and not become obsessed by the destination. My goal isn't to amass possessions or wealth for my old age, but rather experience as much as I possibly can now and throughout all of my life. If I have my choice, I rather amass experiences over goods of fiefs for my old age. We can't take possessions with us when we die, so I'd rather have enriching experiences and fulfilling relationships over possessions any day. And because the warrior doesn't know when that final day will come, but understands that it could be at any time, he or she boldly seeks the most enriching experiences life has to offer, and enjoys even the miniscule moments of the present.

Teacher:

In our culture, we understand the need to have some secure income for our retirement. We do not want to spend our *entire* life working yet, at the same time, we do not wish to be a burden on our children. Perhaps in a different culture, one where children saw the care of their aging parents as a duty, one might be able to make the case that there is no need to seek possessions for old age. But in our modern time in many Western countries, there is every reason to take these precautions.

It would also be good to remember the understanding of the Buddhist ideas on possessions. There was the thought that the clinging to possessions would cause a person to remain on the wheel of life and death, constantly being reborn into a similar life where they would again be given the chance to remove their desire for possessions. This idea may have been at play in Musashi giving this precept to his disciple. Another factor which would be important to consider would be the warrior ethos. Warriors would not have been good at their job if they were making plans for their old age. Dying in battle was an all but foregone conclusion, especially in the age before antibiotics. So, once again we reach a point where the context of the advice makes it less than desirable for our modern times.

This is a precept I must disagree with on the basis that there is a lot more good to be done in our time and our culture in planning for and preparing for our old age. By way of an example, my parents made no plans for their retirement. They owned no property, had no money invested, and were counting on Social Security to see them through. That didn't work out so well...

It turned out to be just enough income to leave them with enough money for about half of each month. They were living rent-free under what can only be called indentured servitude to a landlord. They repaired his other properties in exchange for not needing to pay rent. Obviously, this was a disaster in the making. Once the original landlord died and the properties passed on to the ownership of his son-in-law, the entire deal changed. The new landlord sold the property they lived in and gave them no time to make new arrangements. My father passed away during the process of the sale and my mother was going to be left with nowhere to live until she told me about what had happened. Thankfully I was able to care of everything she needed after that, but the predicament they found themselves in was the direct result of making no real plans.

After this experience, I strongly recommend to everyone that they make detailed plans and work to be sure they have something set aside for a retirement. This precept was set for a different time and a different society.

Ignore it.

Insurance Executive:

I'll certainly try but I'm not certain I can refrain from possessing fiefs.

I think what Musashi is referring to here is our old age—however we want to define that today—should be a time of reflection, fixing past errors, and living out life content with what one has. But too many people continue working for great riches—some clawing for it—late into their advanced years. So many of us are brainwashed by television, internet, shopping malls, and advertising in every other form to keep spending and keep acquiring because it will most certainly bring us happiness. It does, but the emotion is short-lived. Once it passes, the seeker of happiness through material possession once again sets off to acquire more in order to experience a repeat of the short-lived moment of bliss.

I mention elsewhere that I'm a shopper. Alcoholics shouldn't live above a bar and shoppers shouldn't work next to a shopping mall, which I do. Is it tempting? Ooooh yes. Do I fight against the temptation? I like to think most of the time I do and most of the time I win. Of course, there are those times when I don't… But at least I'm trying and at least I understand the lure and psychology coming from the ad agencies.

It helps a little to be mindful of acquiring only those things my husband and I need to function in our daily lives. Anything that goes beyond the needs of sustenance, shelter, clothing, entertainment, and education is usually, when left to ponder before purchasing, not needed. My husband and I have not taken a vow of poverty and we have no plans to work in a cave as Musashi did when writing his great tomes. We choose instead to live comfortably and surround ourselves with things that give us pleasure, comfort, and utility. This means we try not to acquire things we don't need or acquire things only to impress others.

We are both deep into our middle age years now. We continue to work to maintain a comfortable lifestyle and because it gives us satisfaction to help others through our specific jobs. We are blessed to already have those things newly married couples are focused on acquiring. So at this stage on our lives, we get only those things needed for their practicality, and for our particular interests and personal growth.

As we move from middle age into our twilight years (an expression I detest), we want to spend our time on simpler things:

family, friends, art, music, and reflection. If someone wants to give us a million dollars, we wouldn't be rude and refuse them. But until that happens, we aren't going to burn up energy and burn up our remaining years seeking possessions just for the sake of acquiring more things.

Businessman:

To me this precept speaks to stewardship, using our resources wisely while we're here in hopes of leaving a legacy behind that continues to do good things beyond our lifetimes. One of the best examples of this was set by Bill and Melinda Gates. During a vacation to Africa in 1993 the couple began to seriously think about what to do with the enormous wealth they had acquired through Microsoft. They ultimately decided to donate their resources to help those less fortunate, a notion on which the Bill & Melinda Gates Foundation was born.

Bill told reporters, "Well, if you have money, what are you gonna do with it? You can spend it on yourself, you can have, you know, thousands of people holding fans and cooling you off. You can build pyramids and things. You know, I sometimes order two cheeseburgers instead of one. But we didn't have any consumption ideas. And if you don't think it's a favor to your kids to have them start with gigantic wealth, then you've gotta pick a cause." Their foundation's cause is a good one. Their primary focus is currently on eliminating HIV/AIDS, malaria, mother-and-child deaths worldwide. The couple has publically pledged to give away ninety percent of their fortune throughout the rest of their lifetime, donating over $30 billion to their foundation to date.

Leveraging one's wealth toward good deeds is noble, but inspiring others to follow your lead is even better. Since establishing their foundation the couple has successfully signed up over 130 other millionaires and billionaires who have likewise agreed to give away at least half their wealth to charitable causes. Working together with fellow billionaire Warren Buffett, their "The Giving Pledge" project has received the support of luminaries like Paul Allen, Richard Branson, Larry Ellison, George Lucas, Elon Musk, David Rockefeller, and Mark Zuckerberg.

While most of us will never be millionaires let alone billionaires that does not mean that we cannot follow this example. If we don't have excess money we can certainly donate our time to worthwhile causes, both personally and professionally, such as volunteering in the community or taking a position on the board of a charitable foundation. Furthermore, most large enterprises support charitable giving campaigns, either directly or indirectly through United Way or similar agencies. Oftentimes this means that our employers will match whatever donations we make to sanctioned causes, such as 501c3 "nonprofit" charities in the United States, doubling our giving power.

Even where our companies do not sponsor such activities, we can still do good things all by ourselves. For example, on more than one occasion I have carved out time in my annual offsite meetings to gather everyone in my group together and spend a few hours helping out at a local food bank as a teambuilding/community outreach exercise. I have also volunteered as a parent's club officer and fundraiser for my son's school, as a mentor for military veterans entering the civilian workplace, and even as a sideline reporter and photographer for youth football. Martial arts can support the community too. As instructors we help students enhance their self-esteem, develop mental discipline, learn self-defense, and improve their physical conditioning. With a little creativity anyone can find ways to support causes they believe in.

Clearly we need to look out for ourselves and our families first, but in most instances if we are successful in business we will simultaneously build up an excess of resources beyond what we truly need. We owe it to ourselves and our community to be thoughtful about how we spend or invest any surplus. Thoughtful largess can not only help out worthy causes but also make our time on earth more meaningful and rewarding too.

PRECEPT 19

Respect Buddha and the gods without counting on their help

"The gods too are fond of a joke."

— Aristotle

Monk:

Musashi's precept sounds a lot like the maxim, "God helps them who help themselves." It is a great sentiment and you might be surprised to discover that it is not found in the Bible. In fact, it appears to have originated in a document called, *Discourses Concerning Government*, written by Algernon Sydney, a member of British parliament, in 1698. It is also sometimes attributed to Benjamin Franklin, an American founding father, in his work *Poor Richard's Almanac* which was published in 1757. A close derivative expressing the same sentiment can be found in Aesop's tale of *Hercules and the Wagoner*, which was written sometime around 600 BC.

No matter the source, it is quoted often. I have used this phrase too. Years ago I fell back on this sentiment that if I used my wits, worked hard enough, and did the right thing that God would favor me in my endeavors. Of course Musashi says that you should respect the gods. The plural "gods" is completely consistent with his worldview since he lived in time and place where folks believed in a world populated with many, many gods. Whether you are religious or not, working hard, educating yourself, making the most of your natural talents, and doing the right thing are all great traits, ones that should be cultivated. These behaviors will often lead to a good life.

Nevertheless, the idea that you should not depend on God is a quandary. Isn't it a great idea to give oneself up to God? All of the saints have done so and done so completely, seeking the mystical union with the divine, the *Unio Mystica*, the deepest desire of the disciple. By falling completely into the divine the disciple has placed all of their needs into the hands of the God. The mendicant Franciscan's are a Western example. These friars are dependent on others for food and shelter, owning nothing of their own. Not even their habits (uniforms) were theirs to own their minds. This is an extraordinary and profound position. Even riding a horse was rejected by these early friars who chose to walk from place to place. Those that live such lives, they are rare, these people who have totally given themselves over to the favor of God. They live out a deep and profound belief, truly walking the walk as it were...

Musashi held the viewpoint that the gods were going to do whatever the gods were going to do regardless, and one should not prepare themselves based on any god's favor, requested on not. Interesting and imminently practical perspective is it not? Or, is the world full of miracles, both small and large appearing on an ongoing basis, miracles that need only to be recognized. For instance, Saddam Hussein fired 42 SCUD missiles into Israel during the first gulf war in 1991. By way of size comparison, Israel is roughly the size of New Jersey, the fifth smallest state in the United States. Three elderly citizens died of heart attacks, but for the most part this barrage of missiles did virtually no damage. Was that simply good luck or an example of divine intervention? Simply put, it depends on your theological view.

Is it correct to pray to the gods prior to battle? Musashi says that we should depend on our own skills and abilities. In my view why not pray, ask for a blessing for yourself and others, and *then* depend on your skills. It may sound like, "God helps those who help themselves," but it is not. It is casting one's fate to the hands of God, and then doing your best. This may sound like hair-splitting, but I would ask a priest to bless me yet I would not ask a priest to bless my weapon. And then whatever comes, comes. God is incomprehensible and to assume that I can depend on his largess to assure victory is not a good policy any more than for a professional athlete to expect divine intervention on behalf of his team in a championship game.

So I agree with Musashi, but for different reasons.

Warrior:

I agree with this precept much more than the first of the *Twenty-one Precepts of Hojo Soun* which states, "Above all, believe in the gods and Buddhas." Hojo Nagauji (1432 – 1519) was a general of the late *Muromachi* Period who in his later years became a priest, taking the name Soun. His precepts, or rules for the daily life of the common warrior, were written sometime after he became a priest. And while there is a strong tone of self-reliance throughout the precepts, the first stating to "Above all, believe in the gods and Buddhas" seems to reflect his religious trainings and beliefs rather than the more pragmatic stance of Musashi's nineteenth precept. Even the placement of the two within each of their twenty-one precepts seems to reflect quite a difference in the importance of religious beliefs.

I believe that Musashi's pragmatism in not counting on Buddha or the gods to help more adequately serves the warrior than Soun's admonishment. I believe that warriors should act rather than pray. It should be noted that *The Twenty-One Precepts of Hojo Soun* also state, "To worship the gods and Buddhas is the correct conduct for a man." Again, this perspective seems to reflect more on his religious beliefs than Musashi's pragmatism.

In *Living The Martial Way: A Manual for the Way a Modern Warrior Should Think* by Forrest E. Morgan, the chapter on religion and mysticism opens with this quote from Musashi's *The Book Of Five Rings*, "The Way of the warrior does not include other ways, such as Confucianism, Buddhism, certain traditions, artistic accomplishments, and dancing..." The quote is found in *The Earth Book* of the classic text. Musashi then goes on to state that although these are not part of the Way, if you know the Way widely, you will find the Way within everything. Each must pursue his particular Way. For Morgan's purposes, the quote works well for his chapter helping martial artists reconcile their martial arts training with their own personal religious convictions.

However, if you look further, you see that Musashi wrote about these different paths in the Introduction of *The Earth Book*, where he differentiated the paths of the warrior class, the path of Buddha, the path of Confucianism, the path of healing, the path to teach, and so on. He makes it a point that each person specializes in his area of interest and few are inclined to devote themselves to the path of the warrior. Again, we find Musashi looking at things from a very practical viewpoint. It is akin to saying, if you are a doctor, practice medicine; if you are a lawyer practice law; don't do both.*

So what we can discern from reading both the precept above and the relevant passages from *The Book Of Five Rings*, is that Musashi's stoic, disciplined philosophy was more pragmatic than religious. This fits with my own personal philosophy and teaching. I do not mix martial arts and combative training with religious studies. Nor do I believe that a higher power will protect me and that is why I train.

I once had a person tell me that he didn't need self-defense training because Jesus would protect him. For his sake, I hope he never encounters a criminal intent on doing him harm. I'm guessing he never heard the old saying, "God helps those who help themselves." I'm pretty certain Musashi would agree with that saying too.

Teacher:

This precept reminds me of an old joke.

There was once a devout man who found himself nearly stranded in his house as the creek began to flood his property during a rainstorm. As the waters rose, a man driving a four-wheel-drive truck stopped by and offered to take him to safety. The devout homeowner politely refused saying, "No need. The Lord will save me." The waters rose further still. This time a sailor with a boat arrived offering to take the homeowner to safety. Again, he politely refused, "No need. The Lord will save me." The flood water rose further still. Now the man was stuck on the top of his house with water everywhere as far as he could see. A helicopter arrived on the scene and the pilot lowered a ladder to the homeowner offering to fly him to safety. Again, he politely refused, "No need. The Lord will save me!" The helicopter left and the waters continued to rise, drowning the man. As he arrived at the gates of Heaven, he was confused. He said, "Lord? I was devout. I had faith. I waited for you to save me and you let me drown." The Lord replied, "Let you *drown*?! I send a truck, a boat, *and* a helicopter! What more did you want?"

Badum-bum…

Very little is going to be accomplished in your life without

---

* Unless you happen to be my friend Craig, who after a woodworking accident couldn't continue with his career as a heart surgeon and went to law school. But even he didn't do both at the same time…

positive action. You can *want* to lose weight, or make more money, or live in a better neighborhood, but until you actually start taking positive action to make these changes happen, nothing much will take place. Different people have different views on religion. It is not my task here to debate the right or wrong of any particular faith, religion, or ideology. In looking at the precept, what stands out to me is the idea of taking charge of your life, control of your circumstances, and moving forward with *action*.

No one lives your life except you. No one will suffer the disappointments of your failure more than you. No one will know your struggles more than you. And, no one will appreciate your successes more than you will.

Religion is a powerful motivator for some people, yet for others it can become a hindrance. When they reach a point of waiting for God to fix things for them instead of taking the steps needed to make the necessary changes then it becomes a hindrance.

Let us take a simple and fairly common task, getting in shape. If you want to pray that you lose weight and feel that it will make a difference, then pray. But, exercise too! If you feel that God wants you to be healthy, believe that! But, take the other needed steps as well. Go to the gym. Eat right. Get enough sleep. You know the drill… Wishing and wanting and praying are not a detriment to your life. If you feel that they make a difference then by all means wish, want, and pray. But take positive action toward your goals every day as well.

Miracles can happen. But you need to take some personal responsibility as well.

Insurance Executive:

Whether it's the Christian God or Buddha, I take comfort in what each teaches but I'm not one to ask for help every time I have a problem, a dilemma, or have to make a difficult decision. In fact, I rarely ask for anything at all. Actually, I can't think of the last time I did.

I watched a documentary recently about prostitution in a Southeast Asian country. In one scenario, prostitutes were shown praying before the Buddha and asking for lots of customers that night. Are you kidding me? By his own words Buddha isn't a god and is incapable of granting favors for anything, to include wealthy johns. These women have been taught a twisted Buddhism not to mention a twisted view of their own bodies.

187

I like to say I'm a recovering Catholic. I learned all the bells and whistles of Catholicism but it didn't connect with me. Some might say I was led astray by the devil, which I also think is absurd. I have studied Buddhism for a few years and it has connected with me for the simple and appealing reason that it puts me in charge of me, not some invisible deity that allows brutal wars, thousands to starve, children to get cancer, and a terror called ISIS. "What?" Someone will surely exclaim. "You dare judge God?" I sure do.

Am I saying I don't believe in God? Not at all... Well, not as a bearded man sitting on a thrown. I believe there is intelligence behind all existence but I also tend to think this intelligence doesn't really care about us; we are just one part of all that makes up the planet and the universe. I respect the intelligence and I'm in awe of it, but I don't ask it to help me with my report at work or to improve my front kick. In other words, I respect the teachings in the Bible and the teachings of Buddha, but I don't count on God or Buddha to help me.

Writer Louis Kronenberger said, "There seems to be a terrible misunderstanding on the part of many people to the effect that when you cease to believe you may cease to behave." Likewise, I heard a psychologist on a talk show say that he truly believed that if there were no God most people would be good, anyway. Most being the keyword here. Though the world seems to be such an evil place anymore, I still agree with both men and live my life In accordance to what the bible and the Buddha teaches about benevolence and compassion.

I might not believe as I was taught as a child, but I try to be good simply because it's the way I choose to carry out my days. I want to be good for my husband, family, friends, fellow workers, and myself. I like myself when I'm good. It's as simple as that.

I like the expression, "Believe in God but row away from the rocks." You would think with God's hit and miss record people would for sure always "row away from the rocks just in case." But this isn't always the case. As I write this, a man in Dubai allowed his 20-year-old daughter to drown because he was worried about the lifeguards, that is, someone from outside the family, touching her. The father, a large and powerful man, actually blocked the lifeguards from rescuing her to, as he stated later, "To prevent her modesty from being violated."

One can only think he was waiting for God to save her. You would also think anyone with a semblance of intelligence would know there is a risk when swimming in the sea. Combine this with the strict rule of this father's religion that says no one outside of family can touch the girl, perhaps she would be alive today if he had "rowed away from the rocks," in this instance by insisting that she only swim in shallow water.

There was also a case in Saudi Arabia where religious police forced 15 girls to perish in a fire because they were not wearing traditional Islamic head coverings, and therefore not allowed to go outside. Most people are shocked by these incidents. The exception would be those following beliefs to the extent of ignoring, dare I say it, common sense. If I lived to be a thousand years old, I will never believe that God or any divine force would require such nonsense.

Respect whatever religion you follow, but also consider that you have a brain to use to take care of yourself and others.

Businessman:

This is a perfect admonishment. It reminds us that while providence may smile down upon our endeavors there's no guarantee of success. Consequently, we need to become proactive in protecting ourselves and our operations. In business parlance this is called risk management. It is the process of identifying, analyzing, and then either mitigating or accepting sources of uncertainty that might affect our people, products, or organizations.

Why should we care about risk management? Think about the Target, Home Depot, Sony, Nationwide Insurance, and United States Office of Personnel Management data breaches for starters. They made the headlines worldwide, but they were not alone. In fact, a 2015 study by insurance company HSB discovered that 69 percent of businesses had experienced a hacking event during the previous year. Cyber criminals routinely steal sensitive corporate information, financial data, and millions of people's personal information, placing their identities, their credit, and their life-savings in peril. Whenever this happens folks tend to lose their jobs over the breach, either because they let it happen, tried to cover it up, succumbed to blackmail, or because unpalatable actions they took or things they wrote that were never meant to see the light of day were publicized afterward. In some cases their reputations were destroyed to the point where they may never find a decent job again. And, their companies were irreparably harmed as a result of the breach too, spending millions upon millions of dollars to repair the damage.

With ever increasing cyber security risks it is incumbent upon us to understand the value of our data to ourselves as well as to bad guys who might covet or wish to adulterate it, and then put the right technologies, processes, and training plans in place to mitigate the threats to the extent feasible. Since virtually everything is connected to the internet these days it doesn't matter what type of business we are in. Everyone is at risk; even something as mundane as our refrigerators can be the vector that lets the bad guys into our network and from there into our mission critical data. It's not just an IT problem however, we need to safeguard against social engineering scams that can trick folks into voluntarily giving up sensitive information as well as disgruntled employees, customers, or suppliers who might have access to our systems or resources and a desire to do bad things too. As you can see, it's a people, process, *and* technology threat. And, we must continuously assess and defend against new and ever evolving risks.

Hackers are ubiquitous, but they are by no means the only danger that must be taken seriously. The term *force majeure* is French for "superior force," but in practical application it really means "acts of God." It's a legal term that lets parties off the hook for their contractual commitments in the event of catastrophic disruptions such as wars, nuclear accidents, earthquakes, hurricanes, meteor strikes, or other natural disasters. In legalese it's a protection against the unforeseen, but it also a risk that while oftentimes small in likelihood can have catastrophic consequences on our businesses if it comes to fruition. There's no guarantee of perfect safety, it's economically unfeasible, but we can build redundancy into our supply chain, operations, employee base, and IT infrastructure so that if really bad things do happen we will not be shut down and unable to produce the products or services that pay our bills and keep the business afloat every month.

It is incumbent upon all prudent businessmen and women to identify possible risks to our enterprises, evaluate their impact, determine which may be accepted and which must be mitigated to the extent possible, and then figure out how to monitor whether or not they have happened. It's a four-step process that must be repeated continuously: (1) identify the risks, (2) quantify the risks, (3) mitigate the risks, and (4) monitor the risks. In this fashion we evaluate things like strategic, operational, transactional, financial, technology, regulatory, and geopolitical risks, determine our tolerance for uncertainty, and then put plans in place to protect ourselves. Sometimes mitigations are as simple as having an alternate supplier of commodity parts available in case we need them, but other times they are highly complex such as hardening our systems against cyber-attack via network segmentation, enclaves, encryption, and the like which can take millions of dollars and multiple years to put into place. The challenge is to know for certain where we stand and chart a sensible and thoughtful course forward.

There are no guarantees in life or in business, but we can stack the deck in our favor with prudent planning and thoughtful execution of a risk management plan.

PRECEPT 20

You may abandon your own body but you must preserve your honor

"The difference between a moral man and a man of honor is that the latter regrets a discreditable act, even when it has worked and he has not been caught."

— H. L. Mencken

Monk:

Musashi's words are in direct conflict with the world we now have. We live in a time nowadays where somebody can take the most private parts of their life, their most personal acts, and hang them around their neck proudly for all to see. Today the body is placed above honor in virtually everything and practically nobody thinks twice about it. Playing upon lust and desire it is easy to use one's body to gain celebrity for instance, albeit for a flashing moment. Honor is thrown on the trash heap of humanity as we stampede to get a glimpse of someone's naked body part, sex tape, or salacious activity. In a world of celebutantes, it is not the act of the peering that is so weak but rather the inability to control the desire to do so.

So, what then is honor? I like the story we have all heard of about the samurai who was sent to execute a prisoner for some transgression. When the two men met the man who was supposed to be executed made the other angry by spitting in his face and calling out insults. This resulted in the executioner turning and leaving without comment. He did so not out of cowardice or breach of duty, but rather because the execution would have been performed in anger. That was not the task that he'd been sent to do. Consequently he waited until he calmed down and then returned to chop off the other man's head. This is a great example since the outcome was the same but the divergence of intent made all the difference in the world.

Internal honor is something that is very important. I'm not talking about saving face or appearing to do the right things, but rather in knowing that while mysteries may surround man all things are known to the divine. The question then becomes do we not rob, rape, or murder somebody because our moral and ethical code given to us by God tell us that we should not do so, or do we not do it because we're afraid that we'll get caught.

In the early eighties, horrific child molestations by Catholic priests and others associated with some branches of the church came to light. The magnitude was and is incalculable. Those priests who molested their parishioners held no honor. They used their positions of trust within the community to groom their victims and perform egregious acts. They had no ethics, no morals. In fact, they likely had no religion either as surely they must have known not only that they were doing the wrong things but also that God was fully aware of every heinous act whether or not they ever came to light with the secular authorities. Clearly these men did not abandon their bodies in the protection of honor, but rather flipped the concept on its head to satisfy their perverse desires. In doing so they destroyed lives and crushed families. This is an extreme example of what Musashi speaks about with this precept, exactly what he warns against.

What Musashi says throughout the *Dokkodo* is that our essence is the most important thing we own, far beyond any positions, accomplishments, or awards. His admonishment that it is better to forsake our own bodies than to tarnish our sacred honor was as meaningful when he wrote it as it is today. In fact it's arguably a precept that is needed even more now than ever in history, at least in much of the world. The challenge is that it is a deep concept, one that can be very hard to live with. To uphold this precept means that even in the smallest of things you must keep your honor. Calling out a pedophile is easy; we can all agree that their behavior is abominable. Period. There is no gray area, none whatsoever. However, there are places that on a daily basis and in the smallest places of our lives will challenge us to do the right things even when no one is looking. Things like showing up at meetings on time every time, obeying speed limits, or sticking with an exercise routine come to mind, but examples are legion.

This is where the battle for our honor lies. It is in the small, the simple, and the outwardly unknown, the things that the majority of us came face-to-face with on an hour-by-hour, day-by-day basis that mean the most. If we can do all the little things right, the big things often become easy.

Warrior:

I feel the most important part of this precept is the last five words, and in fact it probably should have been written simply as, "You must preserve your honor." I think this is the root of the precept, and it is something I agree with wholeheartedly. As warriors, honor is paramount and something we definitely must preserve.

Honor is a concept found in all warrior groups. From the samurai's *bushido* to the knight's code of chivalry to the code of the West in America's frontier, honor has been central to warriorship. I agree with Forrest Morgan, who wrote in *Living The Martial Way* that, "Warriors are honorable because it's a practical requirement of their profession. They are honorable because it's the most powerful way to live. Most of all, warriors are honorable because to be otherwise is cowardly!"

Musashi's precept reminds me of my father talking to me when I was a boy. He always told me that my word and my name were the only things that couldn't be taken from me, so I better make sure I always kept my word and made my name one to be proud of. Since my father served twenty-two years in the military, two of which were in Vietnam, it's not surprising that this basic lesson he insisted upon consists of the elements of honor found in all warrior cultures.

If we look at the samurai culture, we can find this morality of telling the truth and never going back on your word in the phrase *bushi no ichi-gon*. According to Boye Lafayette De Mente, in *The Japanese Samurai Code: Classic Strategies for Success*, *bushi* means "samurai or warrior" and *ichi-gon* means "one word; a single word." When used together this phrase means that the word of the samurai is as good as gold (to use a Western idiom).

I also think my father told me when I was young and Musashi wrote this for the younger generation because they both knew that young men often give their word freely and without much thought. It is easy to give one's word, and even easier to regret it, but a warrior is expected to honor it regardless. Therefore, it is wise counsel to advise others to take care when giving their word as my father did with me, and as Musashi does with this precept on preserving honor.

To a warrior, honor consists of recognizing obligations and having the courage to do what is right. When you give your word, you obligate yourself to ensure something is done. A warrior doesn't give his or her word lightly, because it means something. When you have the courage to do what is right, you will have a name to be proud of. Therefore, to be honorable, you must know the difference between right and wrong and only take on obligations that are just or right. So while they didn't use the same words, I do believe Musashi's precept of insisting you preserve your honor and my father telling me to make sure I kept my word and make my name one to be proud of were essentially both aimed at keeping obligations and doing the right things to ensure justice. And I agree that these principles of honor are crucial to warriorship.

However, this doesn't mean that all warriors are saints. We all fail in our obligations or ignore justice at times. But just because we have been dishonorable in the past, does not mean we should give up our quest to be honorable in the present and future. It's an ongoing practice, just like the rest of our training. We must be conscious of when we give our word and of those obligations we accept. And when we do give our word and accept an obligation, we must first ensure that it is just and right, and then we must make sure we follow through to its completion. This is how we practice being honorable.

It is much easier to read about, or write about, than to actually live by these principles, and that is why the warrior class has always been a smaller group than the general populace. It might not be easy, but if you are a warrior you must preserve your honor.

Teacher:

The concept of honor runs throughout the martial arts. It is rarely defined in clear and concise terms, but nevertheless it is put forward as an important idea. While I know what honor is, much like St Augustine responded when asked about the nature of time, when pressed for a *definition* of honor, I find it hard to find the right words to explain it.

In some ways honor might be cheapened into a version of caring what others say, feel, or think about us, but I resist this path. There is a small part of the concept of honor that does involve how we are seen by others, but this is more in the area of our personal legacy. This is because once our life is over, we are no longer there to answer questions about what did or did not motivate us to make certain decisions that we made. Actions are remembered, results can carry on, but our motivation remains unknown or is swiftly forgotten.

I think a better concept of honor is in being personally comfortable with all you have done and how you have lived. When you are old, will you be comfortable with how your life unfolded and the decisions you made or are there going to be memories that haunt you? Not just things you regret or wish you had not done, but things which make you feel *ashamed*... This is very different from being concerned over how others might view your life.

Avoiding actions which might bring one to a state of feeling ashamed is probably, to me, at the heart of this precept. Living honorably means never having these moments where you feel that shame over your actions. Your decisions may not have been perfect, or the results of your actions may have been very far removed from what you anticipated or intended, but the decisions were made *by you* according to your personal code and values.

To reach this state, one must live *mindfully*. Each action and choice will be weighed against your concept of right and wrong. In this way, you will make the correct choices and never need to feel such shame.

Of course, this does not mean in any way that you will have a life free from mistakes. No one is perfect so mistakes happen. It is simply impossible to account for every possibility when life is filled with independent variables. But if you can approach life with mindfulness, these mistakes should be fewer in number and when they do occur they will not be caused by selfish oversight. Our errors will be pure and simple mistakes; hence will not be a cause for shame in our old age.

And if one has truly reached a level where they no longer fear death as taught in an earlier precept, then even threats against their life will not cause them to forsake honor.

In this way, I can agree with this precept.

If you have a code of conduct, a set of personal rules and lines which you will not cross, and a set of standards by which you make your decisions, then this precept is not only doable, it can set you on a path to a better place in your life.

Insurance Executive:

As a person and as a martial artist—after all these years they are virtually one and the same—I have developed a self-honor, if you will, to live my life righteously, to respect others, have compassion for others, care about the world, do what is best for my family, and to put in an honest day's work. To this end, I follow my self-imposed discipline to be the best person I can be. I truly expect this of myself, but I realize after having been alive these many years, to not always expect it from others.

My study of self-defense isn't only to protect myself but also to protect my family, friends, and strangers, in short, anyone unable to protect themselves. Additionally, I would use my abilities to protect an animal, whether from a predicament it got into by its own innocence or from a person bent on harming it. In fact, I would love to stop someone from committing a cruel act on an animal. For sure it would require all my self-restraint to use only the necessary force. By virtue of having established this code of honor for myself and by creating a creed that I will be there to protect people and animals unable to protect themselves, I like to think I would sacrifice my own personal safety—my body—to do what I deem right.

Honesty of character and personal integrity is rarely seen these days. As I write this a new presidential race is underway, so the mudslinging is in full force. It's pretty tough to find an ounce of honesty and integrity in the motley crew vying for our votes. You think any of them would jump on a tossed grenade to save a room full of constituents? I don't either. Would I "abandon [my] own body" to protect them? I like to think so.

Living a life of honor is a practice. The word "practice" in this context means to apply my belief and ideas about my personal honor every day. I practice it by figuratively protecting my family and husband by letting them know I love them, helping in any way I can with their problems, striving to make their lives happy, and just simply being available for whatever they need from me. I have yet to physically fight for them, but I like to think my powerful sense of honor will have me charging into the fray no matter what the personal cost to my person.

It's said in war that the best strategy crumbles away when the first shot is fired. Boxer Mike Tyson said, "Everyone has a plan 'till they get punched in the mouth." Likewise, a weak sense of self-respect, self-dignity, and self-honor can quickly crumble in the heat of anger and in the turmoil of violence. It's important, therefore, to ingrain your code of honor and to fix it in place so it remains no matter how tested. Think about it now, when all is well. Think about all aspects so you understand it, believe it profoundly, and act upon it daily. Only then will it be there when the you-know-what hit's the fan.

Businessman:

Once upon a time business was conducted with a handshake. Even today, when it seems that lawyers crawl out of the woodwork every time that anything goes awry and contracts can run thousands of pages to hedge against every conceivable eventuality, there are a few brave companies that do things the old fashioned way. Take McDonald's, for example. Did you know that they do not have a formal contract with their meat suppliers? Think about that, one of the most critical elements of their supply chain, one that nearly brought their competitor Jack-in-the-Box to its knees over food-poisoning concerns, and there's no formal written agreement. Instead, they trust each other to work collaboratively toward outcomes of mutual benefit.

Francesca DeBiase, vice president of strategic sourcing at McDonald's, is quoted as saying, "Many of our strategic suppliers have been working with McDonald's for years, even decades… Over the years our actions and behaviors have shown our suppliers that we conduct business with a high level of integrity. This allows us to operate with a handshake agreement.*"

Integrity, ethics, honor… not words we always associate with business, but ones that we absolutely need to hold in high regard in order to stay in business over the long run. As mentioned previously, enterprises are comprised of individuals. No matter what ethics program is put in place, it's the character of each and every employee—or lack thereof—that counts. Clearly we must preserve our own honor, but we must also take into account the integrity and reputations of those we enter into business with. Actions of our suppliers, employees, and even our customers can all rub off on us by way of association, so it pays to work with only

---

* This quote comes from the book *Vested: How P&G, McDonald's, and Microsoft are Redefining Winning in Business Relationships* by Kate Vitasek, Karl Manrodt, and Jeanne Kling, which describes their business model and contracting philosophy in detail.

those folks we believe we can trust with a handshake deal, ones who say what they mean and mean what they say at all times, even when a formal contract is required.

Before entering into a business relationship with anyone we must do our due diligence. Thankfully with ubiquitous social media it's not that difficult to look into anyone's online presence and determine if we like what we see. For example, the first time I met a consultant from one of our advisory firms she said, "I take it you're Lawrence Kane the author, not Lawrence Kane the Zodiac Killer suspect." Until that day I had no idea that I shared a first and last name with a suspected mass murderer, though thankfully the middle initial is different, we're not the same age, and I look nothing like him. Nevertheless, this incident made me realize that it's useful to Google your name from time to time and see what pops up. And, it's beneficial to do background checks on those we interact with regularly too.

One of the biggest risks of ethics escapes comes from our employees. After all, we hired them so we're responsible and accountable for what they do. One of the potential safeguards to use is in vetting candidates is the behavioral interview. Operating under the assumption that past behaviors can predict future behaviors, we ask a series of open-ended questions designed to draw out how folks acted on previous jobs, asking things like, "Tell me about a time when…" In this fashion we obtain insight into how folks think, communicate, and act. Typically these interviews are conducted by a panel, two or three individuals whose combined perspective yields deep insight into the prospective employee's knowledge, skills, abilities, and cultural fit for the organization. Combined with a thorough background and reference check we can set ourselves up for success in acquiring talent that will benefit our company, representing us in a professional and ethical manner.

Virtually every business uses suppliers, it's imperative because we simply cannot do everything ourselves, but it's also an opportunity for escapes. For example, subcontractors who illicitly dump toxic wastes, exploit underage workers, use conflict minerals, create hazardous working conditions, or engage in other unethical behaviors not only do the wrong things but also taint our image by association. This can have a huge impact on our business.

The "poster child" for ethics escapes was arguably Foxconn, an electronics supplier that made products for Apple, which was accused of creating working conditions so horrific in their Chinese factories that workers started committing suicide on the job by jumping to their deaths.* This adverse publicity quickly had Foxconn and its customers scrambling to do damage control to avoid losing business as a result. We must establish clear expectations for open and ethical business practices to anyone who supports our operations, carefully vet our supply chain, contract only with companies we feel we could do business with on a handshake, and put robust governance in place to make sure that everyone follows through with their commitments.

As Musashi writes, we must preserve our honor. But, we must also safeguard our business interests by vetting those we work with and doing our best to assure that they are trustworthy too.

---

* The article, "1 Million Workers. 90 Million iPhones. 17 Suicides. Who's to Blame?" was published in *Wired Magazine* in February, 2011, with the story subsequently being covered in other publications such as *The New York Times* as well.

PRECEPT 21

Never stray from the Way

"As the fletcher whittles and makes straight his arrows, so the master directs his straying thoughts."

— Buddha

Monk:

Rhythm and ritual are soothing to a child. Any parent can tell you that a disruption in their child's pattern during the day results in behavior within the child that is awkward, disruptive, or just generally out of sorts. Honestly, most adults are not too far removed from stimuli-response behavior too if we look closely. Path and ritual are often so integrated into our existence that they become seamless, smooth. For example, when your coffee vendor sees you coming and starts your "special" cup of coffee, say a quad, two-pump caramel macchiato with soy milk, you are buoyed by the full engagement in your path. All is right and good in the world. These habits help ensure that our pattern in life is smooth, and smooth is not well seen. Like driving to work and not remembering exactly how we got there, we can move on autopilot through our world.

Oddly a path is better seen when the trail is broken. To continue that analogy, if the cup of coffee order is wrong, "This is *not* how I take my coffee, there's whole milk in it!" we spot the break in the pattern. We're disrupted. The ritual actually becomes more visible as it is called out by the person whose path has been interrupted. They actually make a point of, well… pointing out the disruption. Paths have ritualistic expectations. When those expectations are not met, or violated, it is an issue that often attacks the core of the person. This attack may not be not a life-threatening issue, but rather a metaphorical shove to the sense of self that oftentimes feels like it.

Ritual and path create a comfort level, and comfort reduces stress. The ritual assures us we are doing the "correct" things via experience or authority, and the path gives us direction. No biological life is designed for a constant state of alert or stress, it's too psychologically and physically taxing; most life is designed for rest. Being in a state of stress is the opposite of ritual and path. The modern world is a minefield of shifting ritual, and paths, invalidations, and condescension, ad infinitum... Rest and ritual build assurances into the day that allows for a lower ambient state of alertness, a manageable level of stress.

Ritual and path are necessary for human life. Ritual can be religious in nature such as a communal prayer, or as secular as watching a popular television show in the evening. Regardless, it is essential. Every path contains its ritual. The more ingrained the ritual becomes, the more essential it becomes to the path. Consequently the path and the ritual often become confused and incorrectly inseparable.

Alfred Korzybski, a leader in the study of semantics coined the phrase, "The map is not the territory." I will go further and say the ritual is not the territory. The path is not the knowledge.

Musashi took a discipline, the way of the sword, and made it his own by breaking the rules. He broke from his teacher, an incredibly anti-social act in his time and culture. He left his family, again a deep statement especially in a society that placed the family name before the individual name. Musashi decided that one hand on two blades was better that two hands on one blade and began to fight with two swords, clearly unorthodox.

Musashi forged his own path and, as a result, we know of him today. Yet he admonishes us to never stray from the path. Incongruent don't you think? I submit that Musashi was really telling his students was to understand why they were doing what they were doing, to not get distracted with extraneous actions, to focus.

A man once said to a monk, "That was a beautiful prayer, may I come back to the monastery and see your prayer tomorrow." The monk responded, "You have never seen my prayer, you have only seen what I do in preparation of prayer." Never confuse the map for the territory, as the territory of ritual and path is where you live, and for the most part, never seen.

Warrior:

This is a fitting precept to end with, and one that I and every warrior will agree with. I have the audacity to state that all warriors will agree with me and Musashi because I believe that true warriors have something inside that draws them to the way of the warrior. It doesn't matter if you believe in David Grossman's "Sheepdog" analogy or Dan Millman's "Way of the Peaceful Warrior," the simple fact is that some individuals have something inside that draws them toward warriorship.* This may materialize in different ways, and the individuals may sometimes appear to be as different as day and night. But deep inside, they will have a commonality, and that will be the way of the warrior.

When Musashi wrote about the Way, I don't believe he was referring only to his methods of swordsmanship or personal combat. I believe he referred to the Way as a way of life in which every action embodied the physicality and philosophy of warriorship. This includes the arduous physical training a warrior must endure in practice to be able to become victorious on the battlefield, as well as the adherence to the moral codes found in all warrior classes from ancient societies to the creeds found within our modern militaries. The warrior not only must master the technical proficiency of armed and unarmed combat, but the ethical principles taught with the physical techniques to keep one from becoming nothing more than a murdering thug. And, once saturated with both, this "warriorship" then permeates every living fiber down to the warrior's core. It truly is a comprehensive way of life. And in my best Bruce Lee impersonation, it is something you have to "feeeel." To bring up Grossman's analogy again, his "sheep" just won't get it. Even if they can academically understand what I'm talking about, they won't "feeeel" it.

And once you really "feeeel" it, the way becomes a part of you and everything you do. And at that point, it is easy to agree with Musashi's precept that you should never stray from the way. I'd

---

* Lt. Col. David Grossman popularized the theory that there are three kinds of people in the world: (1) sheep, (2) wolves, and (3) sheepdogs, a concept that was used to great effect in the movie *American Sniper*. Sheep are regular, productive, law abiding citizens with little or no capacity for violence. Wolves are, of course, the dregs of society who prey upon the ignorant sheep. Sheepdogs protect the other sheep as well as themselves from the wolves, and are often drawn to careers in military or law enforcement.

like to share a personal example that illustrates how the way becomes a part of everything you do. It was 1990. I'd been out of the army for a year and was just starting my undergraduate studies at the University of Montana. I signed up for a very heavy class load that included a couple of honors classes. The advocate who was helping us at the orientation suggested that I not take such a load, especially as I hadn't been in an academic setting for five years. I looked at her and said, "I'm a sniper, I can do it."

The look on her face revealed that she didn't have a clue what I was talking about, but that I'd said something kind of scary to her. She didn't know that 36 men competed to enter the sniper class I graduated from, and that only 13 made it into that class. Nor did she know that out of those 13, only three graduated as snipers by passing every phase of the course. She had no idea that what it took to become one of those three was beyond anything she'd ever done, or that would ever be required to do at the university. But I knew. I knew because I was one of those 36 on the morning of day one, and then one of the 13 remaining at the end of that first day. I was then one of the three who graduated as a sniper. And how did that help me with my business and other academic classes at UM? I got straight A's that quarter. Those that "feeeel" it will understand.

I'd like to conclude with a quote that has resonated with me since the first time I read it back in 1995. I was reading the excellent book, *In Search of the Warrior Spirit* by Richard Strozzi Heckler. Hidden within those pages was this key to warriorship, "The path of the Warrior is lifelong, and mastery is often simply staying on the path."

Teacher:

Have you ever known someone who seemed to flit about from one interest to the next, filled to the brim with enthusiasm for their latest flavor-of-the-month interest, cause, or hobby? Me too.

This precept speaks to me about a *life's work*. Whether this life's work is a study of a martial art, or music, or the finer points of a long lasting marriage, or *anything* really, when you set on a path (the way), you should do it with tenacity. You should be in it "for the long haul." If you want to be good at anything, then you need hard work over a long period of time, which incidentally is the very definition of *kung fu*, it's Chinese for "hard work."

In any endeavor, there are many off-ramps. You will always feel that you are being presented with reasons to quit and move on to something else. This is especially so in the earlier stages when the fruits of labor are not yet known. When success has arrived, it is easier to keep to the path, but when the struggle is still there and still real then the task is one of determination. When a person is willing to put in the hard work, the early mornings, the late nights, and approach all of it with an attitude that *I will not be denied*, success will come.

In the martial arts, everything that a person could have working against their success I had working against mine. Overweight, uncoordinated, injury-prone, slow healer, slow learner, lazy tendencies, lover of cured pork products, placing of obligations to family ahead of my own wants in my chosen field, low income—you name it, it was on the list. And I still managed to successfully reach black belt rank. And then some...

My success was never because there was something special about me. It was because I refused to quit. That simple. I was going to reach my goals or die trying... and I was reasonably sure that death was not on the line.

At any moment, had I chosen to accept any of the ready-made excuses which were right at my fingertips, I would have failed. When I dislocated my knee two weeks before a rank test, or when I broke a bone in my foot the day before a black belt test, or had I accepted the failure of that test, I would not be where I am now, doing what I do. And, you would be reading the words of someone else.

The excuses to quit are always there, ready and waiting to be accepted. Not just in my life, but in the life of anyone.

Many people live their lives like beaten dogs and never stick their neck out to see what is out there in the world. Their greatest potential lies untapped. What could they have accomplished and contributed to the world if only they'd refused to give in or give up? We will never know. How many cures for diseases went undiscovered because the person with the right set of questions in their head to find the cure was too full of self-doubt to go to school and study medicine? What else have we missed out on because someone quit when things became challenging?

Don't let doubts stop you from taking life as far as you can. Set in your mind that quitting is not an option. If you can see that you have already sacrificed, already taken the hits, already been hurt and beaten, what reason could you possibly have for walking away and not seeing things though to the end?

Insurance Executive:

While this might simply be a clever rhyme, it's more likely referring to the Japanese word "*do*," meaning the "path" or "way." In Japanese, *do* is attached to a number of skills that require years of diligent study, sacrifice, and strict discipline. For example, *karatedo* (the way of the empty hand), *judo* (the gentle way), and *chado* (the way of the tea ceremony) are all used to describe the arduous path required to master the particular skill, and to some degree, any associated philosophies and moral disciplines attached to it.

The path in ancient Japanese culture, and still for many today, is of paramount importance to the mastery of the skill in question, the steadfast development of the practitioner's character, and his or her loyalty to his/her *sensei*, the teacher. Japanese culture has, of course, dramatically changed since Musashi's precepts were written. While there are many Japanese people who strive to retain the old customs, many more have "modernized," so to speak, to ways less severe, freer, and more laid back, if you will.

Our culture in the United States is remote from the ways of old in Japan, and to many of their new ways too, for that matter. For example, while studying with more than one martial arts teacher was rarely done in days of old in Japan, it's quite common in the United States to train with multiple instructors. Case in point, I trained in *taekwondo* for many years earning a black belt, and later switched to American Free Style, a system that combines three fighting arts, earning a black belt in it as well. Before training in *taekwondo*, I earned colored belts in three other fighting styles.

Following the path of any endeavor for an extended period is important to learning it, potentially mastering it. But the absolute of "never straying," especially in these modern times and even more so in the culture of the United States, is virtually impossible. It's not necessary and, perhaps arguably, it might even limit your potential.

Here is another personal example: I have been designing jewelry for many years. If I were making jewelry in the culture and times the precepts were written, I would be a student under the guidance and possibly dictatorship of a master jewelry maker. I would learn everything he had to teach me and, in time, I might also become a master in my own right, but my skill and creativity would be strongly influenced by, and I would argue limited by, the *sensei*'s way.

But today in the United States, I have the advantage of expanding my art beyond just jewelry to include leatherwork, metalwork, painting, and other art forms. Because I can research disciplines off the classical path, I have expanded my interest and skill in other arts, which has made me a better jewelry designer.

Athletics has a term for this: cross training. In my martial arts, for example, training in the Filipino fighting art of *arnis*, in which we practice with 26-inch rattan sticks to attack, block, work practice drills, and spar, has improved my empty-hand skills. Training with body weight exercises and weights has made me stronger in the martial arts while simultaneously increasing my knowledge and control of my body.

To conclude, I respect "the way" as it relates to karate, my art craft, my spiritual life, and to some degree my employment. While I respect it in these areas, I refuse to limit my personal growth in them by never straying from their paths. In fact, I don't think of it as straying at all. I consider it as a way to expand my skill set to not only make me the best I can be at these things, but also help me be a better teacher of them by virtue of my broader knowledge.

Businessman:

There is no "way of business" per say, but to repurpose the admonition a little, martial arts can have significant value for businesspeople. As practitioners we learn how to set and achieve challenging goals, understand strategy, set tactics in motion to accomplish our objectives, and improvise when necessary to stay on target, all of which can be used on the job to help us guide and counsel our teams and organizations toward commercial success. Over time we develop inner strength, becoming calmer and more emotionally resilient than most of our peers too. This can be a significant advantage in stressful times. Those of us who have achieve advanced ranks frequently teach too, which means that we become adept at public speaking, proficient at explaining complicated concepts in everyday language, and develop the intuition to know with certainty when to let disciples struggle in the name of learning as well as when to intervene and lend a helping hand to help them overcome plateaus. All-in-all, few things can prepare us for leadership in business—or in life—better than martial arts.

For example, Jessica Alba is a famous actress but did you know that she is also a highly successful businesswoman? She was recently featured in *Forbes* magazine as having developed a billion dollar business by founding The Honest Company. And, she's also a martial artist, one who has done many of her own movie stunts. Speaking of actors and actresses, Jennifer Aniston, Christian Bale, Jessica Biel, James Caan, Courtney Cox, Robert Downey, Jr., Sean Patrick Flannery, Mel Gibson, Lorenzo Lamas, Adrian Paul, Elvis Presley, Christian Slater, and a host of others all practice (or practiced) martial arts of one kind or another, whether they did action movies or focused on other genres. In fact, martial arts can help folks find success in most any walk of life. German Chancellor Angela Merkel, King Juan Carlos I of Spain, and Russian President Vladimir Putin are all accomplished martial artists. Former Japanese Prime Minister Ryutaro Hashimoto and former United States Presidents Abraham Lincoln, Theodore Roosevelt, and George Washington, were all martial artists was well.* Finally, US Senator Ben Knighthorse Campbell was captain of the 1964 US Olympic Judo team.

Rather than saying never stray from the way, I prefer to say never give up on your training... Physical fitness, mental agility, self-discipline, confidence, and perseverance can all take us far, yet in my mind the most important attribute of martial arts that is directly applicable to the business world is the ability to remain calm under pressure. For example, I work in the aerospace and defense industry. It's a very challenging profession in part because the work comes in waves; we're either swamped and struggling to catch up or downsizing and chasing cost reductions to remain profitable. After the 9/11 attacks air travel plummeted for several years, driving massive layoffs in our sector when our airline customers went into retrenchment mode and orders dried up all around the world.

Although demand for travel and plane orders eventually picked back up, reprioritization of military programs and sequestration cuts in the United States hammered the defense side of the business, so while we do hire for attrition from time-to-time, we've been in an almost continuous layoff cycle for more than a decade.

* This list counts western wrestling and boxing (pugilism) as martial arts.

It's a real challenge to remain optimistic, make well-considered decisions that affect friends and coworkers, and avoid exhaustion in this sort of environment, yet in large part due to my martial arts training I have managed to do so when others have burned out.

So, never stray from the martial arts. Work hard. Train well. And, keep learning.

CONCLUSION

"Every day you may make progress. Every step may be fruitful. Yet there will stretch out before you an ever-lengthening, ever-ascending, ever-improving path. You know you will never get to the end of the journey. But this, so far from discouraging, only adds to the joy and glory of the climb."

— Sir Winston Churchill

Most of life is dead reckoning. "Dead reckoning" is a nautical term that refers to a way of measuring a vessel's path through the open ocean without the use of landmarks, global positioning satellites, the horizon, or even the stars to aid in navigation. For all intents and purposes the captain is blind, but still has a pretty good chance at reaching his or her destination anyway. You see, dead reckoning uses a "fix," that is the ship's last known position, and then calculates where in the world we are based on speed, either estimated or quantified, and the amount of time that has elapsed since the last known measurement was taken. Look at it this way, "We know that an hour ago we left this position traveling due north at a consistent speed of four knots, so looking at the map we should be right about… here."

You can imagine how calculating where we are in the middle of the open ocean via dead reckoning would be very difficult if the speed of the vessel varied from say two knots to maybe seven knots over the course of our journey, a common enough occurrence. Ocean currents impact the process of course, as they speed or slow the vessel, and inclement weather complicates the task even further as wind or waves might divert us from our course and rain, darkness, or the like keep us from validating our assumptions by sighting stars, landmasses, lighthouses, or even other ships. This form of navigation is far from exact, requiring hard-learned skill, attention to detail, and confidence in the sailor's abilities to have any chance for success.

Not so different from navigating our own existence is it? There's no owner's manual for the human body, no navigation chart for the human life, so in many ways this analogy is apt. Life is, in fact, dead reckoning. Much like a sailor's ability to navigate the open sea without instrumentation, our framework of life is based on our experience. Our first set of experiences helps us determine how we see the seas of life. This is based around our family and the impact is undeniable. If our upbringing was healthy and loving we tend to see the world one way, yet if our childhood was violent and unsupportive our worldview would be radically different.

While not as impactful as our parents or siblings, our community plays an important role too, both our public community and our private community. Our public community is constructed from the places we go—school, work, sporting events, restaurants, nightclubs, and the like. All the public places we frequent come with certain codes of conduct, modes of acceptable behaviors for those who attend the venue and interact with others therein. The same thing occurs in private communities. These are comprised of the people we associate with on our own accord, inside or outside public places or organizations. These private communities have rules and methods that are not necessary bad or good, but are not always understood or accepted by the larger public communities.

An example of one of these private communities might be the Society for Creative Anachronism (SCA), a group of people who recreate medieval life, tradecraft, and combat techniques.* They are generally accepted as they don't threaten the larger public community, but let's face it "normal" society doesn't really understand folks who dress up in period costumes, speak "forsoothly," and bash each other with wooden sticks for fun despite any educational value or personal growth members might gain from these events. Similarly, those of us who dress up in a *dogi*, *kung fu* uniform, *hakama*, or *ninja* outfit and practice martial skills that originated during feudal times in some far off land can seem a little odd to folks who have never walked into a *dojo*, *dojang*, or *kwoon*. Throw in a little Japanese, Korean, Chinese,

---

* The Society for Creative Anachronism is an international organization dedicated to researching and re-creating the arts and skills of pre-17th-century Europe. Their "Known World" consists of 20 kingdoms, with over 30,000 members worldwide who dress in clothing reminiscent of the Middle Ages or Renaissance and attend events which feature tournaments, royal courts, feasts, medieval dancing, classes and workshops. Speaking forsoothly is a nod toward the Elizabethan English terminology used at events by most of these historical re-enactors.

Philippines, or wherever our art originated from language and culture and we can seem just as strange as folks who dress up like knights and dames and carry swords and halberds to their events. Nevertheless, we learn about hard work, perseverance, and an appropriate code of conduct in the training hall.

Communities, both public and private, these are the elements the give us our "fix" for the dead reckoning of our lives, the basis on which we chart our course. From there we adjust our "speed" and look at the "map" of our moral and ethical convictions for confirmation that we are on the trajectory that we believe to be in our best interests for achieving our expectations in life.

What about Musashi? In this volume we have gained insight into the path he chose, the teachings he stood for, and how we might interpret them in contemporary times depending on the role we have set for ourselves in life, be it that of the monk, the warrior, the teacher, the businessperson, or whatever fits... Musashi's way was clearly one of stoicism and the use of violence was a means to his end. His stoicism is to be admired, yet his violence when seen from our modern perspective was savage. Judged by his times and values, maybe not...

Allegiance to a path without taking the time to give it thought is as if a person hands over the map and the compass of his or her life to another. That rarely ends well. While we certainly do respect Musashi for the construction of his path in life, for the clarity he brought to it, and for how well it served him and his disciples, we submit that his path is ill-suited to the world in which the majority of us live today. To strictly adhere to his path is intellectually weak, a mismatched framework, and at best a hodgepodge of methods shot through the prism of what we have constructed Musashi to be and not what and who he truly was.

Our starting point on the journey of life has already been fixed by our socialization, yet how we choose to move from that point forward is, of course, our choice. Copying the way of a long-dead man who killed for social advancement and came from a far less than favorable home life is problematic, but much of what he wrote warrants some deep consideration. Obviously there is wisdom in much of what Musashi preached, even when the totality of his teachings are clearly his path and not our own. Finding a path that makes sense for us, that suits our individual needs, and then making it our own is essential to becoming who we truly are.

Scott Ginsberg once said, "There are no cover bands in the Rock and Roll Hall of Fame." Similarly, there were thousands upon thousands of swordsmen who blazed a bloody path to glory in feudal Japan, yet we remember Musashi because he took what had been taught to the masses and made it his own. We all should do as Musashi did, albeit with less dysfunction and a whole lot less bloodshed. We all should question our heroes, our icons. We should choose wisely and with as much awareness as possible in the dead reckoning of our lives. And if, upon reflection, we want to adopt the way of Musashi, well then we need to chart a course that goes beyond his teachings, one that captures the essence of his wisdom, assures it is relevant to contemporary times, yet makes it our own.

We sincerely hope that our interpretations of the *Dokkodo* were illuminating, that we helped you find modern meaning and relevance in Musashi's ancient wisdom. Think deeply on what you've read, judiciously extract those gems that resonate, and then make them your own. Dead reckoning is an inexact science, but those who chart an intentional course, even an imprecise one, can stand head and shoulders above those who aimless drift upon the seas of life. We wish you good journey.

Be safe... and be well.

Don't settle for an ordinary copy of Sun Tzu's Art of War.

SH!T SUN TZU SAID

classic warfare

for the modern mind.

kris wilder • lawrence a kane

Available at
amazon

ABOUT THE AUTHORS

Br. Kris Wilder, OSF

Kris Wilder is the head instructor and owner of West Seattle Karate Academy. He started practicing the martial arts at the age of fifteen. Over the years he has earned black belt rankings in three styles, *Goju-Ryu* karate (5th *dan*), *taekwondo* (2nd *dan*), and judo (1st *dan*), in which he has competed in senior nationals and international tournaments. He is the author of over a dozen books including two *USA Book News* Best Books Award finalists and a *ForeWord Magazine* Book of the Year Award finalist. He also stars in two instructional DVDs.

Kris has been blessed with the opportunity to train under skilled instructors, including Olympic athletes, state champions, national champions, and gifted martial artists who take their lineage directly from the founders of their systems. He teaches seminars worldwide, focusing on growing a person's martial technique and their understanding, whatever their art may be. Kris also serves as a National Representative for the University of New Mexico's Institute of Traditional Martial Arts.

Kris spent about 15 years in the political and public affairs area, working for campaigns from the local to national level. During this consulting career he was periodically on staff for elected officials. His work also involved lobbying and corporate affairs. He is currently a member of The Order of St. Francis (OSF); the OSF is one of many active Apostolic Christian Orders.

Kris lives in Seattle, Washington. You can contact him directly at wskadojo@gmail.com.

Alain Burrese, J.D.

Alain Burrese is an Author, Speaker, and Personal Security, Safety and Self-defense Instructor. He has combined his years of martial art and self-defense training, his military, bouncing and security work, and his formal education which includes a business degree and a law degree into books, DVDs, and programs to help people stay safe and defend themselves if needed. Additionally, he conducts programs and writes about effective communication for conflict resolution and living with the Warrior's Edge.

Alain is the author of seven books which include *Hard-Won Wisdom From The School Of Hard Knocks: How to Avoid A Fight And Things To Do When You Can't Or Don't Want To* and *Lost Conscience: A Ben Baker Sniper Novel*. He has starred in eleven instructional DVDs; including *Streetfighting Essentials*, the *Restraint, Control & Come-A-Long Techniques* set, and the five volume *Lock On: Joint Locking Essentials* series.

Alain's military background includes two years as a paratrooper with an Infantry Battalion in the 82nd Airborne Division at Fort Bragg, N.C., and working as a sniper instructor at the 2nd Infantry Division Scout Sniper School at Camp Casey, South Korea. His martial art background includes training in judo, *taekwondo*, karate, *Hapkido*, and *qigong*. Alain lived in South Korea to train in his primary art of *Hapkido*, a Korean martial art that focuses on self-defense, and he's earned a 5th degree black belt in this martial art.

Alain currently lives in Montana with his wife Yi-saeng and daughter Cosette. He spends his time writing, speaking, teaching, working security, and contributing to *Survive and Defend*, a website that provides information that saves lives. You can learn more about Alain, download his free e-books, and contact him..

Wallace D. Smedley

Wallace has worked for Chuck Norris' KICKSTART KIDS Foundation since 2002. As a part of this work he teaches karate as an alternate Physical Education (P.E.) credit elective class. During his time with KICKSTART KIDS he has had the opportunity to work with more than 1,000 students and that number continues to grow. KICKSTART KIDS is a character education program that uses karate as a tool to recruit and retain students. Working inside of the public school system and side-by-side with other education professionals he had the opportunity to learn how to teach like a teacher while instilling the character strengths that will allow these students to become contributors to society.

Beginning in 2012 he took on the additional responsibilities by accepting a position as an Area Leader for KICKSTART KIDS, which allowed him to also help other KICKSTART KIDS Instructors better implement the teaching methods in the classroom. He also served on a committee that was charged with creating and developing the Character Education Values Curriculum for the Foundation.

He has written hundreds of articles and published several books on the traditional martial arts, practical application of martial arts as well as on the subject of personal safety. His books *Slapping Dragons and Ignorance, Myth and the Martial Arts* were all well received and in 2015 he is releasing *Prelude to a Fight: Personal Safety Before the Physical Violence Begins* and *A Path to a Better Place.*

He lives in the Dallas/Fort Worth area of north Texas and enjoys any free moments with his wife, Daisy, and their children, CJ, Gillian, and Ysabella. He can be reached at smedleymartialarts@gmail.com.

Lisa A. Christensen

Lisa Christensen began training in the martial arts in the mid-1990s, earning black belts in *taekwondo* and American Freestyle Karate. She also earned a brown belt in *kempo*, and has studied kickboxing, *jujitsu*, and *arnis*. She has extensive teaching experience in the martial arts working with adults and children. She began training with her husband, Loren W. Christensen, in 2003 and has appeared in several of his books and DVDs. She has been the principal photographer for numerous martial arts books and magazine articles and is the co-author of *Fight Back: A Woman's Guide to Self-Defense That Works*.

Lisa has worked as a Workers' Comp Claims Examiner for over 30 years. She is certified to adjudicate claims in Oregon and retains an Oregon General Lines Adjuster License. Lisa currently handles Oregon claims for national and regional Oregon accounts, as well as insured and self-insured clients. Lisa has also worked extensively as a jewelry designer and her work is featured on Facebook, ETSY, and her website, www.LAfinery.com.

Lawrence A. Kane, COP-GOV

Lawrence Kane is a Certified Outsourcing Professional in Governance (COP-GOV) and a senior leader at a Fortune® 50 corporation where, among other things, he is responsible for the strategy for a $1.1B per year organization. He architected the IT infrastructure strategy, governed the software asset management process, and established the Sourcing Strategy and Vendor Management organizations. He saved the company well over $2.1B by hiring, training, and developing a high-performance team that creates sourcing strategies, improves processes, negotiates contracts, and benchmarks internal and external supplier performance.

He advances thought leadership in strategic sourcing, benchmarking, and supplier innovation as a frequent speaker at conferences such as Sourcing Industry Group (SIG) and International Association of Outsourcing Professionals (IAOP). His is also a member of the SIG University Advisory Board and the IAOP Training and Certification Committee. He previously worked as a business technology instructor at a technical college for eight years where received student accolades for communicating effectively, demonstrating patience, and fostering a positive learning environment.

A bestselling author, martial artist, and judicious use-of-force expert, his books have earned three *USA Book News* Best Books Award finalists, an *eLit Book Awards* Bronze prize, two *Next Generation Indie Book Awards* finalists, and two *ForeWord Magazine* Book of the Year Award finalists. A founding technical consultant to University of New Mexico's Institute of Traditional Martial Arts, he also has written numerous articles on martial arts, self-defense, countervailing force, and related topics. He has spoken with journalists numerous times, including once where he was interviewed in English by a reporter from a Swiss newspaper for an article that was published in French, and found that oddly amusing.

Since 1970, he has studied and taught traditional Asian martial arts, medieval European combat, and modern close-quarter weapon techniques. Working stadium security part-time for 26 years he was involved in hundreds of violent altercations, but got paid to watch football. Lawrence lives in Seattle, Washington. You can contact him directly at lakane@ix.netcom.com.

OTHER WORKS BY THE AUTHORS

Non-Fiction Books:

1. The Little Black Book of Violence (Kane/Wilder)

   "This book will save lives!" – Alain Burrese, JD, former US Army 2nd Infantry Division Scout Sniper School instructor

   Men commit 80 percent of all violent crimes and are twice as likely to become the victims of aggressive behavior. This book is primarily written for men ages 15 to 35, and contains more than mere self-defense techniques. You will learn crucial information about street survival that most martial arts instructors don't even know. Discover how to use awareness, avoidance, and de-escalation to help stave off violence, know when it's prudent to fight, and understand how to do so effectively.

2. The Big Bloody Book of Violence (Kane/Wilder)

   "Implementing even a fraction of this book's suggestions will substantially increase your overall safety." – Gila Hayes, Armed Citizens' Legal Defense Network

   We could whine about how we live in dangerous times nowadays, but let's face it, all throughout history ordinary people have been at risk of violence in one way or another. Abdicating personal responsibility by outsourcing your safety to others might be the easy way out, but it does little to safeguard your welfare. In this book you'll discover what dangers you face and learn proven strategies to thwart them. Self-defense is far more than fighting skills; it's a lifestyle choice, a more enlightened way of looking at and moving through the world. Learn to make sense of "senseless" violence, overcome talisman thinking, escape riots, avert terrorism, circumvent gangs, defend against home invasions, safely interact with law enforcement, and conquer impossible odds.

3. Dirty Ground (Kane/Wilder)

   "Fills a void in martial arts training." – Loren W. Christensen, Martial Arts Masters Hall of Fame member

   This book addresses a significant gap in most martial arts training, the tricky space that lies between sport and combat applications where you need to control a person without injuring him (or her). Techniques in this region are called "drunkle," named after the drunken uncle disrupting a family gathering. Understanding how to deal with combat, sport, and drunkle situations is vital because appropriate use of force is codified in law and actions that do not accommodate these regulations can have severe repercussions. Martial arts techniques must be adapted to best fit the situation you find yourself in. This book shows you how.

4. Scaling Force (Kane/Miller)

   "If you're serious about learning how the application of physical force works—before, during and after the fact—I cannot recommend this book highly enough." – Lieutenant Jon Lupo, New York State Police

   Conflict and violence cover a broad range of behaviors, from intimidation to murder, and require an equally broad range of responses. A kind word will not resolve all situations, nor will wristlocks, punches, or even a gun. This book introduces the full range of options, from skillfully doing nothing to employing deadly force. You will understand the limits of each type of force, when specific levels may be appropriate, the circumstances under which you may have to apply them, and the potential costs, legally and personally, of your decision.

5. Surviving Armed Assaults (Kane)

   "This book will be an invaluable resource for anyone walking the warrior's path, and anyone who is interested in this vital topic." – Lt. Col. Dave Grossman, Director, Warrior Science Group

   A sad fact is that weapon-wielding thugs victimize 1,773,000 citizens every year in the United States alone. Even martial artists are not immune from this deadly threat. Consequently, self-defense training that does not consider the very real possibility of an armed attack is dangerously incomplete. Whether you live in the city or countryside, you should be both mentally and physically prepared to deal with an unprovoked armed assault at any time. Preparation must be comprehensive enough to account for the plethora of pointy objects, blunt instruments, explosive devices, and deadly projectiles that someday could be used against you. This extensive book teaches proven survival skills that can keep you safe.

6.   The 87-Fold Path to Being the Best Martial Artist (Kane/Wilder)

"Beware! The 87-Fold Path contains unexpected, concise blows to the head and heart... you don't have a chance, but to examine and retool your way of life." – George Rohrer, Executive and Purpose Coach, MBA, CPCC, PCC

Despite the fact that raw materials in feudal Japan were mediocre at best, bladesmiths used innovative folding and tempering techniques to forge some of the finest swords imaginable for their samurai overlords. The process of heating and folding the metal removed impurities, while shaping and strengthening the blades to perfection. The end result was strong yet supple, beautiful and deadly. As martial artists we utilize a similar process, forging our bodies through hard work, perseverance, and repetition. The challenge is that training solely toward physical perfection is not enough. In fact, the more a practitioner knows about physical conflict, the less likely he or she is to engage in violence. Knowing how to fight is important, clearly, yet if you do not find something larger than base violence attached your efforts it becomes unsustainable, your martial arts adventure will eventually come to an end. The 87-Fold Path provides ideas for taking training beyond the physical that are uniquely tailored for the elite martial artist. This makes the martial journey more enjoyable, meaningful, and longer lasting.

7.   How to Win a Fight (Kane/Wilder)

"It is the ultimate course in self-defense and will help you survive and get through just about any violent situation or attack." – Jeff Rivera, bestselling author

More than three million Americans are involved in a violent physical encounter every year. Develop the fortitude to walk away when you can and prevail when you must. Defense begins by scanning your environment, recognizing hazards and escape routes, and using verbal de-escalation to defuse tense situations. If a fight is unavoidable, the authors offer clear guidance for being the victor, along with advice on legal implications, including how to handle a police interview after the altercation.

8. Lessons from the Dojo Floor (Wilder)

"Helps each reader, from white belt to black belt, look at and understand why he or she trains." – Michael E. Odell, Isshin-Ryu Northwest Okinawa Karate Association

In the vein of Dave Lowry, a thought provoking collection of short vignettes that entertains while it educates. Packed with straightforward, easy, and quick to read sections that range from profound to insightful to just plain amusing, anyone with an affinity for martial arts can benefit from this material.

9. Martial Arts Instruction (Kane)

"Boeing trains hundreds of security officers, Kane's ideas will help us be more effective." – Gregory A. Gwash, Chief Security Officer, Boeing

While the old adage, "those who can't do, teach," is not entirely true, all too often "those who can do" cannot teach effectively. This book is unique in that it offers a holistic approach to teaching martial arts; incorporating elements of educational theory and communication techniques typically overlooked in *budo* (warrior arts). Teachers will improve their abilities to motivate, educate, and retain students, while students interested in the martial arts will develop a better understanding of what instructional method best suits their needs.

10. The Way of Kata (Kane/Wilder)

> *"This superb book is essential reading for all those who wish to understand the highly effective techniques, concepts, and strategies that the kata were created to record."* – Iain Abernethy, British Combat Association Hall of Fame member

The ancient masters developed *kata*, or "formal exercises," as fault-tolerant methods to preserve their unique, combat-proven fighting systems. Unfortunately, they also deployed a two-track system of instruction where an outer circle of students unknowingly received modified forms with critical details or important principles omitted. Only the select inner circle that had gained a master's trust and respect would be taught *okuden waza*, the powerful hidden applications of *kata*. The theory of deciphering *kata* applications (*kaisai no genri*) was once a great mystery revealed only to trusted disciples of the ancient masters in order to protect the secrets of their systems. Even today, while the basic movements of *kata* are widely known, advanced practical applications and sophisticated techniques frequently remain hidden from the casual observer. The principles and rules for understanding *kata* are largely unknown. This groundbreaking book unveils these methods, not only teaching you how to analyze your *kata* to understand what it is trying to tell you, but also helping you to utilize your fighting techniques more effectively.

11. The Way of Martial Arts for Kids (Wilder)

> *"Written in a personable, engaging style that will appeal to kids and adults alike."* – Laura Weller, Guitarist, *The Green Pajamas*

Based on centuries of traditions, martial arts training can be a positive experience for kids. The book helps you and yours get the most out of class. It shows how just about any child can become one of those few exemplary learners who excel in the training hall as well as in life. Written to children, it is also for parents too. After all, while the martial arts instructor knows his art, no one knows his/her child better than the parent. Together you can help your child achieve just about anything... The advice provided is straightforward, easy to understand, and written with a child-reader in mind so that it can either be studied by the child and/or read together with the parent.

12. The Way of Sanchin Kata (Wilder)

"This book has been sorely needed for generations!" – Philip Starr, National Chairman, Yiliquan Martial Arts Association

When Karate or *Ti* was first developed in Okinawa it was about using technique and extraordinary power to end a fight instantly. These old ways of generating remarkable power are still accessible, but they are purposefully hidden in *Sanchin kata* for the truly dedicated to find. This book takes the practitioner to new depths of practice by breaking down the form piece-by-piece, body part by body part, so that the very foundation of the *kata* is revealed. Every chapter, concept, and application is accompanied by a "Test It" section, designed for you to explore and verify the *kata* for yourself. *Sanchin kata* really comes alive when you feel the thrill of having those hidden teachings speak to you across the ages through your body. Simply put, once you read this book and test what you have learned, your karate will never be the same.

13. Sensei Mentor Teacher Coach (Wilder/Kane)

"Finally a book that will actually move the needle in closing the leadership skills gap found in all aspects of our society." – Dan Roberts, CEO and President, Ouellette & Associates

Many books weave platitudes, promising the keys to success in leadership, secrets that will transform you into the great leader, the one. The fact of the matter is, however, that true leadership really isn't about you. It's about giving back, offering your best to others so that they can find the best in themselves. The methodologies in this book help you become the leader you were meant to be by bringing your goals and other peoples' needs together to create a powerful, combined vision. Learn how to access the deeper aspects of who you are, your unique qualities, and push them forward in actionable ways. Acquire this vital information and advance your leadership journey today

14. Journey: The Martial Artist's Notebook (Kane/Wilder)

"Students who take notes progress faster and enjoy a deeper understanding than those who don't. Period." – Loren W. Christensen, martial arts Masters Hall of Fame inductee

As martial arts students progress through the lower ranks it is extraordinarily useful for them to keep a record of what they have learned. The mere process of writing things down facilitates deeper understanding. This concept is so successful, in fact, that many schools require advanced students to complete a thesis or research project concurrent with testing for black belt (or equivalent) rank, advancing the knowledge base of the organization while simultaneously clarifying and adding depth to each practitioner's understanding of his or her art. Just as Bruce Lee's notes and essays became *Tao of Jeet Kune Do*, perhaps someday your training journal will be published for the masses, but first and foremost this notebook is by you, for you. It contains both structured and unstructured blank pages for you to take notes and make sketches that enhance your training experience. As an added bonus, there are 125 thought-provoking martial arts quotes too. This is where the deeper journey on your martial path begins...

15. The Way to Black Belt (Kane/Wilder)

"It is so good I wish I had written it myself." – Hanshi Patrick McCarthy, Director, International Ryukyu Karate Research Society

Cut to the very core of what it means to be successful in the martial arts. Earning a black belt can be the most rewarding experience of a lifetime, but getting there takes considerable planning. Whether your interests are in the classical styles of Asia or in today's Mixed Martial Arts, this book prepares you to meet every challenge. Whatever your age, whatever your gender, you will benefit from the wisdom of master martial artists around the globe, including Iain Abernethy, Dan Anderson, Loren Christensen, Jeff Cooper, Wim Demeere, Aaron Fields, Rory Miller, Martina Sprague, Phillip Starr, and many more, who share more than 300 years of combined training experience. Benefit from their guidance during your development into a first-class black belt.

16. 101 Safety and Self-Defense Tips (Burrese)

Learn from the top experts on safety and self-defense in the field. This book is a compilation of lessons from 101 different books dealing with violence and survival. Besides learning from the included lessons, the book provides and list and samples to assist you in building your own safety and self-defense library. Learn from Loren Christensen, Kelly McCann, Rory Miller, Ira Lipman, Lawrence Kane, Kris Wilder, Michael Janich, Sammy Franco, Marc "Animal" MacYoung, Juval Aviv, Massad Ayoob, Peyton Quinn, Sanford Strong and more…

17. Hard Won Wisdom from the School of Hard Knocks (Burrese)

The author's actual experiences provide the backbone for this realistic look at self-defense. Barroom brawls, street fights, and barracks ruckuses combined with bouncing, security, and bodyguard work taught the author the realities of fighting and street violence. This informative and entertaining guide contains loads of serious lessons and practical advice on fighting and violence and gives you the knowledge you'll need to prevail in a physical encounter (including how to be aware of and avoid an impending fight). Burrese covers the physical aspects of self-defense such as punching, kicking and other related training, but more importantly, he covers the little discussed aspects of self-defense and fighting.

18. How to Protect Yourself by Developing a Fighter's Mindset (Burrese)

The Fighter's Mindset is the foundation to build your safety and self-defense strategies upon. You must have the proper mindset to stay safe, aware, and avoid potential danger; and you must have the proper mindset to escape to safety or attack back if you are assaulted or attacked. Learn how and why you must be aware, be decisive, be courageous, be willing, be vicious, be determined, be cool and believe in yourself. He even shares why being nice is a safety and self-defense strategy. Filled with practical advice and quotations from many leading experts, this guide to developing a fighter's mindset will be the cornerstone to your safety and self-defense. It will increase your safety and ability to defend yourself if ever attacked.

19. Tough Guy Wisdom (Burrese)

The first volume of the ultimate collection of "tough guy" movie quotes and trivia. The movie lines you love, along with the settings, the actors/actresses in the scenes, movie trivia, and interesting facts about the actors who said them. For action movie buffs and tough guy film aficionados, the Tough Guy Wisdom series will "Make your day!"

20. Tough Guy Wisdom II (Burrese)

Volume two of the Tough Guy Wisdom series. The movie lines you love, along with the settings, the actors/actresses in the scenes, movie trivia, and interesting facts about the actors who said them. For action movie buffs and tough guy film aficionados, the Tough Guy Wisdom series will "Make your day!"

21. Tough Guy Wisdom III (Burrese)

Volume three of the Tough Guy Wisdom series. The movie lines you love, along with the settings, the actors/actresses in the scenes, movie trivia, and interesting facts about the actors who said them. For action movie buffs and tough guy film aficionados, the Tough Guy Wisdom series will "Make your day!"

22. Fight Back (Christensen)

Some "experts" say that you should be submissive when attacked at home or by a stranger. You won't find that advice here, although you might use it as a ruse before you claw your assailant's eyes and annihilate his groin. Your ultimate goal is to get away but you don t achieve that by being meek and docile. You get away by drawing on that hard-wired survival instinct to attack him like an enraged lioness protecting its babies. Learn exactly what you need to survive an attack in your home or on the street.

23. Slapping Dragons (Smedley)

All too often, martial artists surrender their intellectual freedom and opt instead to accept without thinking the strange and unbelievable claims made by so-called masters and experts in the martial arts. Wallace Smedley takes a close look at the claims and asks important questions about the basis for such acceptance. Some of the claims are harmless, but some can get you killed if you follow them, and so questions need to be asked. Often, asking questions on the subjects can be compared to slapping a dragon, but Smedley claims that there are times when Slapping Dragons is exactly what we need to do. This book contains expanded articles comprised from the best of wallacesmedley.com as well as new material.

24. Ignorance, Myth and Martial Arts (Smedley)

Within the martial arts a person will find outrageous claims, and subtle lies. There are tales of ancient masters who had powers usually reserved for Superman or Santa Clause, but there are also instructors who use misleading marketing tactics to entice students to pay to be safe. Few instructors actually tell students that the best way to be safe is to be nice to people and not act like a raving ding-dong anytime someone rubs you the wrong way. One will also find absurd practices and a near brainwashing process where you surrender your critical thinking in favor of herd mentality. It is easy to not question the instructor, or the procedures and policies of the class and organization. There is a much more difficult road in questioning, but questions must be asked.

Fiction Books:

1. Blinded by the Night (Kane)

"Kane's expertise in matters of mayhem shines throughout." – Steve Perry, bestselling author

Richard Hayes is a Seattle cop. After 25 years with the PD he thinks he knows everything there is to know about predators. The dregs of society like rapists, murderers, gang bangers, and child molesters are just another day at the office. Commonplace criminals become the least of his problems when he goes hunting for a serial killer and runs into a real monster. The creature not only attacks him, but merely gets pissed off when he shoots it. In the head. Twice! Surviving that fight is only the beginning. Richard discovers that the vampire he destroyed was the ruler of an eldritch realm he never dreamed existed. By some archaic rule, having defeated the monster's sovereign in battle, Richard becomes their new king. Now he is responsible for a host of horrors who stalk the night, howl at the moon, and shamble through the darkness. But, why would these creatures willingly obey a human? When it comes to human predators,

Richard is a seasoned veteran, yet with paranormal ones he is but a rookie. He must navigate a web of intrigue and survive long enough to discover how a regular guy can tangle with supernatural creatures and prevail. One mistake and things surely won't end well...

2. Legends of the Masters (Wilder/Kane)

"It is a series of (very) short stories teaching life lessons. I'm going to bring it out when my nephews are over at family dinners for good discussion starters. A fun read!" – Angela Palmore

Storytelling is an ancient form of communication that still resonates today. An engaging story told and retold shares a meaningful message that can be passed down through the generations. Take fables such as *The Boy Who Cried Wolf* or *The Tortoise and the Hare*, who hasn't learned a thing or two from these ancient tales? *Legends of the Masters* retools Aesop's lesser-known fables, reimagining them to meet the needs and interests of modern martial artists. Reflecting upon the wisdom of yesteryear in this new light will surely bring value for practitioners of the arts today.

3. Lost Conscience (Burrese)

After a tragic school shooting, former army sniper, turned attorney, Ben Baker must decide between what's legal and what's right. Together with long-time friend, and former sniper buddy, Frank Senich, the two seek justice against a child trafficking ring. The pair must draw on their military sniping skills and their expertise in hand-to-hand combat to see their mission to its end. A mission that includes meth addicts breaking into Baker's house; long range sniping; confrontations with the County Attorney and Attorney General; and battles with a former SEAL sniper, truck stop thugs, child abductors, and a pair of giants, one of whom was kicked out of professional wrestling for injuring too many wrestlers. Along the way, in order to succeed, and more importantly survive, Ben Baker must lose his conscience.

DVDs:

1. <u>121 Killer Appz</u> (Wilder/Kane)

    "Quick and brutal, the way karate is meant to be." – Eric Parsons, Founder, Karate for Life Foundation

    You know the *kata*, now it is time for the applications. *Gekisai (Dai Ni)*, *Saifa*, *Seiyunchin*, *Seipai*, *Kururunfa*, *Suparinpei*, *Sanseiru*, *Shisochin*, and *Seisan kata* are covered. If you ever wondered what purpose a move from a *Goju Ryu* karate form was for, wonder no longer. This DVD contains no discussion, just a no-nonsense approach to one application after another. It is sure to provide deeper understanding to your *kata* practice and stimulate thought on determining your own applications to the *Goju Ryu* karate forms.

2. <u>Sanchin Kata: Three Battles Karate Kata</u> (Wilder)

    "A cornucopia of martial arts knowledge." – Shawn Kovacich, endurance high-kicking world record holder (as certified by the Guinness Book of World Records)

    A traditional training method for building karate power *Sanchin kata*, or Three Battles Sequence, is an ancient form that can be traced back to the roots of karate. Some consider it the missing link between Chinese kung fu and Okinawan karate. *Sanchin kata* is known to develop extraordinary quickness and generate remarkable power. This program breaks down the form piece by piece, body part by body part, so that the hidden details of the *kata* are revealed. Regular practice of *Sanchin kata* conditions the body, trains correct alignment, and teaches the essential structure needed for generating power within all of your karate movements. Many karate practitioners believe that *Sanchin kata* holds the key to mastering the traditional martial arts. Though it can be one of the simplest forms to learn, it is simultaneously one of the most difficult to perfect. This DVD complements the book <u>The Way of Sanchin Kata</u>, providing in-depth exploration of the form, with detailed instruction of the essential posture, linking the spine, generating power, and demonstration of the complete *kata*.

3.   <u>Scaling Force</u> (Miller/Kane)

   "Kane and Miller have been there, done that and have the t-shirt. And they're giving you their lessons learned without requiring you to pay the fee in blood they had to in order to learn them. And that is priceless." – M. Guthrie, Federal Air Marshal

   Conflict and violence cover a broad range of behaviors, from intimidation to murder, and they require an equally broad range of responses. A kind word will not resolve all situations, nor will wristlocks, punches, or even a gun. Rory Miller and Lawrence A. Kane explain and demonstrate the full range of options, from skillfully doing nothing to applying deadly force. You will learn to understand the limits of each type of force, when specific levels may be appropriate, the circumstances under which you may have to apply them, and the potential cost of your decision, legally and personally. It is vital to enter this scale at the right level, and to articulate why what you did was appropriate. If you do not know how to succeed at all six levels, there are situations in which you will have no appropriate options. More often than not, that will end badly. This DVD complements the book <u>Scaling Force</u>.

4.   <u>Lock On: Joint Locking Essentials Volume 1</u>: Wrist Locks (Burrese)

   Joint locks can be some of the most difficult techniques to learn and master. That is until now. This series is a comprehensive guide to joint locks and one of the most complete programs available for practical joint locking information, with detailed instruction on the mechanics of each lock, proper execution, and various applications to enable the viewer to learn the essentials of applying joint locks in any situation. Volume 1 focuses on wrist locks, with deep insight to supplement hands-on instruction. If you want to take your joint locking ability to the next level, you must have this DVD.

5.   <u>Lock On: Joint Locking Essentials Volume 2</u>: Arm Bars & Elbow Locks (Burrese)

   Joint locks can be some of the most difficult techniques to learn and master. That is until now. This series is a comprehensive guide to joint locks and one of the most complete programs available for practical joint locking information, with detailed instruction on the mechanics of each lock, proper execution, and various applications to enable the viewer to learn the essentials of applying joint locks in any situation. Volume 2 contents include basic arm bars, elbow breaks, armpit clamps, grappling, and more.

6. Lock On: Joint Locking Essentials Volume 3: Shoulder Locks (Burrese)

    Joint locks can be some of the most difficult techniques to learn and master. That is until now. This series is a comprehensive guide to joint locks and one of the most complete programs available for practical joint locking information, with detailed instruction on the mechanics of each lock, proper execution, and various applications to enable the viewer to learn the essentials of applying joint locks in any situation. Volume 3 contents include an explanation of the shoulder, raising arm locks, pulling shoulder locks, various chicken wing locks, figure four locks, and more.

7. Lock On: Joint Locking Essentials Volume 4: Finger Locks (Burrese)

    Joint locks can be some of the most difficult techniques to learn and master. That is until now. This series is a comprehensive guide to joint locks and one of the most complete programs available for practical joint locking information, with detailed instruction on the mechanics of each lock, proper execution, and various applications to enable the viewer to learn the essentials of applying joint locks in any situation. Volume 4 contents include an explanation of the finger, handshake techniques, pressing fingers down, forcing fingers up behind the back, escapes from various holds, and more.

8. Lock On: Joint Locking Essentials Volume 5: Combining Locks & Lock Flow Drills (Burrese)

    Joint locks can be some of the most difficult techniques to learn and master. That is until now. This series is a comprehensive guide to joint locks and one of the most complete programs available for practical joint locking information, with detailed instruction on the mechanics of each lock, proper execution, and various applications to enable the viewer to learn the essentials of applying joint locks in any situation. Volume 5 provides detailed instruction on the four corner throw (*shionage* in Japanese), a lock that exploits both the wrist and shoulder. Then, Burrese provides instruction on how to go from one lock to another, building to three and four lock combinations, and concluding with longer series of flow drills.

9. Restraint, Control & Come-A-Long Techniques Volume 1 (Burrese)

Restrain, control, and take people outside with techniques specific to bouncers, security professionals and law enforcement. Learn how to use joint locks and pain compliant techniques to control and move people. Burrese instructs on how to make your joint locks, holds, and take downs more effective when working positions that require you to go "hands on." Everyone who might need to control others needs to learn the techniques Alain teaches in this program. Additionally, even though designed for law enforcement and security professionals, this DVD set is also an invaluable tool for any martial artist who wants to make joint-locking techniques street effective. Volume 1 includes communication, cone of power, arm bar, lower back wrist lock, goose neck, chicken wing, standing center lock, applications, and more.

10. Restraint, Control & Come-A-Long Techniques Volume 2 (Burrese)

Restrain, control, and take people outside with techniques specific to bouncers, security professionals and law enforcement. Learn how to use joint locks and pain compliant techniques to control and move people. Volume 2 includes spinning a person, combat breathing, thumb grab goose neck, split finger goose neck, fingers behind back hold, over the top chicken wing, four corner throw, figure four lock, rolling a subject over, pressure points, applications, and more.

11. Chokes and Sleeper Holds Proven Techniques for Both Competition and the Street (Burrese)

Chokes and sleeper holds are some of the most powerful and effective ways of stopping a fully resisting attacker. Take away a person's consciousness and you take away the ability to fight. This information packed DVD will provide you with the tools to apply chokeholds and sleeper holds quickly and correctly, making you a formidable person to be reckoned with. Learn how to properly apply these chokes and sleeper holds and you'll have powerful tools added to your arsenal. Learn how to end a fight in seconds with techniques like these: rear naked choke, side shoulder sleeper, guillotine choke, front collar choke, one hand chokes, uniform or jacket techniques, and much more.

12. Streetfighting Essentials (Burrese)

Real street fights are serious trouble the kind of trouble that most martial arts don't prepare you for. So what do you do when a street thug approaches, wanting to make you his next victim? Learn how to blend the proven hand techniques of boxing and hapkido's devastating throws and kicks into a street fighting system that is sure to keep you on top and put your opponent on the pavement. Burrese begins by teaching you the tools of the trade including killer punches, hammer fists, palm heels, elbows, knees, kicks and throws. Then, through chillingly realistic scenarios and slow motion photography, he shows you how to apply these tools against the kinds of punches, grabs, weapon attacks and gang attacks you'll really encounter on the street. This DVD is a comprehensive self-defense system that bridges the gap between martial arts theory and brutal street fighting reality.

13. Hapkido Hoshinsul: The Explosive Korean Art of Self Defense (Burrese)

Hapkido is a traditional Korean martial art that translates as "The Way of Coordinated Power." Unlike the more popular and sport-oriented *taekwondo*, *hapkido* is a pure fighting art that combines powerful striking and kicking methods with devastating joint locks, throws and breaks. Learn the secrets of hapkido's effective techniques including how to use its fundamental wrist, elbow and shoulder locks to defend against a variety of street attacks. Drawing from his own real-world experience, Burrese shows how to adapt these techniques to the needs of the bouncer, security specialist or law enforcement officer.

14. Hapkido Cane: Big Stick Fighting from the Dojo to the Street (Burrese)

An often misunderstood but potentially deadly weapon, the cane is one of the few self-defense tools you can take virtually anywhere no matter what level of security you're facing. Learn how to maximize the combative use of the cane, turning it from just a leg support to an invaluable part of your arsenal. Stripping away the flashy martial arts moves to leave behind the bare essentials of big stick fighting, Burrese teaches you the rapid, vicious strikes that take advantage of the cane's size and heft, and then transitions seamlessly into brutal combinations of striking and blocking that will have your opponent wishing he'd never mistaken you for an easy mark. From there, he shows hooking and grabbing techniques that enable you to move into joint locks, chokes and stick submissions relying on street-proven principles of movement, not fancy dojo dancing. Whether you carry a cane out of necessity or choice, this video will give you information on big stick fighting you can use to keep yourself safe on the street.

Printed in Great Britain
by Amazon

67235829R00158